Effective English

COMPREHENSION

Read Fast, Understand Better!

Published by:
Lotus Press : Publishers & Distributors

Effective English
COMPREHENSION

Read Fast, Understand Better!

Rahul Chawla

4735/22, Prakash Deep Building
Ansari Road, Darya Ganj,
New Delhi-110002

LOTUS PRESS Publishers & Distributors
Unit No. 220, Second Floor, 4735/22,
Prakash Deep Building, Ansari Road,
Daryaganj, New Delhi- 110002
Ph.: 32903912, 23280047, 098118-38000
E-mail: lotus_press@sify.com

Effective English Comprehension

Read Fast, Understand Better

ISBN 978-81-8382-258-9

Published by: **Lotus Press**, New Delhi.
Printed at: Concept Imprint, Delhi.

PREFACE

Reading can be challenging, particularly when the material is unfamiliar, technical or complex. Moreover, for some readers, who are not well conversant with the language, comprehension is always challenging. They may understand each word separately, but linking them together into meaningful ideas often doesn't happen as it should.

The sole reason of reading is comprehension. If readers can read the words but do not understand what they are reading, they are not really reading. Comprehension refers to the ability to go beyond the words, understand the ideas and the relationships between ideas conveyed in a text. Good readers are both purposeful and active. They have a purpose for reading.

Reading is a complex process that develops over time. Although the basics of reading—word recognition and fluency—can be learned in a few years, reading to learn subject matter does not occur automatically once one has learned to read. Text comprehension should be emphasized from the beginning, rather than waiting until one has mastered the basics of reading.

The focus of this book is on improving English comprehension. It also stresses on techniques that help readers improve their ability to comprehend text quickly and easily.

The book lists reading comprehension strategies. Indeed, the use of the effective reading comprehension strategies is perhaps the most important means to helping readers improve comprehension and learning from text.

This volume provides an overview of reading comprehension strategies and strategy interventions that have been shown empirically to be effective in helping readers to overcome comprehension challenges. The book also includes practice exercise for all age groups. It is an ideal reference for learners as well as others who pursue to improve their English comprehension.

Author

CONTENTS

Chapter 1

Introduction to English Comprehension

Reading Comprehension

Reading is all about information. It's not about the number of words you read, but the amount of value you extract from them. The key to improved reading comprehension isn't moving your eyes across a page more quickly. It's about creating a mental framework that helps you process words and ideas.

With a bit of practice, anyone can read faster and more productively. The steps outlined here will help you to extract the maximum amount of information in the least amount of time.

Nearly all speed reading courses recommend doing a pre-reading survey. The purpose is to gain a better understanding of the content and structure of the material. You'd be amazed how often people read through an entire book, only to realise that the information they need isn't there. Pre-reading will make your reading more efficient by creating a mental map. Have a look at some of these tips to help you read with speed and understand with ease.

Define Your Purpose

Take a general look at the text in your hand. Now that you have a general grasp of the material, you need to define a purpose. What information are you hoping to gain? This sounds like a simple question, but sometimes it isn't. Different readers can have drastically different objectives. If you don't define a purpose, it's likely you'll get bogged down by unimportant sections or ignore crucial ones. By clarifying what you need to know, you'll be able to distinguish the important from the irrelevant and allocate your attention accordingly.

Create questions the reading should answer

In addition to a general purpose, it's also helpful to write down specific questions. This focuses your mind on a set of objectives and gives you a way to measure comprehension. By writing down questions, you create a set of mental cues. Whenever you spot an important keyword in the text, you'll become aware of the question it relates to and your mind will start looking for an answer.

Take notes or highlight important concepts

One of the best ways to embed something in your memory is to write it down. When you read an important point, make a note of it on a separate piece of paper, inside the margin, or use a highlighter. This will help you remember what you read and make the important sections easy to find when you review the text.

Importance of Reading

Reading is a vital skill required to develop one's understanding of the English language. It's really important that you start reading as soon as possible because this is a skill that will prove integral to your everyday life should you choose to live in an English speaking environment.

For example, if a student is travelling in another country they may need to be able to read a timetable, a road sign or even the instructions for their new bicycle.

One needs to develop a plethora of skills including understanding the key concepts of a piece of literature and effectively scanning their text.

When choosing practice texts, try to choose topics which you are already interested in.

General reading activities

When learning to read English you need to ensure that your talk time is high. Activities are a great way to do this and they will help you to work out how you have understood from the text you have been reading.

- Do-it-yourself question – can be done in groups or pairs. Students write comprehension questions for other students to answer.
- Come up with a title for a story.
- Summarize a story.
- Continue the story – students offer suggestions as to what happens next.
- Preface to the story – students offer suggestions as to what happened before the story began.
- Revision – students are given the pictures from a storyboard of the text and have to put them in order.
- Fill in the gap – students are given a text with certain words missing and have to fill them in appropriately.
- Correct mistakes – students are given two texts and through asking each other questions they identify and correct any mistakes.
- Discussion about themes present in the text.

Additional pre-reading activities

When reading a text with a class or a group of people, it's usually a good idea to do one or more pre-reading activities to get their attention and raise their interest. This will ensure that the students are interested in the reading exercise and it will also give all the opportunity to be introduced to new vocabulary that will help them understand the text better.

- Give the students the title of the text you are going to be looking at and let them suggest ideas as to what will happen in the story.
- Rearrange the words in the title of a text for your students to put back into the correct order.
- Pre-teach necessary vocabulary, if you are working with new or particularly difficult language, to help students understand the text.

Additional activities to be carried out during the reading of text

Asking students to simply read the text is often much less effective than working through the text with your students. In some cultures when faced with something they don't know, be it a word or a tense, they will just stop and it's important that you pick up on this as quickly as possible so you don't waste any time. Using activities as you read through the text is a good way of doing this.

- Rearrange paragraphs or sentences of the text for students to put back in the correct order.
- Give the students pictures of events in the story which students put in order as they read the text.
- Give the students a text containing deliberate mistakes for the students to identify.
- Omit words in a text, giving the students a list of words with which to fill in the gaps.
- Replace certain words with a picture to help students work out what the missing word is.

Additional post-reading activities

You should always follow up your reading activities with a post-reading activity. This will give students the opportunity to practice their reading and will reiterate what you have taught them in the lesson. Most importantly, however, it will give the exercise a sense of meaning so that your students feel they have achieved something.

- Students create tasks such as filling in the gaps, for other students.
- Students write a letter from, or a conversation between characters in the text.
- Students each assume a role of a character in the text and act out all or part of the text.

Introduction to Reading

Reading is a complex developmental challenge that we know to be intertwined with many other developmental accomplishments: attention, memory, language, and motivation, for example, Reading is not only a cognitive psycholinguistic activity but also a social activity.

Being a good reader in English means that one has gained functional knowledge of the principles of the English alphabetic writing system. Young children gain functional knowledge of the parts, products, and uses of the writing system from their ability to attend to and analyse the external sound structure of spoken words.

Understanding the basic alphabetic principle requires an awareness that spoken language can be analysed into strings of separable words, and words, in turn, into sequences of syllables and phonemes within syllables.

Beyond knowledge about how the English writing system works, though, there is a point in a student's growth when we expect 'real reading' to start. Children are expected, without help, to read some unfamiliar texts, relying on the print and drawing meaning from it. There are many reasons why children have difficulty learning to read. These issues and problems led to the initiation of this study.

Development Before Kindergarten: The First Five Years

Learning to read and write begins long before the school years, as the biological, cognitive, and social precursors are put into place. One of the most important preconditions for literacy is the integrity of a child's health and sensory organs, since the window for the establishment of such skills as language is relatively brief.

The child's intelligence, as long as it is in the normal range, does not have much of an impact on the ease of learning to read. The capacity to learn to read and write is related to children's age-related developmental timetables, although there is no clear agreement on the precise chronological or mental age nor on a particular developmental level that children must reach before they are 'ready' to learn to read and write.

Children gain an increasingly complex and de contextualized understanding of the world as their brains develop during their first years of life. As they grow and gain experience, new neural connections are established at irregular rates, with spurts and plateaus. Although this process is orderly, it is variable among individual children due to differences in both biological and experiential influences.

Children who become successful readers tend to exhibit age-appropriate sensory, perceptual, cognitive, and social skills as they progress through the preschool years. Through the interaction of maturation and experience, they become increasingly adept at mastering physical dexterity and locomotion, at categorizing and constructing relationships between physical objects, at remembering facts and events over time, at engaging in imaginative play, at forming social relationships, and so forth.

Of course, many factors in an infant's life can affect development, ranging from maternal mental and physical health to conditions of housing, temperament, nutrition, and emotional stress and support. Although all these can have an impact on later literacy development via their impact on general development, we focus in this chapter on factors that differentially affect reading. Counting, number concepts, letter names and shapes, phonological awareness, interest in literacy, and cooperation with peers are some of the preschool accomplishments that are of particular relevance to later academic challenges.

Developing Reading Activities

Developing reading activities involves more than identifying a text that is 'at the right level', writing a set of comprehension questions for students to answer after reading, handing out the assignment and sending students away to do it. A fully-developed reading activity supports students as readers through prereading, while-reading, and post-reading activities.

While choosing reading tasks, keep in mind that the reader should be able to recall of all the information in a text is an unrealistic expectation. Reading activities that are meant to increase communicative competence should be success oriented and build up students' confidence in their reading ability.

Construct the reading activity around a purpose that has significance for the students

Make sure students understand what the purpose for reading is: to get the main idea, obtain specific information, understand most or the entire message, enjoy a story, or decide whether or not to read more. Recognizing the purpose for reading will help students select appropriate reading strategies.

Define the activity's instructional goal and the appropriate type of response

In addition to the main purpose for reading, an activity can also have one or more instructional purposes, such as practicing or reviewing specific grammatical constructions, introducing new vocabulary, or familiarizing students with the typical structure of a certain type of text.

Check the level of difficulty of the text

The factors listed below can help you judge the relative ease or difficulty of a reading text for a particular purpose and a particular group of students.

- How is the information organized? Does the story line, narrative, or instruction conform to familiar expectations? Texts in which the events are presented in natural chronological order, which have an informative title, and which present the information following an obvious organisation (main ideas first, details and examples second) are easier to follow.
- How familiar are the students with the topic? Remember that misapplication of background knowledge due to cultural differences can create major comprehension difficulties.
- Does the text contain redundancy? At the lower levels of proficiency, listeners may find short, simple messages easier to process, but students with higher proficiency benefit from the natural redundancy of authentic language.
- Does the text offer visual support to aid in reading comprehension? Visual aids such as photographs, maps, and diagrams help students preview the content of the text, guess the meanings of unknown words, and check comprehension while reading.

Remember that the level of difficulty of a text is not the same as the level of difficulty of a reading task. Students who lack the vocabulary to identify all of the items on a menu can still determine whether the restaurant serves steak and whether they can afford to order one.

Use pre-reading activities to prepare students for reading

The activities you use during pre-reading may serve as preparation in several ways. During pre-reading you may:

- Assess students' background knowledge of the topic and linguistic content of the text.

- Give students the background knowledge necessary for comprehension of the text, or activate the existing knowledge that the students possess.
- Clarify any cultural information which may be necessary to comprehend the passage.
- Make students aware of the type of text they will be reading and the purpose(s) for reading.
- Provide opportunities for group or collaborative work and for class discussion activities.

Here are some sample pre-reading activities:

- Use the title, subtitles, and divisions within the text to predict content and organisation or sequence of information.
- Look at pictures, maps, diagrams, or graphs and their captions.
- Talk about the author's background, writing style, and usual topics.
- Skim to find the theme or main idea and eliciting related prior knowledge.
- Review vocabulary or grammatical structures.
- Read over the comprehension questions to focus attention on finding that information while reading.
- Construct semantic webs (a graphic arrangement of concepts or words showing how they are related).
- Do guided practice with guessing meaning from context or checking comprehension while reading.

Pre-reading activities are most important at lower levels of language proficiency and at earlier stages of reading instruction. As students become more proficient at using reading strategies, you will be able to reduce the amount of guided pre-reading and allow students to do these activities themselves.

Match while-reading activities for the purpose for reading

In while-reading activities, students check their comprehension as they read. The purpose for reading determines the appropriate type and level of comprehension.

- When reading for specific information, students need to ask themselves, have I obtained the information I was looking for?
- When reading for pleasure, students need to ask themselves, Do I understand the story line/sequence of ideas well enough to enjoy reading this?
- When reading for thorough understanding (intensive reading), students need to ask themselves, Do I understand each main idea and how the author supports it? Does what I'm reading agree with my predictions, and, if not, how does it differ? To check comprehension in this situation, students may
    - stop at the end of each section to review and check their predictions, restate the main idea and summarize the section;
    - use the comprehension questions as guides to the text, stopping to answer them as they read.

■■■

CHAPTER 2

Beginner's Reading Comprehension

Reading Strategies for Upstart Child

Prior Knowledge

What readers bring to the printed page affects their comprehension. Some insist that the prior knowledge of readers is the single most important component in the reading process.

Some claim that the printed page of the writer merely serves to stimulate ideas already in readers' heads and may cause, at best, only highlighting and possible restructuring of these ideas in a fresh way. Others believe that the text is simply a blueprint from which readers build their own meaning.

Because current theories of comprehension recognize the importance if not the primacy of prior knowledge, activation of this must be included in the comprehension process.

Prior knowledge refers to all the knowledge which readers have acquired through their lives. Some theorists use the term prior knowledge synonymously with *world knowledge, background knowledge, memory storage,* or *experiential background.*

Schema Theory

Of all the recent research and speculation about the comprehension process, that associated with schema theory seems to have had the most unique impact. Because of its influence, it is important to define and review it.

Schema theory is a theory about knowledge, about how knowledge is represented, and about how that representation facilitates the use of knowledge in various ways. According to schema theorists, all knowledge is packaged into units called schemata, and embedded into these units of knowledge is information on how this knowledge is to be used.

Each separate schema is a device for representing knowledge of a concept, along with specifications for relating it to an appropriate network of connections that seem to hold all components of that particular concept.

Individuals acquire schemata through their experiences - both real and vicarious. As individuals have more experiences, they refine, reshape, correct, and restructure their schemata. As adult's, schema for the word *teacher* is seldom the same as it is for a first grader. Through life experiences, schema adjustments are made as adults continue having more experiences with teachers. One of the major problems involved in comprehension is that all people hardly ever share the same schemata; one of the problems in reading comprehension is that readers do not always old the same schemata as do the writers.

Strategies to Activate Prior Knowledge

Brainstorming: In these sessions, teachers ask students to examine together the title of the selection they are about to read. The teacher lists on the board all the information that comes to mind as students read the title. These pieces of information are then used to further recall, and in the process considerable knowledge will be activated.

Class Discussions: Class discussions and informal talks in and out of class all serve as techniques to discover more about what students bring to their reading. Over a period of time, teachers can begin to get some idea as to what their students know and can adjust how much time needs to be spent on background information.

Semantic Mapping: Students still use brainstorming strategies in semantic mapping; however this strategy is organized and controlled by the teacher. As students offer their personal ideas about a topic, the teacher writes these ideas on the board. In brainstorming, all ideas are written on the board. In semantic mapping, ideas are organised on the board underheadings. The diagram represents the information elicited from the students but created in such a way that qualities and relationships are evident. During active reading, students may also use semantic maps. As they read, they include new information on their maps. During post-reading, students can use their maps as a review of information gained.

Prequestions: Whenever teachers or students decided on questions to be answered by reading, they are activating prior knowledge. These questions tend to focus attention and provide for purposeful reading. Teachers can accomplish this by preparing questions in advance of reading. This will help in guiding students as they complete their reading assignment. The teacher can also help students develop their own questions which will help them establish purpose and focus attention.

Visual Aids: Pictures and other visual material can activate a students' prior knowledge. If a student has some schema for *fossils,* a simple picture may serve to retrieve appropriate knowledge. Thus a teacher may share this photograph of a fossil before students read a science textbook chapter on fossils. The picture serves to activate the students' schemata on fossils.

Advance Organisers: Advance organizers are specific types of cognitive organizers. They are a means of helping students relate the new reading material to something they already know. If material can be related to the learner's background and experiences, it can be meaningful. When these organizers are skilfully prepared, these help to activate knowledge students possess while at the same time helping them to see it in relation to the material they are about to read. Many textbooks provide well-written advance organizers within their books to guide students. If these are not available, teachers may create their own. Several ideas of uses of graphic organizers have been included within the various strategy sections.

Increasing Prior Knowledge

Accretion: Accretion involves putting new information into schemata already possessed. Each time something new is taught or even referred to it in class, traces of it are left in students' memory. Hopefully, over time and through enough classroom discussion and experience, the students' schema will become more fully formed and this will help them to better understand the text.

Tuning: Tuning happens when students reshape and modify information until it works for the them. Tuning involves only minor changes in schemata.

Reconstruction: Reconstruction represents major changes in schemata. When students learn something that goes against what they have previously thought to be true, reconstruction takes place. New schemata must be built to replace existing schemata. Reconstructing is the most difficult step in schemata adjustments because existing schemata tends to get in the way

Strategies to Increase Prior Knowledge

Build on What They Already Know: Question students as to what they already know regarding the assigned selection. Expand on the terms and information they already understand. Elicit a large number of associations from the students to the prior knowledge they already possess and help them see the connections.

Increase Background Information: Increase the amount of background information by providing more in-depth ideas regarding the topic. This will help the students understand the selection at a higher level.

Real-Life Experiences: Actual experience is the best way to develop and refine the schemata that make up readers' prior knowledge. To impact a student's memory, they must see, touch, use, and experience real objects or situations. If possible, provide any real-life experiences that have to do with the assignment. Even something done on a small level will help with students' understanding.

Vicarious Experiences Through Wide Reading: Wide reading is important in providing students with information about people, places, events and situations. Even though direct experience is preferred, many times it is not possible. However, experiences lived vicariously through reading can produce tremendous results.

Additional Pre-reading Strategies

Overviews: Discussing information about the selection or assignment prior to reading must take place. This may take the form of class discussions, printed previews, photographs, outlines, or films. Never give an assignment before this step has been completed. Spend enough time before the students begin the assignment to insure understanding of it.

Vocabulary Previews: Unfamiliar key words need to be taught to students before reading so that new words, background information, and comprehension can improve together.

List all words in the assignment that may be important for students to understand. Arrange words to show the relationships to the learning task. Add words students probably already understand to connect relationships between what is known and the unknown. Share information with students. Verbally quiz them on the information before assigned reading begins.

Structural Organisers: Before reading an assignment, basic frameworks which are included in the text should be pointed out such as cause-effect or problem-solution. It can be beneficial to call attention to specific plans of paragraph or text organisation such as signal words, main idea sentences, highlighted phrases, headings and subtitles. A review of skimming techniques might also be appropriate as these various areas are covered.

A Purpose for Reading: When students have a purpose for reading a selection, they find that purpose not only directs their reading towards a goal, but helps to focus their attention. Purposes may come from teacher directed questions, questions from class discussions or brainstorming, or from the individual student. Along with the question, it is a good idea to pose predictions of the outcome and problems which need to be solved. These may be generated by the student or the teacher, but the teacher should use these to guide students in the needed direction for the assigned selection.

Author Consideration: Depending upon the content area, a discussion of the author of the particular work can be helpful to the understanding of it. What is the author trying to say? What is his point of view and his reason for writing the particular work?

Practice Exercises

Christmas Present

David wants to buy a Christmas present for a very special person, his mother. David's father gives him Rs 500 a week pocket money and David puts Rs 200 a week into his bank account. After three months David takes Rs 2000 out of his bank account and goes to the shopping mall. He looks for a perfect gift.

Suddenly he sees a beautiful brooch in the shape of his favourite pet. He says to himself, "My mother loves jewelry, and the brooch costs only Rs 1700." He buys the brooch and takes it home. He wraps the present in Christmas paper and places it under the tree. He is very excited and he is looking forward to Christmas morning to see the joy on his mother's face.

But when his mother opens the present she screams with fright because she sees a spider.

1. What does David want to buy his Mother?

a) a special birthday present

b) a Christmas present

c) a spider ring

Ans. a Christmas present.

2. Who does David get his money from?

a) his pet

b) is mother

c) his father

Ans. his father.

3. How much money does David take to the mall?

a) Rs 2000

b) Rs 500

c) Rs 1700

Ans. Rs. 2000.

4. What does David buy his mother?

a) a ring

b) a brooch

c) a spider

Ans. a brooch.

5. What does David do with the present when he takes it home?

a) he gives it to his mother

b) he wraps it in Christmas paper

c) he is very excited

Ans. he wraps it in Christmas paper.

6. Why does David's mother scream?

a) because the present is beautiful

b) because she doesn't like Christmas presents

c) because she thinks she sees a real spider

Ans. because she thinks she sees a real spider.

7. Why does David buy a spider brooch?
   a) spiders are his favourite pet
   b) he loves Christmas
   c) to scare his mother

   Ans. spiders are his favourite pet.

8. Where does David put the present on Christmas Eve?
   a) under his pillow
   b) under a spider
   c) under the Christmas tree

   Ans. under the Christmas tree.

Two Sisters and the Cat

Mrs Bhatia and Mrs Kapoor are sisters. Mrs Bhatia lives in a house in Duncan and Mrs. Kapoor lives in a condominium in Victoria. One day Mrs Bhatia visited her sister. When her sister answered the door, Mrs Bhatia saw tears in her eyes. "What's the matter?" she asked. Mrs. Kapoor said "My cat Sammy died last night and I have no place to bury him".

She began to cry again. Mrs. Bhatia was very sad because she knew her sister loved the cat very much. Suddenly Mrs Bhatia said "I can bury your cat in my garden in Duncan and you can come and visit him sometimes." Mrs. Kapoor stopped crying and the two sisters had tea together and a nice visit.

It was now five o'clock and Mrs Bhatia said it was time for her to go home. She put on her hat, coat and gloves and Mrs Kapoor put the dead Sammy into a shopping bag. Mrs. Bhatia took the shopping bag and walked to the bus stop. She waited a long time for the bus so she bought a newspaper. When the bus arrived, she got on the bus, sat down and put the shopping bag on the floor beside her feet. She then began to read the newspaper. When the bus arrived at her bus stop, she got off the bus and walked for about two minutes. Suddenly she remembered she had left the shopping bag on the bus.

1. Where does Mrs. Kapoor live?
   a) in a condominium in Duncan
   b) in a condominium in Victoria
   c) in a house in Duncan

   Ans. in a condominium in Victoria.
2. Why is Mrs Kapoor upset?
   a) because her sister came to see her cat
   b) because her cat died.
   c) because Mrs. Bhatia was sad.

   Ans. because her cat died.
3. What did Mrs. Bhatia do ?
   a) Take the cat with her on the bus.
   b) Put her gloves in the shopping bag
   c) Prepare dinner for her sister.

   Ans. take the cat with her on the bus.
4. Who did Sammy the cat live with?
   a) Mrs. Bhatia
   b) Mrs. Kapoor
   c) Mrs. Bhatia and Mrs Kapoor.

   Ans. Mrs. Kapoor
5. What time did Mrs. Bhatia go home?
   a) When the bus arrived.
   b) At 5 pm
   c) After she walked for two minutes.

   Ans. At 5 pm.

6. How did Mrs. Bhatia go home?
 a) Walked for two minutes before she caught the bus.
 b) Read a newspaper on the bus.
 c) Took a bus.

 Ans. Took a bus.

7. What did Mrs. Bhatia forget ?
 a) The newspaper
 b) Her handbag
 c) The shopping bag

 Ans. The shopping bag.

Ferdinand Magellan's Explorations

In the sixteenth century, an age of great marine and terrestrial exploration, Ferdinand Magellan led the first expedition to sail around the world. As a young Portuguese noble, he served the king of Portugal, but he became involved in the quagmire of political intrigue at court and lost the king's favour. After he was dismissed from service to the king of Portugal, he offered to serve the future Emperor Charles V of Spain.

A papal decree of 1493 had assigned all land in the New World west of 50 degrees W longitude to Spain and all the land east of that line to Portugal. Magellan offered to prove that the East Indies fell under Spanish authority. On September 20, 1519, Magellan set sail from Spain with five ships. More than a year later, one of these ships was exploring the topography of South America in search of a water route across the continent. This ship sank, but the remaining four ships searched along the southern peninsula of South America. Finally, they found the passage they sought near a latitude of 50 degrees S. Magellan named this passage the Strait of All Saints, but today we know it as the Strait of Magellan.

One ship deserted while in this passage and returned to Spain, so fewer sailors were privileged to gaze at that first panorama of the Pacific Ocean. Those who remained crossed the meridian we now call the International Date Line in the early spring of 1521 after ninety-eight days on the Pacific Ocean. During those long days at sea, many of Magellan's men died of starvation and disease.

Later Magellan became involved in an insular conflict in the Philippines and was killed in a tribal battle. Only one ship and seventeen sailors under the command of the Basque navigator Elcano survived to complete the westward journey to Spain and thus prove once and for all that the world is round, with no precipice at the edge.

1. The sixteenth century was an age of great ___exploration.

   a) cosmic

   b) land

   c) mental

   d) common man

   e) none of the above

   Ans. land.

2. Magellan lost the favour of the king of Portugal when he became involved in a political ___.

   a) entanglement

   b) discussion

   c) negotiation

   d) problems

   e) none of the above

   Ans. entanglement.

3. The Pope divided New World lands between Spain and Portugal according to their location on one side or the other of an imaginary geographical line 50 degrees west of Greenwich that extends in a ___ direction.

   a) north and south

b) crosswise

c) easterly

d) south east

e) north and west

Ans. north and south.

4. One of Magellan's ships explored the ___ of South America for a passage across the continent.

a) coastline

b) mountain range

c) physical features

d) islands

e) none of the above

Ans. physical features.

5. Four of the ships sought a passage along a southern ___.

a) coast

b) inland

c) body of land with water on three sides

d) border

e) answer not available

Ans. body of land with water on three sides.

6. The passage was found near 50 degrees S of ___.

a) Greenwich

b) The equator

c) Spain

d) Portugal

e) Madrid

Ans. The equator.

7. In the spring of 1521, the ships crossed the ___ now called the International Date Line.

a) imaginary circle passing through the poles

b) imaginary line parallel to the equator

c) area

d) land mass

e) answer not found in article

Ans. imaginary circle passing through the poles.

Madam Marie Curie

Marie Curie was one of the most accomplished scientists in history. Together with her husband, Pierre, she discovered radium, an element widely used for treating cancer, and studied uranium and other radioactive substances. Pierre and Marie's amicable collaboration later helped to unlock the secrets of the atom.

Marie was born in 1867 in Warsaw, Poland, where her father was a professor of physics. At the early age, she displayed a brilliant mind and a blithe personality. Her great exuberance for learning prompted her to continue with her studies after high school. She became disgruntled, however, when she learned that the university in Warsaw was closed to women. Determined to receive a higher education, she defiantly left Poland and in 1891 entered the Sorbonne, a French university, where she earned her master's degree and doctorate in physics.

Marie was fortunate to have studied at the Sorbonne with some of the greatest scientists of her day, one of whom was Pierre Curie. Marie and Pierre were married in 1895 and spent many productive years working together in the physics labouratory. A short time after they discovered radium, Pierre was killed by a horse-drawn wagon in 1906. Marie was stunned by this horrible misfortune and endured heartbreaking anguish. Despondently she recalled their close relationship and the joy that they had shared in scientific research. The fact that she had two young daughters to raise by herself greatly increased her distress.

Curie's feeling of desolation finally began to fade when she was asked to succeed her husband as a physics professor at the Sorbonne. She was the first woman to be given a professorship at the world-famous university. In 1911, she received the Nobel Prize in chemistry for isolating radium. Although Marie Curie eventually suffered a fatal illness from her long exposure to radium, she never became disillusioned about her work. Regardless of the consequences, she had dedicated herself to science and to revealing the mysteries of the physical world.

1. The Curies' ____ collaboration helped to unlock the secrets of the atom.

a) friendly

b) competitive

c) courteous

d) industrious

e) chemistry

Ans. friendly.

2. Marie had a bright mind and a __ personality.

a) strong

b) lighthearted

c) humorous

d) strange

e) envious

Ans. light hearted.

3. When she learned that she could not attend the university in Warsaw, she felt___.

a) hopeless

b) annoyed

c) depressed

d) worried

e) none of the above

Ans. annoyed.

4. Marie ___ by leaving Poland and traveling to France to enter the Sorbonne.

a) challenged authority

b) showed intelligence

c) behaved

d) was distressed

e) answer not available in article

Ans. challenged authority.

5. _____she remembered their joy together.

a) Dejectedly

b) Worried

c) Tearfully

d) Happily

e) Sorrowfully

Ans. dejectedly.

6. Her ____ began to fade when she returned to the Sorbonne to succeed her husband.

a) misfortune

b) anger

c) wretchedness

d) disappointment

e) ambition

Ans. wretchedness.

7. Even though she became fatally ill from working with radium, Marie Curie was never ____.

a) troubled

b) worried

c) disappointed

d) sorrowful

e) disturbed

Ans. disappointed.

Mount Vesuvius

Mount Vesuvius, a volcano located between the ancient Italian cities of Pompeii and Herculaneum, has received much attention because of its frequent and destructive eruptions. The most famous of these eruptions occurred in A. D. 79.

The volcano had been inactive for centuries. There was little warning of the coming eruption, although one account unearthed by archaeologists says that a hard rain and a strong wind had disturbed the celestial calm during the preceding night. Early the next morning, the volcano poured a huge river of molten rock down upon Herculaneum, completely burying the city and filling in the harbour with coagulated lava.

Meanwhile, on the other side of the mountain, cinders, stone and ash rained down on Pompeii. Sparks from the burning ash ignited the combustible rooftops quickly. Large portions of the city were destroyed in the conflagration. Fire, however, was not the only cause of destruction. Poisonous sulphuric gases saturated the air. These heavy gases were not buoyant in the atmosphere and therefore sank toward the earth and suffocated people.

Over the years, excavations of Pompeii and Herculaneum have revealed a great deal about the behaviour of the volcano. By analysing data, much as a zoologist dissects a specimen animal, scientist have concluded that the eruption changed large portions of the area's geography. For instance, it turned the Sarno River from its course and raised the level of the beach along the Bay of Naples. Meteorologists studying these events have also concluded that Vesuvius caused a huge tidal wave that affected the world's climate.

In addition to making these investigations, archaeologists have been able to study the skeletons of victims by using distilled water to wash away the volcanic ash. By strengthening the brittle bones with acrylic paint, scientists have been able to examine the skeletons and draw conclusions about the diet and habits of the residents. Finally, the excavations at both Pompeii and Herculaneum have yielded many examples of classical art, such as jewelry made of bronze, which is an alloy of copper and tin.

The eruption of Mount Vesuvius and its tragic consequences have provided us with a wealth of data about the effects that volcanoes can have on the surrounding area. Today volcanologists can locate and predict eruptions, saving lives and preventing the destruction of cities and cultures.

1. Herculaneum and its harbour were buried under ___lava.

a) liquid

b) solid

c) flowing

d) gas

e) answer not available

Ans. solid.

2. The poisonous gases were not ___ in the air.

a) able to float

b) visible

c) able to evaporate

d) invisible

e) able to condense

Ans. able to float.

3. Scientists analysed data about Vesuvius in the same way that a zoologist ___ a specimen.

a) describes in detail

b) studies by cutting apart

c) photographs

d) chart

e) answer not available

Ans. studies by cutting apart.

4. ____have concluded that the volcanic eruption caused a tidal wave.

a) Scientist who study oceans

b) Scientist who study atmospheric conditions

c) Scientist who study ash

d) Scientist who study animal behaviour

e) None of the above

Ans. Scientist who study atmospheric conditions.

5. Scientist have used ___water to wash away volcanic ash from the skeletons of victims.

a) bottled

b) volcanic

c) purified

d) sea

e) fountain

Ans. purified.

The Trojan War

The Trojan War is one of the most famous wars in history. It is well known for the ten-year duration, for the heroism of a number of legendary characters, and for the Trojan horse. What may not be familiar, however, is the story of how the war began.

According to Greek myth, the strife between the Trojans and the Greeks started at the wedding of Peleus, King of Thessaly, and Thetis, a sea nymph. All of the gods and goddesses had been invited to the wedding celebration in Troy except Eris, goddesses of discord. She had been omitted from the guest list because her presence always embroiled mortals and immortals alike in conflict.

To take revenge on those who had slighted her, Eris decided to cause a skirmish. Into the middle of the banquet hall, she threw a golden apple marked "for the most beautiful." All of the goddesses began to haggle over who should possess it. The gods and goddesses reached a stalemate when the choice was narrowed to Hera, Athena, and Aphrodite. Someone was needed to settle the controversy by picking a winner. The job eventually fell to Paris, son of King Priam of Troy, who was said to be a good judge of beauty.

Paris did not have an easy job. Each goddess, eager to win the golden apple, tried aggressively to bribe him.

"I'll grant you vast kingdoms to rule, " promised Hera. "Vast kingdoms are nothing in comparison with my gift," contradicted Athena. "Choose me and I'll see that you win victory and fame in war." Aphrodite outdid her adversaries, however. She won the golden apple by offering Helen, Zeus' daughter and the most beautiful mortal, to Paris. Paris, anxious to claim Helen, set off for Sparta in Greece.

Although Paris learned that Helen was married, he accepted the hospitality of her husband, King Menelasu of Sparta, anyway. Therefore, Menelaus was outraged for a number of reasons when Paris departed, taking Helen and much of the king's wealth back to Troy. Menelaus collected his loyal forces and set sail for Troy to begin the war to reclaim Helen.

1. Eris was known for ___both mortals and immortals.

a) scheming against

b) involving in conflict

c) feeling hostile toward

d) ignoring

e) comforting

Ans. involving in conflict.

2. Each goddess tried ___to bribe Paris.

a) boldly

b) effectively

c) secretly

d) carefully

e) answer not stated

Ans. boldly.

3. Athena ___ Hera, promising Paris victory and fame in war.

a) denied the statement of

b) defeated

c) agreed with

d) restated the statement

e) questioned the statement

Ans. denied the statement of.

The Start of Flight

Many great inventions are greeted with ridicule and disbelief. The invention of the airplane was no exception. Although many people who heard about the first powered flight on December 17,1903, were excited and impressed, others reacted with peals of laughter. The idea of flying an aircraft was repulsive to some people. Such people called Wilbur and Orville Wright, the inventors of the first flying machine, impulsive fools. Negative reactions, however, did not stop the Wrights. Impelled by their desire to succeed, they continued their experiments in aviation.

Orville and Wilbur Wright had always had a compelling interest in aeronautics and mechanics. As young boys they earned money by making and selling kites and mechanical toys. Later, they designed a newspaper-folding machine, built a printing press, and operated a bicycle-repair shop. In 1896, when they read about the death of Otto Lilienthal, the brother's interest in flight grew into a compulsion.

Lilienthal, a pioneer in hang-gliding, had controlled his gliders by shifting his body in the desired direction. This idea was repellent to the Wright brothers, however, and they searched for more efficient methods to control the balance of airborne vehicles. In 1900 and 1901, the Wrights tested numerous gliders and developed control techniques. The brothers' inability to obtain enough lift power for the gliders almost led them to abandon their efforts.

After further study, the Wright brothers concluded that the published tables of air pressure on curved surfaces must be wrong. They set up a wind tunnel and began a series of experiments with model wings. Because of their efforts, the old tables were repealed in time and replaced by the first reliable figures for air pressure on curved surfaces. This work, in turn, made it possible for them to design a machine that would fly. In 1903, the Wrights built their first airplane, which cost less than one thousand dollars. They even designed and built their own source of propulsion–a lightweight gasoline engine. When they started the engine on December 17, the airplane pulsated wildly before taking off. The plane managed to stay aloft for twelve seconds, however, and it flew one hundred twenty feet.

By 1905, the Wrights had perfected the first airplane that could turn, circle, and remain airborne for half an hour at a time. Others had flown in balloons or in hang gliders, but the Wright brothers were the first to build a full-size machine that could fly under its own power. As the contributors of one of the most outstanding engineering achievements in history, the Wright brothers are accurately called the fathers of aviation.

1. The idea of flying an aircraft was ___to some people.

a) boring

b) distasteful

c) exciting

d) needless

e) answer not available

Ans. distasteful.

2. People thought that the Wright brothers had ____.

a) acted without thinking

b) been negatively influenced

c) been too cautious

d) had not given enough thought

e) acted in a negative way

Ans. acted without thinking.

3. The Wright's interest in flight grew into a ____.

a) financial empire

b) plan

c) need to act

d) foolish thought

e) answer not in article

Ans. need to act.

4. Lilenthal's idea about controlling airborne vehicles was ___the Wrights.

a) proven wrong by

b) opposite to the ideas of

c) disliked by

d) accepted by

e) opposed by

Ans. disliked by.

5. The old tables were __ and replaced by the first reliable figures for air pressure on curved surfaces.
   a) destroyed
   b) canceled
   c) multiplied
   d) discarded
   e) not used

   Ans. canceled.

6. The Wrights designed and built their own source of ____.
   a) force for moving forward
   b) force for turning around
   c) turning
   d) force to going backward
   e) none of the above

   Ans. force for moving forward.

Floods

Floods are second only to fire as the most common of all natural disasters. They occur almost everywhere in the world, resulting in widespread damage and even death. Consequently, scientists have long tried to perfect their ability to predict floods. So far, the best that scientists can do is to recognise the potential for flooding in certain conditions. There are a number of conditions, from deep snow on the ground to human error, that cause flooding.

When deep snow melts it creates a large amount of water. Although deep snow alone rarely causes floods, when it occurs together with heavy rain and sudden warmer weather it can lead to serious flooding. If there is a fast snow melt on top of frozen or very wet ground, flooding is more likely to occur than when the ground is not frozen. Frozen ground or ground that is very wet and already saturated with water cannot absorb the additional water created by the melting snow. Melting snow also contributes to high water levels in rivers and streams. Whenever rivers are already at their full capacity of water, heavy rains will result in the rivers overflowing and flooding the surrounding land.

Rivers that are covered in ice can also lead to flooding. When ice begins to melt, the surface of the ice cracks and breaks into large pieces. These pieces of ice move and float down the river. They can form a dam in the river, causing the water behind the dam to rise and flood the land upstream. If the dam breaks suddenly, then the large amount of water held behind the dam can flood the areas downstream too.

Broken ice dams are not the only dam problems that can cause flooding. When a large human-made dam breaks or fails to hold the water collected behind it, the results can be devastating. Dams contain such huge amounts of water behind them that when sudden breaks occur, the destructive force of the water is like a great tidal wave. Unleashed dam waters can travel tens of kilometres, cover the ground in metres of mud and debris, and drown and crush everything and creature in their path.

Although scientists cannot always predict exactly when floods will occur, they do know a great deal about when floods are likely, or probably, going to occur. Deep snow, ice-covered rivers, and weak dams are all strong conditions for potential flooding. Hopefully, this knowledge of why floods happen can help us reduce the damage they cause.

1. Which of the following words are natural disasters?

   a) Flood

   b) Earthquake

   c) Airplane Crash

   d) Typhoon

   Ans. Flood, Earthquake, Typhoon.

2. Which of the following are included as causes for floods in the reading passage?

a) droughts

b) large lakes

c) poorly built roads

d) melting snow

Ans. melting snow.

3. How does deep snow cause flooding?

a) melting snow causes flooding

b) too much rain causes flooding

c) sudden warm temperatures combined with heavy rains causes flooding

d) freezing water causes flooding

Ans. melting snow causes flooding.

4. A broken human-made dam is compared to what?

a) a tsunami

b) a tidal wave

c) a broken ice dam

d) overflowing

Ans. tidal wave.

5. Which of the following best describes how a frozen river can cause a flood.

a) The ice in the river melts too quickly and causes a flood.

b) The ice in the river cracks causing the water to overflow.

c) The ice in the river cracks into pieces that eventually create a dam causing the water to overflow.

d) The water behind the ice dam collects and when the dam breaks, it causes flooding upstream.

Ans. The ice in the river cracks into pieces that eventually create a dam causing the water to overflow.

6. How far can dam water travel when it is unleashed from a broken dam?
   a) less than 10 kilometres
   b) tens of kilometres
   c) thousands of kilometres
   d) tens of thousands of kilometres downstream

   Ans. tens of kilometres.
7. Why does saturated ground contribute to flooding problems?
   a) the ground cannot absorb more moisture
   b) the ground is too hard, so the water runs off
   c) the ground forms a kind of dam
   d) it remains frozen

   Ans. the ground cannot absorb more moisture.
8. What kinds of problems can floods cause?
   a) death
   b) widespread damage
   c) destruction of plants and animals
   d) all of the above

   Ans. all of the above.
9. What is the most common natural disaster?
   a) flood
   b) fire
   c) wind damage
   d) rain

   Ans. fire.
10. How does melting snow cause problems related to flooding?
    a) it makes the rivers run too fast

b) it makes the water too cold

c) it causes pieces of ice to block the river

d) it makes the level of the river rise

Ans. it makes the level of the river rise.

Stress

There is a famous expression in English: "Stop the world, I want to get off!" This expression refers to a feeling of panic, or stress, that makes a person want to stop whatever they are doing, try to relax, and become calm again. 'Stress' means pressure or tension. It is one of the most common causes of health problems in modern life. Too much stress results in physical, emotional, and mental health problems.

There are numerous physical effects of stress. Stress can affect the heart. It can increase the pulse rate, make the heart miss beats, and can cause high blood pressure. Stress can affect the respiratory system. It can lead to asthma. It can cause a person to breathe too fast, resulting in a loss of important carbon dioxide. Stress can affect the stomach. It can cause stomach aches and problems digesting food. These are only a few examples of the wide range of illnesses and symptoms resulting from stress.

Emotions are also easily affected by stress. People suffering from stress often feel anxious. They may have panic attacks. They may feel tired all the time. When people are under stress, they often overreact to little problems. For example, a normally gentle parent under a lot of stress at work may yell at a child for dropping a glass of juice. Stress can make people angry, moody, or nervous.

Long-term stress can lead to a variety of serious mental illnesses. Depression, an extreme feeling of sadness and hopelessness, can be the result of continued and increasing stress. Alcoholism and other addictions often develop as a result of overuse of alcohol or drugs to try to relieve stress. Eating disorders, such as anorexia, are sometimes caused by stress and are often made worse by stress. If stress is allowed to continue, then one's mental health is put at risk.

It is obvious that stress is a serious problem. It attacks the body. It affects the emotions. Untreated, it may eventually result in mental illness. Stress has a great influence on the health and well-being of our bodies, our feelings, and our minds. So, reduce stress: stop the world and rest for a while.

1. Which of the following is not a common problem caused by stress?

a) physical problems

b) anecdotal problems

c) mental problems

d) emotional problems

Ans. anecdotal problems.

2. According to the essay, which of the following parts of the body does not have physical problems caused by stress.

a) the arms

b) the stomach

c) the lungs

d) the heart

Ans. the arms.

3. Choose the best answer to explain how alcoholism is caused by stress.

a) alcohol is used to relieve stress

b) alcohol is popular

c) alcohol is a chemical

d) alcohol is similar to medicine

Ans. alcohol is used to relieve stress.

4. Which of the following is not caused by long-term stress?

a) bloating

b) addiction

c) anorexia

d) alcoholism

Ans. bloating.

5. Stress can affect the heart by _________.

a) decreasing the pulse rate

b) causing asthma

c) a loss of carbon dioxide

d) causing breathing problems

Ans. decreasing the pulse rate.

6. Symptoms of emotional stress include _________.

a) feeling joyous

b) feeling hungry

c) feeling thirsty

d) feeling tired

Ans. feeling tired.

Butterflies

Butterflies are some of the most interesting insects on the planet Earth. There are more than seventeen thousand different kinds of butterflies! Butterflies come in all shapes and sizes..

Butterflies go through four main stages of life. The first stage is the egg stage followed by the larva stage. As a larva, or caterpillar, the future butterfly eats as much as possible. As it grows, it sheds it outer skin, or exoskeleton. This may happen four or five times. After a few weeks, the caterpillar enters the next stage of its life, the chrysalis stage. In the chrysalis, the caterpillar will liquefy into a soup of living cells. Then, it will reorganize into a butterfly and the metamorphosis is complete. In later parts of the chrysalis stage, you can see the forming butterfly through the chrysalis.

When the butterfly emerges from the chrysalis, it pumps its wings to send blood through them so that it can fly. Most butterflies only live a couple of weeks, just enough time to drink flower nectar and to mate. Some, like the Monarch Butterfly, however, may live many months.

1. In what stage does the metamorphosis happen?
   a) butterfly
   b) egg
   c) caterpillar
   d) chrysalis

   Ans. chrysalis.

2. What is the second stage of life for a butterfly?
   a) larva
   b) butterfly
   c) egg
   d) chrysalis

   Ans. larva

3. Why does the butterfly shed its skin?
   a) the butterfly is coming.
   b) it is hungry
   c) to defend itself against predators
   d) it is growing

   Ans. it is growing

4. Which of the following is NOT true?
   a) caterpillars turn into a liquid in the chrysalis
   b) butterflies must wait until blood drains into their wings before flying.

c) most butterflies live a short time

d) the butterfly may shed its skin 8 or 9 times

Ans. the butterfly may shed its skin 8 or 9 times

5. Which is true?

a) there is only one kind of butterfly in the world.

b) there are more than a thousand different kinds of butterflies in the world.

c) there are less than a thousand different kinds of butterflies in the world.

d) there are about a thousand different kinds of butterflies in the world.

Ans. there are more than a thousand different kinds of butterflies in the world.

Buffalo Hunters

The great herds of buffalo that roamed the plains were essential for all parts of Sioux life and society. For most Sioux villages, 'home' was wherever the herds of buffalo roamed.

Before the introduction of the horse, Sioux warriors would hunt the buffalo by dressing up as wolves as tricking them into running off of cliffs and ledges. They would also dress up in buffalo skins and make crying sounds like a baby buffalo. When an adult buffalo went to investigate, the warriors would kill it with spears and arrows.

The Sioux Indians used the entire buffalo following a kill. The buffalo hide was used for making tepees, clothes, moccasins, and robes. The hair was used to make rope and the horns were used as cups and dishes. Children fashioned sleds out of buffalo ribs, and buffalo fat was used as glue. Most importantly, buffalo meat provided food for the entire village. Much of the buffalo meat that was collected was cooked, dried, and pounded into pemmican (sort of like modern-day beef jerky).

1. Buffalo hair was used to make ________________.
   a) rope
   b) basket
   c) coat
   d) cloth

   Ans. rope

2. Buffalo ribs were used to make ________________.
   a) houses
   b) sleds
   c) boxes
   d) furniture

   Ans. sleds

3. Buffalo meat was not.....
   a) cooked
   b) fried
   c) dried
   d) pounded

   Ans. fried

4. Which of the following statements is true?
   a) the Sioux Indians were totally dependent on the buffalo.
   b) the Sioux Indians were not dependent on the buffalo.
   c) the Sioux Indians were somewhat dependent on the buffalo.
   d) the Sioux Indians were fairly dependent on the buffalo.

   Ans. the Sioux Indians were totally dependent on the buffalo.

5. What likely changed after the Sioux became familiar with the horse?
   a) the way buffalo meat was cooked and prepared.

b) hunting techniques

c) the way in which the buffalo was used for clothing

d) buffalo as the main source of food for the Sioux.

Ans. hunting techniques

6. Buffalo hides were not used for ....

a) tepees

b) moccasins

c) cups

d) robes

Ans. cups

7. A Sioux hunter dressing up as a wolf in an attempt to scare a buffalo is an example of ......

a) selfishness

b) selflessness

c) worship

d) imitation

Ans. imitation

8. The introduction of the horse probably made the Sioux more _______________.

a) efficient at hunting

b) effective in battle

c) mobile

d) all of the above

Ans. all of the above

9. Which of the following best describes the hunting techniques of the Sioux before the introduction of the horse?

a) resourceful

b) ravenous

c) selfish

d) strange

Ans. resourceful

10. In which of the following places would you be likely to find a buffalo herd?

a) open field

b) forest

c) swamp

d) beach

Ans. open field

Great White Sharks

The Great White Shark is the largest predatory shark, and is probably the most well-known and feared shark. The Great White Shark is gray or bluish above and white below. The largest Great Whites can reach lengths of 22 feet and weigh up to 5,000 pounds. Most are between 13 and 16 feet and weigh 1,500-2,400 pounds. The Great White has massive teeth, which are positioned in rows and serrated. When the Great White attacks, it bites its prey and shakes it head back and forth. The serrated teeth act as a saw and literally tear the victim apart. The Great White Shark often swallows many of its own teeth in an attack.

The Great White Shark normally feeds on fish, seals, dolphins, porpoises, otters, and turtles. It is thought to locate its prey by electrosense and by smell. Like all sharks, Great Whites have special pores called Ampullae of Lorenzini, which enable them to detect the electromagnetic fields radiated by moving organisms. Great Whites can detect voltage as small as one half billionth of a volt.

Great Whites employ several hunting techniques depending on the prey. Most of the time, the shark will remain still underwater before ambushing its prey from underneath. In the case of hunting some kinds of seals, the impact of the shark is so powerful that it knocks both the shark and the seal clear out of the water. With larger prey such as elephant seals, the shark will simply take a huge bite out of it and wait for it to bleed to death. When hunting dolphins, the shark will attack from above, presumably to avoid detection from the dolphin's echolocation.

Range/Habitat: Great White Sharks are most commonly observed throughout the world's sub-arctic coastal waters, though they likely spend most of their time in the open ocean. Highest concentrations are found in the waters off the coast of South Africa, Australia, California, and Mexico. The Great White Shark is also found in the Adriatic and Mediterranean Seas. They generally prefer water between 54 and 75 degrees Fahrenheit.

A Great White Shark has never been observed giving birth, however pregnant females have been caught. The Great White Shark is known to be ovoviviparous (young develop in eggs within the mother's body). Females give birth to eight or nine pups that are about five feet in length upon birth. Great Whites reach reproductive maturity when the male is about 12 feet long and the female about 13 feet long. It is thought that Great White Sharks live up to 40 years in the wild, but this estimate may be too low.

Despite the fear of Great White Sharks, at least in part generated by Steven Spielberg's 1975 movie, Jaws, Great White Sharks do not target humans as prey. Most attacks are attributed to mistaken identity. Sharks can easily mistake humans for seals. Many human injuries caused by Great White Sharks are cases of test-biting. If a shark is unsure about a floating object, it often gives it a test bite to determine what kind of object it is. While such bites do little damage to buoys and other objects, they obviously can inflict serious damage on the human body.

1. Which of the following is least likely?

a) finding a 15 foot long Great White Shark.

b) find a Great White Shark hunting a porpoise

c) find a Great White Shark that weighs 2,000 pounds

d) finding a Great White Shark in 85 degree (Fahrenheit) water.

Ans. finding a Great White Shark in 85 degree (Fahrenheit) water.

2. The maximum weight of MOST Great White Sharks is ____________ pounds.

a) 24,000

b) 4,200

c) 2,400

d) 5,000

Ans. 2,400

3. Select all of the following that are normal parts of the Great White Shark's diet.

a) seals

b) fish

c) dolphins

d) humans

Ans. Seals, Fish, Dolphins

4. The ______________________________ are specialized pores that allow a shark to detect magnetic fields of moving organisms.

a) echolocation

b) ampullae of Lorenzini

c) serrations

d) electomagnets

Ans. ampullae of Lorenzini

5. What does ovoviviparous mean?

a) it refers to animals whose young develop outside the mother's body.

b) it refers to animals that lay eggs

c) it refers to animals that do not lay eggs

d) it refers to animals whose young develop in eggs within the mother's body.

Ans. it refers to animals whose young develop in eggs within the mother's body.

6. You would have something in common with the Great White Shark if you.....

a) have four brothers and four sisters

b) spend most of your time near the shore

c) lived to be 80 years old

d) located your food by sound

Ans. have four brothers and four sisters

7. In which of the following places would you have the best chance to see a Great White Shark?

a) Mississippi River

b) Antarctica

c) Mediterranean Sea

d) coastal South Africa

Ans. coastal South Africa

8. Sharks often mistake humans for ________________.

a) seals

b) fish

c) reptiles

d) submarines

Ans. seals

9. Which of the following is NOT true?

a) Great White Sharks can detect prey by smell or by magnetic field.

b) Great White Sharks employ different hunting techniques depending on the prey they are stalking.

c) Great White Sharks often target humans as prey.

d) Great White Sharks swallow their own teeth during attacks.

Ans. Great White Sharks often target humans as prey.

10. Which of the following may or may not be true?

a) Great White Sharks have a life span of 40 years.

b) Great White Sharks have serrated teeth that act like saws.

c) Newborn Great White Sharks are about five feet in length.

d) The Great White Shark is actually only white on its underparts.

Ans. Great White Sharks have a life span of 40 years.

■■■

Chapter 3

Transitional Reading Comprehension

The level of one's understanding of a printed word is termed as **reading comprehension**.

Adept reading relies on a person's capability to make out words without delay and with no difficulty. If one has a trouble in recognising words, a person is said to be utilizing too much of their capacity in processing to read single words, which hinders with their aptitude to understand what they are reading.

Many instructors believe that a child ought to learn to understand or comprehend printed words even prior to reading it on their own and comprehension or understanding an instruction more often than not starts at a very early stage of learning.

On the other hand, other educators believe that what this reading means is utterly rearward for the young kids. They disagree that the kids ought to learn on how to make sense of the words in a text by means of phonics first before they can comprehend or understand the storyline itself.

The job of reading comprehension exercises is to make sure that the reader comprehends what he or she is reading. Kids and adults alike are clever at hiding when they do not comprehend, so when you are teaching somebody to read, you should always test for comprehension once in a while. This is a vital aspect in teaching reading comprehension skills.

You can take help of fluent English speakers in your friend circle. Ask them to inquirr straightforward questions or queries after paying attention to your aloud reading session.

Presuming a student has just finished reading a passage about Mahatma Gandhi's contribution towards the making of a free India. Parents or teachers then can inquire questions like "Who was Mahatma Gandhi?" or "Was he a spiritual leader or a freedom fighter? How did he unite Indians?"

The student's answer can give the discernment on whether their child had understood the passage that he or she was reading.

For kids, having their parents read a newspaper article with or to them is an outstanding technique to facilitate them perk up their vocabulary intellectual capacity and at the same time give them the opportunity to start thinking regarding the public issues during the day. But always be cautious about the type of newspaper you are going to choose.

Reading is a necessary skill, but being illiterate is not uncommon anymore in today's world. As a matter of fact, according to reports, as many as thirty percent of people are illiterate. They are incapable in reading and writing sufficiently well to complete an application for employment or have the ability to read a training handbook. Most often than not, those people who does not have the capability to read do not do well in life.

School educators can also get reading comprehension training in able to learn on how to perk up their literacy in their respective workplace. If you have not so good reading skills, this might spoil your work performance.

Reading comprehension training is also a big help to students. There are lots of interactional programmes in reading that can aid people in practicing their skills in reading. Reading comprehension training is particularly helpful in facilitating those students who do not speak English in learning how to read the

English language. The subjects are also intended to assist students in building their reading comprehension of the English written language.

Those people who are able to read can have a lot of opportunities than those who does not know how. They will have the chance to get good jobs and play a part in activities. Reading can improve employment potentials and it can also enrich lives.

Tips for Reading Comprehension

A **successful reading comprehension** is a result of the person's proficiency in phonics, vocabulary, the fluency, and being adept in reading comprehension. A person that has an excellent comprehension skill is said to be a reader, with a capability to interrelate the terms by comprehending its entire implication and its notion. Therefore, having an adept reading comprehension can make a distinction between readers which are considered active from readers who are said to be passive (these are those people are reading the words without really understanding the meaning).

Students are easily perturbed when they cannot understand or comprehend what they reading thus, they turn out to be less motivated to study or read anymore. An educator should devise and lecture using various strategies to facilitate students seal up those gaps in their comprehension. The critical test for a teacher is discerning precisely which approach is helpful and most advantageous to teach, in view of the fact that every student requires diverse strategies.

A beneficial method to teach and emphasise reading strategies is by making use of vivid visual aids. A graphic organizer appeals to a diversity of various aptitudes and it is imperative for students to make out the relationship among the visual aid and the reading selection.

By discovering or finding out techniques of teaching strategies which are not direct, a professor then ought to have taught the students something and giving them the notion of knowledge. Homework or assignment regarding reading strategies ought to serve as a supplementary reinforcement and is supposed to be reasonably associated and those that surface logically from the studied lesson.

Listening Comprehension Exercises

Students often become bored despite of innovative attempts at trying to improve their reading and comprehension ability. At such a stage, teachers, educators and friends need to waken their attention.

You could make use of a learning exercise or activity that would truly rouse your students up. There are lots of **listening comprehension exercises** offered but not all are suited for everyone.

Majority of the human population find music irresistible. It had always been a part of the people's existence from nativity and beyond. When we were still babies, we were lulled to sleep by our caretaker's lullabies. As little kids we had played, sang and danced to a numerous nursery songs. As teens, we are addicted to the music of famous singers nationwide. As grown-ups, each type of publicity we heed, each extraordinary occasion we experience, have music. Music suffuses TV, cinema, plays, and even to daily hearsays. When we work out, when we have fun and even till our last breath, music is always present to highlight or modify each disposition and sentiment. Hence, why not comprise music and a song in learning, too?

Below are some factors that contribute to listening comprehension of a song.

1. Making use of new words, sayings and expressions.
2. The articulation and enunciation of the music artist.
3. The usage of grammar and its structure.

However, when choosing a song to teach there are still criteria involved.

1. Make use of songs that are quite famous with your students.
2. The songs should have comprehensible and clear lyrics. Song

with vague and incomprehensible lyrics is the worst because nobody will understand it and it will forfeit your purpose in the goal of having listening comprehension.

3. The songs ought to have a very suitable subject matter for the people listening to it. Those songs with any sort of downbeat idea should not be brought up. There are lots of constructive, cheerful, and even amusing songs offered. Utilize these.

Music spread through almost each facet of our being. Students love it. It includes several helpful essentials for reading comprehension exercises and it is quite fun. Hence, having music and songs incorporated with English classes is one of the best ways to enhance listening comprehension.

Reading Comprehension (also known as Critical Reading) questions test your ability to understand a passage and answer question on the basis of what is stated and implied in the passage. You need to read the passage first so that you can identify the main idea of the passage and appreciate features such as the author's tone and attitude as well as the organisation of the passage.

There are actually three main levels or strands of comprehension—primary, interpretive and critical comprehension.

The first level, primary comprehension, is the most obvious. Comprehension at this level involves surface meanings. At this level, teachers can ask students to find information and ideas that are explicitly stated in the text.

The second level or strand is interpretive or referential comprehension. At this level, students go beyond what is said and read for deeper meanings. They must be able to read critically and analyse carefully what they have read. Students need to be able to see relationships among ideas, for exmple how ideas go together and also see the implied meanings of these ideas. It is also obvious that before our students can do this, they have to first understand the ideas that are stated (literal comprehension). Interpretive or referential comprehension includes thinking processes such as drawing conclusions, making generalisations and predicting outcomes. At this level, teachers can ask more challenging questions such as asking students to do the following:

- Re-arrange the ideas or topics discussed in the text.
- Explain the author's purpose of writing the text.
- Summarize the main idea when this is not explicitly stated in the text.
- Select conclusions which can be deduced from the text they have read.
- Finally, the third level of comprehension is critical reading whereby ideas and information are evaluated. Critical evaluation occurs only after our students have understood the ideas and information that the writer has presented. At this level, students can be tested on the following skills:
  - The ability to differentiate between facts and opinions.
  - The ability to recognise persuasive statements .
  - The ability to judge the accuracy of the information given in the text.

General Strategies for Reading Comprehension

1. Try to read the whole text of the passage once, if possible.

   Many people think you should just skim the passage or read the first lines of every paragraph, and not to read the passage. We believe this is an error: if you misunderstand the main idea of the passage, you will certainly get at least some of the questions wrong. Give the passage one good read, taking no more than 3 minutes to read all of the text. Do not read the passage more than once – that wastes too much time. If you have not understood it completely, try to answer the questions anyway.

   Note: this point of reading the whole passage is important for test-takers whose first language is not English, provided that they can read the passage in 3 minutes or less.

2. Make brief notes on the text on your scrap paper.

   Write down a couple of words on A) the Main Idea or Primary Purpose, B) Organization/Structure of the passage, and C) the Tone or Attitude of the author (if applicable). You just need a few words for each of these areas, and altogether it should not take longer than 30 seconds to write down.

3. Remember that the tone or attitude of the passage is usually respectful and moderate, never going to extremes of praise nor criticism.

4. Look out for structural words that tell you the important ideas or transitions in a passage.

For example:

- Continue the Idea Words: Similarly, Moreover, Additionally, In the same way, Likewise
- Conclusion Words: Thus, Therefore, Hence, So, In summary, In conclusion
- Contradiction or Contrast Words: Nevertheless, Nonetheless, However, But, Although, Though, Even though, Notwithstanding, Yet, Despite, In spite of, On the one hand...on the other hand, While, Unlike

5. Go back to the text of the passage for the answers.

   Many test-takers fail to return to the text of the passage to look for the correct answers. They rely solely on their memories and understanding of the passage after having read or skimmed it.. Go back to the text to look for information to answer the questions. Nine times out of ten, the answer lies within the passage.

Main Idea/Primary Purpose Questions

Many people believe there is no difference between the main or central idea of the passage and the primary purpose of the author of the passage. This is simply not true. Let's take a look at the subtle but important difference between them:

Main Idea

The question might look something like this:

- "Which of the following best states the central idea of the passage?"
- "Which of the following most accurately states the main idea of the passage?"
- "Which of the following is the principal topic of the passage?"
- "The main topic of the passage is...."

Primary Purpose

The question might look like this:

- "The primary purpose of this passage is to..."
- "The primary purpose of the passage as a whole is to..."
- "The primary focus of this passage is on which of the following?"
- "The main concern of the passage is to..."
- "In the passage, the author is primarily interested in...."
- "The passage is chiefly concerned with..."

Strategy

Main Idea: Look in the first and last paragraphs for the main idea. Any conclusion words like therefore, thus, so, hence, etc. that you see are most likely introducing the main idea. The correct answer will say the same thing as it says in the text, but using different words. The Main Idea is not always stated explicitly in the passage – in fact, more likely than not, it is not stated explicitly. Therefore, in order to answer this type of question when it is more implicit follow these tips:

1. Re-read the first line of every passage, and the last line of the first and last paragraphs. This should give you the general structure or outline of the argument, with which you can answer the Main Idea question.

2. After determining the general structure or content of the argument, eliminate answer choices that are too broad or too specific, i.e. answer choices that go beyond the content of the passage, or that deal with content only discussed in one paragraph of the passage.
3. Make brief notes – a couple of words- regarding the Main Idea on the text on your scrap paper while you read.

Primary Purpose: What is the author trying to do? What is his intention? If he is evaluating a theory, then the answer could be something like 'Discuss an interpretation'. Note that the correct answer would deal with 'an interpretation', because the author is only dealing with one theory. If the Primary Purpose is to criticise 2 new books, then his intention or his primary purpose might be to 'Critique new studies'. Again, as in Main Idea questions, re-read the first line of every passage, and the last line of the first and last paragraphs. This should give you the general structure or outline of the argument, with which you can answer the Primary Purpose question.

Note: A good main idea or primary purpose does not go beyond the scope of the passage, nor does it limit itself to discussing only one part of the passage.

Explanation

This is a Primary Purpose question, so we have to determine what the author is trying to do or say in this passage. So, let's read the first and last lines of a passage in order to get an idea of the primary purpose. The first line says 'Great news for Star Trek fans: warp drives that can propel starships around the Galaxy faster than the speed of light may be possible after all—with a little help from Dr Who'. The last line is a quote by a physicist that says "Of course, there are still some basic questions—like how does one go about constructing this Tardis space-time—but it puts the concept of space warps back on the agenda." From both these sentences, we get the idea of space travel, faster than light travel and space warps – maybe this is a discussion of faster than light space travel. Does that match what you have already read? Yes, basically this is a discussion of the theoretical state of play in the area of faster-than-light space travel. In a question asked, do any of the answer choices match that? Yes; even if the wording is somewhat different from how we are wording it, the idea might be almost exactly thesame.

Another way of getting to the answer is through elimination of obviously incorrect answer choices. We can eliminate some options because of a wrong idea presented or an extreme opinion highlighted. Read the passage again if you have any doubts regarding the answer to be chosen.

Reading Comprehension Exercises

Each reading passage in this section is followed by questions based on the content of the reading passage. Read the passage carefully and chose the best answer to each question. The questions are to be answered on the basis of what is stated or implied in the passage.

Man and Weapons

Man is not destined to vanish. He can be killed, but he cannot be destroyed, because his soul is deathless and his spirit is irrepressible. Therefore, though the situation seems dark in the context of the confrontation between the superpowers, the silver lining is provided by amazing phenomenon that the very nations which have spent incalculable resources and energy for the production of deadly weapons are desperately trying to find out how they might never be used. They threaten each other, intimidate each other and go to the brink, but before the total hour arrives they withdraw from the brink.

1. The main point from the author's view is that

a) Man's soul and spirit can not be destroyed by superpowers.

b) Man's destiny is not fully clear or visible.

c) Man's soul and spirit are immortal.

d) Man's safety is assured by the delicate balance of power in terms of nuclear weapons.

e) Human society will survive despite the serious threat of total annihilation.

Ans. (e).

2. The phrase 'Go to the brink' in the passage means

a) Retreating from extreme danger.

b) Declare war on each other.

c) Advancing to the stage of war but not engaging in it.

d) Negotiate for peace.

e) Commit suicide.

Ans. (c).

3. In the author's opinion:

a) Huge stockpiles of destructive weapons have so far saved mankind from a catastrophe.

b) Superpowers have at last realised the need for abandoning the production of lethal weapons.

c) Mankind is heading towards complete destruction.

d) Nations in possession of huge stockpiles of lethal weapons are trying hard to avoid actual conflict.

e) There is a Silverlining over the production of deadly weapons.

Ans. (d).

4. 'Irrepressible' in the passage means

a) incompatible

b) strong

c) oppressive

d) unrestrainable

e) unspirited

Ans. (d).

5. A suitable message by the passage would be
   a) Destruction of mankind is in evitable.
   b) Man's desire to survive inhibits use of deadly weapons.
   c) Mounting cost of modern weapons.
   d) Threats and intimidation between super powers.
   e) Cowardly retreat by man

   Ans. (b).

Air and Water

Disequilibrium at the interface of water and air is a factor on which the transfer of heat and water vapour from the ocean to the air depends. The air within about a millimeter of the water is almost saturated with water vapour and the temperature of the air is close to that of the surface water. Irrespective of how small these differences might be, they are crucial, and the disequilibrium is maintained by air near the surface mixing with air higher up, which is typically appreciably cooler and lower in water vapour content. The turbulence, which takes its energy from the wind mixes the air. As the speed of wind increases, so does the turbulence, and consequently the rate of heat and moisture transfer. We can arrive at a detailed understanding of this phenomenon after further study. The transfer of momentum from wind to water, which occurs when waves are formed is an interacting-and complicated phenomenon. When waves are made by the wind, it transfers important amounts of energy-energy, which is consequently not available for the production of turbulence.

1. **This passage principally intends to:**
   a) resolve a controversy
   b) attempt a description of a phenomenon
   c) sketch a theory
   d) reinforce certain research findings

e) tabulate various observations

Ans. (b).

2. The wind over the ocean usually does which of the following according to the given passage?

i. Leads to cool, dry air coming in proximity with the ocean surface.

ii. Maintains a steady rate of heat and moisture transfer between the ocean and the air.

iii. Results in frequent changes in the ocean surface temperature.

a) i. only

b) ii. only

c) i. and ii. only

d) ii. and iii. only

e) i., ii., and iii.

Ans. (a).

3. According to the author the present knowledge regarding heat and moisture transfer from the ocean to air as

a) revolutionary

b) inconsequential

c) outdated

d) derivative

e) incomplete

Ans. (e).

4. According to the given passage, in case the wind was to decrease until there was no wind at all, which of the following would occur?

a) The air, which is closest to the ocean surface would get saturated with water vapour.

b) The water would be cooler than the air closest to the ocean surface.

c) There would be a decrease in the amount of moisture in the air closest to the ocean surface.

d) There would be an increase in the rate of heat and moisture transfer.

e) The temperature of the air closest to the ocean and that of the air higher up would be the same.

Ans. (a).

Use of Antibiotics

The Food and Drug Administration has formulated certain severe restrictions regarding the use of antibiotics, which are used to promote the health and growth of meat animals. Though the different types of medicines mixed with the fodder of the animals kills many microorganisms, it also encourages the appearance of bacterial strains, which are resistant to anti-infective drugs.

It has already been observed that penicillin and the tetracyclines are not as effective therapeutically as they once used to be. This resistance to drugs is chiefly caused due to tiny circlets of genes, called plasmids, which are transferable between different species of bacteria. These plasmids are also one of the two kinds of vehicles on which molecular biologists depend on while performing gene transplant experiments. Existing guidelines also forbid the use of plasmids, which bear genes for resistance to antibiotics, in the labouratories. Though congressional dabate goes on as to whether these restrictions need to be toughened with reference to scientists in their labouratories, almost no congressional attention is being paid to an ill advised agricultural practice, which produces deleterious effects.

1. In the present passage, the author's primary concern is with:

a) The discovery of methods, which eliminate harmful microorganisms without generating drug-resistant bacteria.

b) Attempting an explanation of the reasons for congressional inaction about the regulation of gene transplant experiments.

c) Portraying a problematic agricultural practice and its serious genetic consequences.

d) The verification of the therapeutic ineffectiveness of anti-infective drugs.

e) Evaluation of the recently proposed restrictions, which are intended to promote the growth of meat animals.

Ans. (c).

2. As inferred from the above passage, the mutual transfer of plasmids between different bacteria can result in which of the following?

a) Microorganisms, which have an in-built resistance to drugs

b) Therapeutically useful circlets of genes

c) Penicillin like anti-infective drugs

d) Viruses used by molecular biologists

e) Carriers for performing gene transplant experiments.

Ans. (a).

3. According to the above passage the author believes that those who favour the stiffening of restrictions on gene transplant research should logically also.

a) Approve and aid experiments with any plasmids except those, which bear genes for antibiotic resistance.

b) Inquire regarding the addition of anti-infective drugs to livestock feeds.

c) Oppose the using of penicillin and tetracyclines in order to kill microorganisms.

d) Agree to the development of meatier live-stock through the use of antibiotics.

e) Approve of congressional debate and discussion regarding science and health issues.

Ans. (b).

4. The attitude the author has with reference to the development of bacterial strains that render antibiotic drugs in effective can best be described as

a) indifferent

b) perplexed

c) pretentious

d) insincere

e) apprehensive

Ans. (e).

Black Fiction and Criticism

Roger Rosenblatt's book Black Fiction, manages to alter the approach taken in many previous studies by making an attempt to apply literary rather than sociopolitical criteria to its subject. Rosenblatt points out that criticism of Black writing has very often served as a pretext for an expounding on Black history. The recent work of Addison Gayle's passes a judgement on the value of Black fiction by clearly political standards, rating each work according to the ideas of Black identity, which it propounds.

Though fiction results from political circumstances, its author react not in ideological ways to those circumstances, and talking about novels and stories primarily as instruments of ideology circumvents much of the fictional enterprise. Affinities and connections are revealed in the works of Black fiction in Rosenblatt's literary analysis; these affinities and connections have been overlooked and ignored by solely political studies.

The writing of acceptable criticism of Black fiction, however, presumes giving satisfactory answers to a quite a few questions. The most important of all, is there a sufficient reason, apart from the racial identity of the authors, for the grouping together of Black authors? Secondly, what is the distinction of Black fiction from other modern fiction with which it is largely contemporaneous? In the work Rosenblatt demonstrates that Black fiction is a distinct body of writing, which has an identifiable, coherent literary tradition. He highlights recurring concerns and designs, which are independent of chronology in Black fiction written over the past eighty years. These concerns and designs are thematic, and they come form the central fact of the predominant white culture, where the Black characters in the novel are situated irrespective of whether they attempt to conform to that culture or they rebel against it.

Rosenblatt's work does leave certain aesthetic questions open. His thematic analysis allows considerable objectivity; he even clearly states that he does not intend to judge the merit of the various works yet his reluctance seems misplaced, especially since an attempt to appraise might have led to interesting results. For example, certain novels have an appearance of structural diffusion. Is this a defeat, or are the authors working out of, or attempting to forge, a different kind of aesthetic? Apart from this, the style of certain Black novels, like Jean Toomer's Cane, verges on expressionism or surrealism; does this technique provide a counterpoint to the prevalent theme that portrays the fate against which Black heroes are pitted, a theme usually conveyed by more naturalistic modes of expressions?

Irrespective of such omissions, what Rosenblatt talks about in his work makes for an astute and worthwhile study. His book very effectively surveys a variety of novels, highlighting certain fascinating and little-known works like James Weldon Johnson's Autobiography of an Ex-Coloured Man. Black Fiction is tightly constructed, and levelheaded and penetrating criticism is exemplified in its forthright and lucid style.

1. The author of the passage raises an objection to criticism of Black fiction like that by Addison Gayle as it:

a) Highlights only the purely literary aspects of such works

b) Misconceive the ideological content of such fiction

c) Miscalculate the notions of Black identity presented in such fiction

d) Replaces political for literary criteria in evaluating such fiction

e) Disregards the reciprocation between Black history and Black identity exhibited in such fiction.

Ans. (d).

2. The primary concern of the author in the above passage is:

a) Reviewing the validity of a work of criticism

b) Comparing various critical approaches to a subject

c) Talking of the limitations of a particular kind of criticism

d) Recapitulation of the major points in a work of criticism

e) Illustrating the theoretical background of a certain kind of criticism.

Ans. (a).

3. The author is of the opinion that Black Fiction would have been improved had Rosenblatt:

a) Undertaken a more careful evaluation of the ideological and historical aspects of Black Fiction

b) Been more objective in his approach to novels and stories by Black authors

c) Attempted a more detailed exploration of the recurring themes in Black fiction throughout its history

d) Established a basis for placing Black fiction within its own unique literary tradition

e) Calculated the relative literary merit of the novels he analysed thematically.

Ans. (e).

4. Rosenblatt's discussion of Black Fiction is:

a) Pedantic and contentious
b) Critical but admiring
c) Ironic and deprecating
d) Argumentative but unfocused
e) Stilted and insincere.

Ans. (b).

5. According to the given passage the author would be LEAST likely to approve of which among the following?

a) Analysing the influence of political events on the personal ideology of Black writers
b) Attempting a critical study, which applies sociopolitical criteria to the autobiographies of Black authors
c) A literary study of Black poetry that appraises the merits of poems according to the political acceptability of their themes
d) Studying the growth of a distinct Black literary tradition within the context of Black history
e) Undertaking a literary study, which attempts to isolate aesthetic qualities unique to Black fiction.

Ans. (c).

6. From the following options, which does the author not make use of while discussing Black Fiction?

a) Rhetorical questions
b) Specific examples
c) Comparison and contrast
d) Definition of terms
e) Personal opinion.

Ans. (d).

7. The author makes a reference to James Weldon Johnson's Autobiography of an Ex-coloured Man most probably to:

a) Highlight the affinities between Rosenblatt's method of thematic analysis and earlier criticism

b) Elucidate regarding the point made regarding expressionistic style earlier in the passage

c) Qualify the assessment of Rosenblatt's book made in the first paragraph of the passage

d) Demonstrate the affinities among the various Black novels talked of by Rosenblatt's literary analysis

e) Present a specific example of one of the accomplishments of Rosenblatt's work.

Ans. (e).

Biological Evolution

Some modern anthropologists hold that biological evolution has shaped not only human morphology but also human behaviour. The role those anthropologists ascribe to evolution is not of dictating the details of human behaviour but one of imposing constraints – ways of feeling, thinking, and acting that "come naturally" in archetypal situations in any culture. Our "frailties"– emotions and motives such as rage, fear, greed, gluttony, joy,lust, love-may be a very mixed assortment quality: we are, as we say, "in the grip" of them. And thus they give us our sense of constraints.

Unhappily, some of those frailties our need for ever-increasing security among them are presently maladaptive. Yet beneath the overlay of cultural detail, they, too, are said to be biological in direction, and therefore as natural to us as are our appendixes. We would need to comprehend throughly their adaptive origins in order to understand how badly they guide us now. And we might then begin to resist their pressure.

1. The author implies that control to any extent over the "frailties" that constrain our behaviour is though to presuppose

a) That those frailties and adaptive are recognised as currently beneficial and adaptive

b) That there is little or no overlay of cultural detail that masks their true nature

c) That there are cultures in which those frailties do not "come naturally" and from which such control can be learned

d) A full understanding of why those frailties evolved and of how they function now

e) A thorough grasp of the principle that cultural detail in human behaviour can differ arbitrarily from society to society.

Ans. (d).

2. It can be inferred that in his discussion of maladaptive frailties the author assumes that

a) Evolution does not favour the emergence of adaptive characteristics over the emergence of maladaptive ones

b) Any structure or behaviour not positively adaptive is regarded as transitory in evolutionary theory

c) Maladaptive characteristics, once fixed, make the emergence of other maladaptive characteristics more likely

d) The designation of a characteristic as being maladaptive must always remain highly tentative

e) Changes in the total human environment can outpace evolutionary change.

Ans. (e).

3. The primary purpose of the passage is to present

a) A position on the foundations of human behaviour and on what those foundations imply

b) A theory outlining the parallel development of human morphology and of human behaviour

c) A diagnostic test for separating biologically determined behaviour patters from culture – specific detail

d) An overview of those human emotions and motive's that impose constraints on human behaviour

e) A practical method for resting the pressures of biologically determined drives.

Ans. (a).

4. Which of the following most probably provides an appropriate analogy from human morphology for the "details" versus "constraints" distinction made in the passage in relation to human behaviour?

a) The ability of most people to see all the colours of the visible spectrum as against most peoples inability to name any but the primary colours

b) The ability of even the least fortunate people to show compassion as against people's inability to mask their feelings completely

c) The ability of some people to dive to great depths as against most people's inability to swim long distance

d) The psychological profile of those people who are able to delay gratification as against people's inability to control their lives completely

e) The greater lung capacity of mountain peoples that helps them live in oxygen-poor air as against people's inability to fly without special apparatus.

Ans. (e).

Evolution

The existence of mammals on the earth can be traced back to at least the Triassic time. The rate of development was retarded, till evolutional change suddenly accelerated in the oldest Paleocene. This resulted in an increase in average size, larger mental capacity, and special adaptations for different modes of life, during the Eocene time. Further improvement was seen during the Oligocene Epoch, with the appearance of some new lines and extinction of others. The Miocene and Pliocene times are especially significant as they mark the culmination of various groups and a continued approach toward modern characters. It is in the Miocene time that the mammals reached their peak with reference to variety and size.

The ability of the mammals to adapt to various modes of life finds a parallel in the reptiles of the Mesozoic time, and apart form their greater intelligence, the mammals apparently have not done much better than the corresponding reptilian forms. Undoubtedly the bat is a better flying animal than the pterosaur, but at the same time the dolphin and whale are hardly more fish like than the ichthyosaur. Quite a few of the swift-running mammals inhabiting the plains, like the horse and the antelope, must excel any of the dinosaurs. Although the tyrannosaur was a more weighty and robust carnivore than perhaps any carnivorous mammal, the lion and the tiger, by virtue of their superior brain are far more efficient and dangerous beasts of prey. It is significant to note that various species of mammals gradually adapted themselves to various kinds of lifestyles, some took to grazing on the plains and were able to run swiftly (horse, deer, bison), others started living in rivers and swamps (hippopotamus, beaver), inhabiting trees (sloth, monkey), burrowing underground (rodent, mole), feeding on flesh (tiger, wolf), swimming in the water (dolphin, whale, seal), and flying in the air (bat). Human beings on account of their superior brain have been able to harness mechanical methods to conquer the physical world and adapt to any set of conditions.

Such adaptation to different conditions leads to a gradual change in form and structure. This is a biological characteristic of the youthful, plastic stage of a group. It is seen that early in its evolutional cycle animals possess the capacity for change, but as the animal progresses in its cycle becoming old and fixed, this capacity for change disappears. The generalised types of organisms retain longest the ability to make adjustments when required, and it is from them that new, fecund stocks take origin-certainly not from any specialised end products. With reference to mammals, we see their birth, plastic spread in many directions, increased specialisation, and in some cases, extinction; this is a characteristic of the evolution of life, which can be seen in the geologic record of life.

1. From the following, choose another appropriate title for the above passage?
 a) From Dinosaur to Man
 b) Adaptation and Extinction
 c) The Superior Mammals
 d) The Geologic Life Span
 e) Man, the Vanquisher of the Physical World.

 Ans. (b).

2. According to the passage the chronological order of the geologic periods is:
 a) Paleocene, Miocene, Triassic, Mesozoic
 b) Paleocene, Triassic, Mesozoic, Miocene
 c) Miocene, Paleocene, Triassic, Mesozoic
 d) Mesozoic, Oligocene, Paleocene, Miocene
 e) Mesozoic, Paleocene, Eocene, Miocene

 Ans. (e).

3. From the above passage, we can infer that, the pterosaur
 a) resembled the bat
 b) was a Mesozoic mammal
 c) was a flying reptile
 d) inhabited the seas
 e) evolved during the Miocene period

 Ans. (c).

4. As inferred from the passage, the largest number of mammals were found in which of the following periods?

a) Triassic period

b) Eocene period

c) Oligocene epoch

d) Pliocene period

e) Miocene period

Ans. (e).

5. Among the following statements, which statement, if true, would weaken the argument put forth in the first sentence of Paragraph 1?

a) It has been found that the tryannosaur had a larger brain, than was previously known.

b) Within the next thousand years, mammals will become extinct.

c) Recently certain forms of flying ichthyosaurs have been discovered.

d) It has now been proved, that the tiger is more powerful than the carnivorous reptiles.

e) It is now possible to double human mental capacity, by the use of certain recently developed computers.

Ans. (a).

6. It is clear from the passage, that the evidence used to discuss the life of past time periods

a) was developed by Charles Darwin

b) was unearthed by the author

c) has been negated by more recent evidence

d) was never truly established

e) is based on fossilized remains

Ans. (e).

7. As inferred from the passage, which of the following proverbial expressions is the author most likely to agree with?

a) It's a cruel world.

b) All the world's a stage.

c) The more things change, the more they remain the same.

d) Footprints in the sands of time.

e) A short life, but a merry one.

Ans. (d).

Pterosaurs and their Fossils

For a period of more than two centuries paleontologists have been intrigued by the fossilized remains of pterosaurs, the first flying vertebartes. The issues, which puzzle them, are how these heavy creatures, having a wingspan of about 8-12 metres managed the various problems associated with powered flight and whether these creatures were reptiles or birds.

Perhaps the least controversial assertion about the pterosaurs is that they were reptiles. Their skulls, pelvises, and hind feet are reptilian. The anatomy of their wings suggests that they did not evolve into the class of birds. In pterosaurs a greatly elongated fourth finger of each forelimb supported a winglike membrane. The other fingers were short and reptilian, with sharp claws. In birds the second finger is the principal strut of the wing, which consists primarily of feathers. If the pterosaurs walked on all fours, the three short fingers may have been employed for grasping. When a pterosaurs walked or remained stationary, the fourth finger, and with it the wing, could only urn upward in an extended inverted V- shape along each side of the animal's body.

In resemblance they were extremely similar to both birds and bats, with regard to their overall body structure and proportion. This is hardly surprising as the design of any flying vertebrate is subject to aerodynamic constraints. Both the pterosaurs and the birds have hollow bones, a feature that represents a savings in weight. There is a difference, which is that the bones of the birds are more massively reinforced by internal struts.

Although scales typically cover reptiles, the pterosaurs probably had hairy coats. T.H. Huxley reasoned that flying vertebrates must have been warm-blooded because flying implies a high rate of metabolism, which in turn implies a high internal temperature. Huxley speculated that a coat of hair would insulate against loss of body heat and might streamline the body to reduce drag in flight. The recent discovery of a pterosaur specimen covered in long, dense, and relatively thick hair like fossil material was the first clear evidence that his reasoning was correct.

Some paleontologists are of the opinion that the pterosaurs jumped from s dropped from trees or perhaps rose into the light winds from the crests of waves in order to become airborne. Each theory has its associated difficulties. The first makes a wrong assumption that the pterosaurs hind feet resembled a bat's and could serve as hooks by which the animal could hang in preparation for flight. The second hypothesis seems unlikely because large pterosaurs could not have landed in trees without damaging their wings. The third calls for high aces to channel updrafts. The pterosaurs would have been unable to control their flight once airborne as the wind from which such waves arose would have been too strong.

1. As seen in the above passage scientists generally agree that:

a) the pterosaurs could fly over large distances because of their large wingspan.

b) a close evolutionary relationship can be seen between the pterosaurs and bats, when the structure of their skeletons is studied.

c) the study of the fossilized remains of the pterosaurs reveals how they solved the problem associated with powered flight.

d) the pterosaurs were reptiles.

e) Pterosaurs walked on all fours.

Ans. (d).

2. The view that, the pterosaurs rose into light winds from the

crest of the waves to become airborne, is viewed by the author as

a) revolutionary

b) unlikely

c) unassailable

d) probable

e) outdated.

Ans. (b).

3. As inferred from the passage, the skeleton of a pterosaur is distinguishable from that of a bird by the

a) length of its wingspan

b) hollow spaces in its bones

c) anatomic origin of its wing strut

d) evidence of the hooklike projections on its hind feet

e) location of the shoulder joint joining the wing to its body.

Ans. (c).

4. From the viewpoint of T.H.Huxley, as given in the passage, which of the following statements is he most likely to agree with?

a) An animal can master complex behaviours irrespective of the size of it's brain.

b) Environmental capabilities and physical capabilities often influence the appearance of an animal.

c) Usually animals in a particular family group do not change their appearance dramatically over a period of time.

d) The origin of flight in vertebrates was an accidental development rather than the outcome of specialisation or adaption.

e) The pterosaurs should be classified as birds, not reptiles.

Ans. (b).

5. According to the passage which of the following is a characteristic of the pterosaurs?

a) The pterosaurs were not able to fold their wings when not in use

b) Like the bats, they hung upside down from branches

c) They flew in order to capture prey

d) They can be said to be an earlier stage in the evolution of the birds

e) They lived principally in a forest like habitat.

Ans. (a).

6. The organisation of the last paragraph of the passage can best be described as:

a) New data is introduced in order to support a traditional point of view

b) Three explanations are put forth and each of them is disputed by means of specific information

c) An outline of three hypotheses are given and evidence supporting each of them is given

d) Description of three recent discoveries is presented, and their implications for future study are projected

e) The material in the earlier paragraphs is Summarised and certain conclusions are from it.

Ans. (b).

7. According to the passage, some scientists believe that pterosaurs

a) Lived near large bodies of water

b) Had sharp teeth for tearing food

c) Were attacked and eaten by larger reptiles

d) Had longer tails than many birds

e) Consumed twice their weight daily to maintain their body temperature.

Ans. (a).

Athenian Culture

Certain scraps of evidence bear out those who hold a very high opinion of the average level of culture among the Athenians of the great age. Pericles's funeral speech is undoubtedly the most famous evidence from Athenian literature, that its level was indeed high. However, Pericles was a politician, and it is possible that he was flattering his audience. We know that thousands of Athenians sat hour after hour in the theater listening to the plays of the great Greek dramatists. The Greek plays, particularly the tragedies, maintained an extremely high intellectual level throughout, with no letdowns, no concessions to the lowbrows or to the demands of "realism", like the gravediggers scene in Shakespeare's Hamlet. The music and dancing seen in these plays were also of an equally high level. The best modern parallel can be seen in the restrained, difficult opera of the 18th century. The comparison is no doubt dangerous, but can you imagine almost the entire population of an American city (in suitable installments, of course) sitting through performances of Mozart's Don Giovanni or Gluck's Orpheus? Perhaps the Athenian masses went to these plays because of a lack of other amusements. They could at least understand something of what went on, since the subjects were part of their folklore. Undoubtedly the theme of grand opera is not part of the folklore of the American people.

1. From the passage it is evident that the author seems to question the sincerity of

a) politicians

b) playwrights

c) opera goers

d) "low brows"

e) gravediggers

Ans. (a).

2. According to the author the average American

a) Enjoys Hamlet

b) Loves folklore

c) Is not able to understand grand opera

d) Seeks a high cultural level

e) Lacks entertainment.

Ans. (c).

3. From the passage, we can say that the author's attitude toward Greek plays is one of

a) Qualified approval

b) Grudging admiration

c) Studied indifference

d) Partial hostility

e) Great respect.

Ans. (e).

4. The author makes a suggestion that Greek plays

a) Were demanding on the actors

b) Flattered their audiences

c) Were focussed on a limited audience

d) Were dominated by music and dancing

e) Stimulated their audiences.

Ans. (e).

Nonconformist Manhood

Everyone conforms to infancy, infancy conforms to nobody, so that one babe commonly makes four or five out of the adults who prattle and play to it. So God has armed youth and puberty and manhood no less with its own piquancy and charm, and made it enviable and gracious and its claims not to be put by, if it will stand by itself. Do not think the youth has no force, because he cannot speak to you and me. Hark! In the next room his voice is sufficiently clear and emphatic. It seems he knows how to speak to his contemporaries. Bashful or bold, then, he will know how to make us seniors very unnecessary.

The healthy attitude of human nature can be seen in the nonchalance of boys who are sure of a dinner, and would disdain as much as a lord to do or say aught to conciliate one. A boy is in the parlor what the pit is in the playhouse; independent, irresponsible, looking out from his corner on such people and facts as pass by, he tries and sentences them on their merits, in the swift, summary way of boys, as good, bad, interesting, silly, eloquent, troublesome. He never cumbers himself regarding consequences, about interests and he gives an independent, genuine verdict. You should court him: he will not court you. But the man is, as it were, clapped into jail by his consciousness. As soon as he has once acted or spoken with eclat, he is a committed person, watched by the sympathy or the hatred of hundreds, whose affections must now enter into his account. There is no Lethe for this. Ah, that he could pass again into his neutrality.

These are the voices, which we hear in solitude, but they grow faint and inaudible as we enter into the world. Everywhere society is conspiring against the manhood of every one of its members. Society is joint stock company, in which members agree, for the better securing of his bread to each shareholder, to surrender the liberty and culture of the eater. The virtue in most request is conformity. It is averse to self-reliance. What it loves is names and customs and not realities and creators.

Whosoever is a man has to be a nonconformist. He who would gather immortal palms must not be hindered by the name of goodness, but must explore if it be goodness. Nothing is at last sacred but the integrity of your own mind.

No law can be sacred to me but that of my nature. Good and bad are but names very readily transferable to that to this; the only right is what is after my constitution, the only right is what is after me constitution, the only wrong what is against it. A man is to carry himself in the presence of all opposition as if every thing were titular and ephemeral but he. I am ashamed to think how easily we capitulate to badges and names, to large societies and dead institutions. Every decent and well-spoken individual affects and sways me more than is right. I ought to go upright and vital, and speak the rude truth in all ways.

I shun father and mother and wife and brother, when my genius calls me. I would write on the lintels of the doorpost, whim. I hope it is somewhat better than whim at last, but we cannot spend the day in explanation. Except me not to show cause why I seek or why I exclude company.

Then, again, do not tell me, as a good man did not to-day, of my obligation to put all poor men in good situations. Are they my poor? I tell thee, thou foolish philanthropist, that I grudge the dollar, the time, the cent, I give to such men as do not belong to me and to whom I do not belong. There is a class of person to whom by all spiritual affinity I am bought and sold; for them I will go to prison, if need be; but your miscellaneous popular charities; the education at collage of fools; the building of meeting house to the vain end to which many now stand; alms to sots; and the thousandfold Relief Societies; – though I confess with shame I sometimes succumb and give the dollar, it is a wicked dollar which by and by I shall have the manhood to withhold.

If you refuse to conform, you can experience the displeasure of the world. Hence, a man should know how to estimate a sour face. The by standers look askance on him in the public street or in the friend's parlour. In case this aversion originates from contempt and resistance similar to his own, it might result in a sad countenance; but the sour faces of the multitude, like their sweet faces, have no deep cause, but are caused by reasons as diverse as the direction of the wind and what he reads in the newspapers. Yet is the discontent of the multitude more formidable than that of the senate and the collage.

Another factor, which frightens us from self trust in our consistency; a reverence for our past act or word, because the eyes of others have no other data for computing our orbit than our past acts, and we are loath to disappoint them.

But why should you keep your head over your shoulder? Why drag about this corpse of your memory, lest you contradict somewhat you have stated in this or that public place? Suppose you should contradict yourself; what then?

This is a rather silly consistency in our minds, which is adored by little statesmen and philosophers and divines. Uniformly a great soul has almost nothing to do, he could just occupy himself with his shadow on the wall. Speak what you think now in hard words; and to-morrow speak what tomorrow thinks in hard words again, though it contradict everything you said to-day. "Ah, so you shall be sure to be misunderstood." - Is it so bad, then, to be misunderstood? Pythagoras was misunderstood, and Socrates, and Jesus, and Luther, and Copernicus, and Galileo, and Newton, and every pure and wise spirit that ever took flesh. What can be considered to be truly great is to be misunderstood.

1. Which of the following statements would best describe the main theme of the above passage?

a) "A foolish consistency is the hobgoblin of little mind."

b) "Eternal youth means eternal independence."

c) "Whoso would be a man must be a nonconformist."

d) "Colleges are designed to educate fools."

e) "Infancy conforms to nobody."

Ans. (c).

2. When is the period during which we are most nonconformist?

a) infancy

b) puberty

c) youth

d) manhood

e) old age

Ans. (a).

3. In his statement "What can be considered to be truly great is to be misunderstood" the author means:

a) One should refrain from saying, what one exactly means

b) Being misunderstood, equals being great

c) All great man have always been misunderstood

d) Even though a person might be considered inconsistent, he shouldn't hesitate to change his mind if he feels the need to.

e) It is seldom, that nice people succeed.

Ans. (d).

4. As inferred from the passage, the refusal of young people to cater to accept public opinion is:

a) A feature of the rebelliousness of youth

b) A healthy attitude of human nature

c) A manifestation of deep- seated immaturity

d) Simply bad manners

e) Part of growing up

Ans. (b).

5. "Society is a joint-stock company etc." is one way which the author shows

a) The anti-culture attitude of the public

b) Society is highly organised and structured

c) The self-rejection of society

d) The lack of room for solitude in our world

e) The public's interest in the stock market.

Ans. (c).

6. " I would write on the lintels of the doorpost, whim." What does the author mean by this statement:

a) That one should renounce his immediate family

b) That signposts have an important educational function in our society

c) That an impulsive action may have a subsequent rational explanation

d) That one must never be held responsible for what one says and does

e) That everyone should do foolish things occasionally.

Ans. (c).

7. Which of the following statements best Summarises the spirit and sense of the above passage?

a) "Nothing is at last sacred but the integrity of your own mind."

b) "With consistency, a great soul; has simply nothing to do."

c) "Do not think the youth has no force, because cannot speak to you and me."

d) "The virtue in most request is conformity."

e) "A man must know how to estimate a sour force."

Ans. (a).

Wakefield Master

Furthermore, insofar as any conclusion about its author can be drawn from five or six plays attributed to him, the Wakefield Master is without exception considered to be a man of sharp contemporary observation. He was, probably clerically educated, as indicated by his Latin and music, his Biblical and patristic lore. Even today he is remembered for his his quick sympathy for the oppressed and forgotten man, his sharp eye for character, a ready ear for colloquial, vernacular turns of speech and a humor alternately rude and boisterous, coarse and happy. Therefore in spite of his conscious artistry as can be seen in his feeling for intricate metrical and stanza forms, he is regarded as a kind of medieval Steinbeck, indignantly angry at, uncompromisingly and even brutally realistic in presenting the plight of the agricultural poor.

It is now fairly accepted to regard the play as a kind of ultimate point in the secularization of the medieval drama. Therefore more stress has been laid on it as depicting realistically humble manners and pastoral life in the bleak of the west riding of Yorkshire on a typically cold night of December 24th. After what are often regarded as almost "documentaries" given in the three successive monologues of the three shepherds, critics go on to affirm that the realism is then intensified into a burlesque mock-treatment of the Nativity. Finally as a sort of epilogue or after-thought in deference to the Biblical origins of the materials, the play slides back into an atavistic mood of early innocent reverence. In actuality, the final scene is the culminating scene and also the raison etre of the introductory "realism."

Superficially the present play supports the conventional view of its mood of secular realism. At the same time, the "realism" of the Wakefield Master is of a paradoxical turn. His wide knowledge of people, as well as books indicates no cloistered contemplative but one in close relation to his times. Still, that life was after all a predominantly religious one, a time which never neglected the belief that man was a rebellious and sinful creature in need of redemption. So deeply (one can hardly say "naively" of so sophisticated a writer) and implicitly religious is the Master that he is less able (or less willing) to present actual history realistically than is the author of the Brome Abraham and Isaac. His historical sense is even less realistic than that of Chaucer who just a few years before had done for his own time "costume romances," such as The Knight's Tele, Troilus and Cressida, etc. Furthermore, used highly romantic materials, which could excuse his taking liberties with history.

1. Of the following statements, which is not true of Wakefield Master?

   a) He and Chaucer were contemporaries.

   b) Wakefield Master is remembered as having written five or six realistic plays.

   c) His plays realistically portray the plight of the country folk of his day.

   d) His writing was similar to that of John Steinbeck.

   e) He was an accomplished artist.

   Ans. (d).

2. The word 'patristic' in the first paragraph is used to mean:

   a) patriotic

   b) superstitious

   c) folk

   d) relating to the Christian Fathers

   e) realistic

   Ans. (d).

3. The statement about the "secularization of the medieval drama" (opening sentence of the second paragraph) refers to the

   a) Introduction of religious themes in the early days

   b) Presentation of erudite material

   c) Use of contemporary materials

   d) Return to early innocent reverence at the end of the play

   e) Introduction of mundane matters in religious plays

   Ans. (e).

4. From the following what would the writer be expected to do in the subsequent paragraphs:

   a) Make a justification for his comparison with Steinbeck

b) Put forth a view point, which would take up the thought of the second paragraph

c) Point out the anachronisms in the play

d) Discuss the works of Chaucer

e) Talk about the lack of realism in the works of the Wakefield Master.

Ans. (b).

Classical Indian Dances

Classical Indian dances are among the most graceful and beautiful in the world. Dancers use their eyes, hands, arms, legs, hips, knees, waist and feet to express various emotions like love, anger, hatred and amazement. They dance to vocal and instrumental accompaniment. There are five major styles of Indian classical dance: 1) Bharatanatyam, 2) Kathak, 3) Odissi, 4) Kathakali, and 5) Manipuri. Though these dances were developed in different regions of India, they share the common thread of telling stories of Hindu gods.

Bharatanatyam is a style of dance from the south of India. It is probably one of the oldest styles of Indian classical dance. A solo dancer performs it. Kathak is a style of dance of north India and was created in the courts of the Mughal rulers. It involves energetic footwork and expressive eye movements.

Traditional Indian dance, in particularly Bharatanatyam and Odissi, is an artistic yoga (natya yoga), for revealing the spiritual through the corporeal. Bharatanatyam is the most widely practised of Indian traditional dances worldwide, as it is the style that most faithfully adheres to the Bible of the traditional Indian dance, the Natya Shastra, and most comprehensively embodies it. It is also the most ancient of all the traditional dance forms in India.

In the first half of the 19th century much of traditional Indian dance of Bharatanatyam was redefined by the contributions of four talented brothers known today as the Tanjore Quartet:

Chinniah, Sivanandam, Ponniah and Vadivelu. Styles of traditional Indian dance of Bharatanatyam were preserved in practice mostly by the guru's and performers of the Isai Velalar community of Tamil Nadu. The Tanjore Quartet organised all the basic traditional Indian dance of Bharatanatyam movements of pure dance into a progressive series, adavus.

Each adavu is a basic unit taught in systematic order and then combined with others to produce choreographed traditional Indian dance of Bharatanatyam sequences based upon the rhythmic pattern of a musical composition. The brothers composed new music specifically for traditional Indian dance of Bharatanatyam, and introduced a different sequence of items which integrated various aspects of dance and music into a carefully coordinated, aesthetically sound progression. This infusion of creative energy marks the early 19th century as one of the most innovative periods in the history of traditional Indian dance. In the 20th century, such prominent personalities as Mangudi Dorairaja Iyer and Krishna Iyer made their significant contributions. The social status and image of traditional Indian dance was restored by Rukminidevi Arundale, the founder of Kalakshetra, who started teaching a simplified, Kalakshetra style invented by her after having learnt some of the Pandanallur style of traditional Indian dance of Bharatanatyam in a record 3 years' time. Traditional Indian dance has undergone much change but is still deeply rooted in the spiritual Hindu heritage. Contemporary traditional Indian dancers are both male and female artists. While most learn it as a hobby, very few make it their career and a lifestyle, as it is extremely demanding and complex in terms of dedication and daily practice. While most university degree courses offer mainly a theoretical base in traditional Indian dance, there are institutions that offer certificate and diploma courses with the focus on the practical skills.

Most of the contemporary choreographers and dancers may use some of the formal traditional Indian dance technique or its elements to stage ballets presenting various themes such as nationalism, unity of religions, the sanctity of the environment, the animal rights activism, the greatness of a king or a political party, or even the delightfulness of Coca-Cola. In Vande Mataram, a dance festival organised under the auspices of Natyarangam, a project of Narada Gana Sabha in 1997 in Chennai, there was a host of topics: evils of the current education system, the caste and reservation systems, threat of nuclear weapons, AIDS, the population explosion, corruption in politics, bribery, religious fanaticism, secularism, the greed for riches, the Chinese aggression, the Dandi March, literacy, agriculture, mechanisation, industrialisation. Most recently, some dancers of Nrityanjali Academy (Andhra Pradesh) managed to draw their divine inspiration even from Condom Songs.

The true traditional Indian dance, it has to be stated clearly, is not a vulgar form of entertainment but a sacred ritual that is supposed to bring the rasanubhava (catharsis, or spiritual upliftment) to the rasika (audience) and the dancer.

1. Indian classical dancers dance to________.

a) Vocal accompaniment

b) Instrumental accompaniment

c) Emotions

d) Both A and B

e) None of these

Ans. Both A and B

2. Traditional Indian dance, in particularly Bharatanatyam and Odissi, is ________.

a) Exercise for the mind

b) Artistic Yoga

c) Meditation

d) Amusement

e) Song & Dance Sequence

Ans. Artistic Yoga

3. Identify the odd one out.

a) Kathakali

b) Odissi

c) Kathak

d) Manipuri

e) Salsa

Ans. Salsa

Investment and Consumption

There was in increase of about 10% in the investment in the public sector, like electricity, irrigation quarrying, public services and transport; even though the emphasis leaned towards transport and away from the other sectors mentioned. A 16-17% growth in investment, including a 30% increase in investment in business premises has been recorded in trade and services. Although there continued to be a decline in the share of agriculture in total gross investment in the economy, investment grew by 9% in absolute terms, largely spurred on by a 23% expansion of investment in agriculture equipment. Housing construction had 12% more invested in it in 1964, not so much owing to increase demand, as to fears of impending new taxes and limitation of building.

There was a rise of close to 11% in the total consumption in real terms during 1964 and per capita personal consumption by under 7%, as in 1963. The undesirable trend towards a rapid rise in consumption, evident in previous years, remains unaltered. Since at current prices consumption rose by 16% and disposable income by 13%, there was evidently a fall in the rate of saving in the private sector of the economy. Once again a swift advance in the standard of living was indicated in consumption patterns. Though fruit consumption increased, expenditure on food, especially bread and staple items, declined significantly. There was a continuing increase in the outlay on furniture and household equipment, health, education and recreation. The greatest proof of altered living standards was the rapid expansion of expenditure on transport (including private cars) and personal services of all kinds, which occurred during 1964. The changing composition if purchased durable goods demonstrated the progressive affluence of large sectors of the public. On the one hand increased purchase of automobiles and television sets were registered, a point of saturation was rapidly being approached for items like the first household radio, gas cookers, and electric refrigerators.

1. It is possible to to conclude from this passage, that the people of the country were

a) spending more money than they earn

b) investing and consuming at an accelerated pace

c) saving more money than previously

d) spending their money wisely

e) lacking in necessities

Ans. (b).

2. According to the author the trend towards a rapid rise in consumption is "undesirable" as:

a) there was an increase in the expenditure on frills and luxuries

b) the people were affluent

c) there was a rise in the standard of living

d) people were eating less

e) people were saving less

Ans. (e).

3. It is possible to conclude that the United States is not the discussed country as:

a) there was a decline in the expenditures for food

b) From the statement that the saturation point was rapidly being approached for first household radios

c) there is no mention of military expenditures

d) the people were affluent

e) the people were not saving their money

Ans. (b).

4. The area, which saw the greatest expenditure of investment funds was

a) The public sector

b) Business premises

c) Housing construction

d) Agricultural equipment

e) A field which cannot be determined.

Ans. (e).

Recognition and Interpretation

Visual recognition involves storing and retrieving memories. Neural activity, triggered by the eye, forms an image in the brains memory system that constitutes an internal representation of the viewed object. When an object is encountered again, it is matched with its internal representation and thereby recognized. Controversy surrounds the question of whether recognition is a parallel, one-step process or a serial, step-by-step one. Psychologists of the Gestalt school maintain that object are recognised as wholes in a parallel procedure:, the internal representation is matched with the retinal image in a single operation. Other psychologists have proposed that internal representation features are matched serially with an object's features. Although some experiments show that, as an object become familiar, its internal representation becomes more familiar, its internal representation becomes more holistic and the recognition process correspondingly more parallel, the weight of evidence seems to support the serial hypothesis, at least for objects that are not notably simple and familiar.

1. It can be inferred from the passage that the matching process in visual recognition is
   a) Not a natural activity.
   b) Not possible when an object is viewed for the very first time.
   c) Not possible if a feature of a familiar object is changed in same way.
   d) Only possible when a retinal image is received in the brain as a unitary whole.
   e) Now fully understood as a combination of the serial and parallel process.

   Ans. (a).
2. In terms of its tone and form, the passage can best be characterised as
   a) A biased exposition
   b) A speculative study
   c) A dispassionate presentation
   d) An indignant denial
   e) A dogmatic explanation.

   Ans. (c).
3. The author is primarily concerned with
   a) Explaining how the brain receives images.
   b) Synthesizing hypotheses of visual recognition.
   c) Examining the evidence supporting the serial recognition hypothesis.
   d) Discussing visual recognition and some hypotheses proposed to explain it.
   e) Reporting on recent experiments dealing with memory systems and their relationship to neural activity.

   Ans. (b).

4. According to the passage, Gestalt psychologists make which of the following suppositions about visual recognition?
   i. A retinal image is in exactly the same form as its internal representation.
   ii. An object is recognised as a whole without any need for analysis into component parts.
   iii. The matching of an object with its internal representation occurs in only one step.
   a) ii. only
   b) iii. only
   c) i. and iii. only
   d) ii. and iii. only
   e) i., ii. and iii.

   Ans. (d).

The Fourth Dimension

According to Albert Einstein the non-mathematician, is seized by a mysterious shuddering when he hears of 'four-dimensional' things, he is seized by a feeling, which is very similar to the thoughts awakened by the occult. And at the same time the statement that the world in which we live is a four-dimensional space - time continuum is quite a common place statement.

This might lead to an argument regarding the use of the term "commonplace" by Einstein. Yet the difficulty lies more in the wording than the ideas. Einstein's concept of the universe as a four-dimensional space-time continuum becomes plain and clear, when what he means by "continuum" becomes clear. A continuum is something that is continuous, A ruler, for example, is a one-dimensional space continuum. Most rulers are divided into inches and fractions, scaled down to one-sixteenth of an inch.

Will it be possible to conceive a ruler, which is calibrated to a millionth or billionth of an inch. In theory there is no reason why the steps from point to point should not be even smaller. What distinguishes a continuum is the fact that the space between any two points can be sub-divided into an infinite number of smaller divisions.

A railroad track is a one-dimensional space continuum and on it the engineer of a train can describe his position at any time by citing a single co-ordinate point – i.e., a station or a milestone. A sea captain, however, has to worry about two dimensions. The surface of the sea is a two-dimensional continuum and the co-ordinate points by which sailor fixes his positions in his two dimensional continuum are latitude and longitude. An airplane pilot guides his plane through a three-dimensional continuum, hence he has to consider not only latitude and longitude, but also his height above the ground. The continuum of an airplane pilot constitutes space as we perceive it. In other words, the space of our world is a three-dimensional continuum.

Just indicating its position in space is not enough while describing any physical event, which involves motion. How position changes in time also needs to be mentioned. Thus to give an accurate picture of the operation of a New York-Chicago express, one must mention not only that it goes from New York to Albany to Syracuse to Cleveland to Toledo to Chicago, but also the times at which it touches each of those points. This can be done either by means of a timetable or a visual chart. If the miles between New York and Chicago are plotted horizontally on a piece of ruled paper and the hours and minutes are plotted vertically, then a diagonal line properly drawn across the page illustrates the progress of the train in two-dimensional space-time continuum. This type of graphic representation is familiar to most newspaper readers; a stock market chart, for example, pictures financial events in a two-dimensional dollar-time continuum. Similarly for the best picturization of the flight of an airplane from New York to Los Angeles a four-dimensional space-time continuum is essential. The latitude, longitude and altitude will only make sense to the traffic manager of the airline if the time co-ordinate is also mentioned.

Therefore time is the fourth dimension. If a flight has to be looked at, perceived as a whole, it wouldn't work if it is broken down into a series of disconnected take-offs, climbs, glides, and landing, it needs to be looked at and perceived as a continuous four-dimensional space-time continuum curve.

1. In order to explain a difficult topic, the author use
   a) Simply phrased definition's
   b) An incessant metaphor
   c) A plain writing style
   d) Familiar images
   e) A quotation from Einstein

   Ans. (d).

2. The significant feature of a continuum, according to the passage, revolves around
   a) The divisibility of the interval between any two points.
   b) An ordinary ruler's calibre for marking.
   c) Its unending curve.
   d) Its lucid from providing comprehensibility to the non - scientists as well.
   e) Its variety of co-ordinates.

   Ans. (a).

3. The purpose of this passage is to highlight the point that
   a) Plots and sea captains have something in common
   b) Stock market charts may be helpful to physicists
   c) The fourth dimension is time
   d) Non-mathematician's are often afraid of the commonplace
   e) There is a marked quality to distance

   Ans. (c).

4. According to the passage, an airlines traffic manager depends upon all of the following EXCEPT
   a) latitude
   b) altitude
   c) the time co-ordinate
   d) longitude
   e) the continuous curve in co four

   Ans. (e).

5. The underlying tone of this selection is
   a) persuasive
   b) deferential
   c) candid
   d) instructive
   e) gently condescending

   Ans. (d).

6. According to the author if on wishes portray a physical event in which motion plays a role-one has to
   a) Make use of a time-table
   b) Indicate how position changes in time
   c) Be conversant with the scientist's theories
   d) Describe it graphically
   e) Be aware of altitude, latitude and longitude

   Ans. (b).

7. The sea-captain's example has been cited in order to
   a) Help understand a two-dimensional continuum
   b) Set up a logical progression
   c) Simplify what ever is too elaborate

d) Mitigate the gap between the engineer and pilot

e) To sustain out interest in the reading of the passage.

Ans. (a).

Oceans

From the 197 million square miles, which make up the surface of the globe, 71 per cent is covered by the interconnecting bodies of marine water; the Pacific Ocean alone covers half the Earth and averages near 14,000 feet in depth. The portions which rise above sea level are the continents –Eurasia, Africa; North America, South America, Australia, and Antarctica. The submerged borders of the continental masses are the continental shelves, beyond which lie the deep-sea basins.

The ocean are deepest not in the center but in some elongated furrows, or long narrow troughs, called deeps. These profound troughs have a peripheral arrangement, notably around the borders of the pacific and Indian oceans. The position of the deeps, like the highest mountains, are of recent origin, since otherwise they would have been filled with waste from the lands. This is further strengthened by the observation that the deeps are quite often, where world-shaking earthquakes occur. To cite an example, the “tidal wave” that in April, 1946, caused widespread destruction along Pacific coasts resulted from a strong earthquake on the floor of the Aleutian Deep.

The topography of the ocean floors is none too well known, since in great areas the available soundings are hundreds or even thousands of miles apart. However, the floor of the Atlantic is becoming fairly well known as a result of special surveys since 1920. A broad, well-defined ridge-the Mid-Atlantic ridge-runs north and south between Africa and the two Americas and numerous other major irregularities diversify the Atlantic floor. Closely spaced soundings show that many parts of the oceanic floors are as rugged as mountainous regions of the continents. Use of the recently perfected method of submarine topography.

During world war II great strides were made in mapping submarine surfaces, particularly in many parts of the vast Pacific basin.

Most of the continents stand on an average of 2870 feet above sea level. North America averages 2300 feet; Europe averages only 1150 feet; and Asia, the highest of the larger continental subdivisions, averages 3200 feet. Mount Everest, which is the highest point in the globe, is 29,000 feet above the sea; and as the greatest known depth in the sea is over 35,000 feet, the maximum relief (that is, the difference in altitude between the lowest and highest points) exceeds 64,000 feet, or exceeds 12 miles. The continental masses and the deep-sea basins are relief features of the first order; the deeps, ridges, and volcanic cones that diversify the sea floor, as well as the plains, plateaus, and mountains of the continents, are relief features of the second order. The lands are unendingly subject to a complex of activities Summarised in the term erosion, which first sculptures them in great detail and then tends to reduce them ultimately to sea level. The modelling of the landscape by weather, running water, and other agents is apparent to the keenly observant eye and causes thinking people to speculate on what must be the final result of the ceaseless wearing down of the lands. Much before there was any recognizable science as geology, Shakespeare wrote "the revolution of the times makes mountains level."

1. The peripheral furrows or deeps are found

a) only in the pacific and Indian oceans

b) near earthquakes

c) near the shore

d) in the center of the ocean

e) to be 14,000 feet in depth in the pacific.

Ans. (c).

2. The largest ocean is the

a) Atlantic

b) pacific
c) Aleutian deep
d) arctic
e) Indian.

Ans. (b).

3. We may conclude from this passage that earthquakes
a) Occur more frequently in newly formed land or sea formations
b) Are caused by the weight of the water
c) Cause erosion
d) Occur in the deeps
e) Will ultimately "make mountains level".

Ans. (a).

4. The highest mountains are
a) oldest
b) in excess of 12 miles
c) near the deeps
d) relief features of the first order
e) of recent origin.

Ans. (e).

5. The science of geology was started
a) By the Greeks
b) During world war II
c) April 1946
d) After 1600
e) In 1920

Ans. (d).

6. The highest point on North America is

a) 2870 feet above sea level
b) not mentioned in the passage
c) higher than the highest point in Europe
d) 2300 feet above sea level
e) in Mexico.

Ans. (b).

7. The deeps are subject to change caused by
a) erosion
b) soundings
c) earthquakes
d) waste
e) weathering

Ans. (c).

8. The continental masses
a) Rise above sea level
b) Consist of six continents
c) Are relief features of the second order
d) Are partially submerged
e) Comprise 29 per cent of the earth's surface.

Ans. (d).

Nahuatl

A clear answer to whether the languages of the ancient American peoples were made use of for expressing abstract universal concepts can be sought in the case of Nahuatl, which like Greek and German, is a language that allows the formation of extensive compounds. By combining radicals or semantic elements, single compound words can express complex conceptual relations, often of an abstract universal character.

The tlamatinime ("those who know") were able to use this rich stock of abstract terms to express the nuances of their thought. They also availed themselves of other forms of expression with metaphorical meaning, some probably original, some derived from Toltec coinages. Of these forms the most characteristic in Nahuatl is the juxtaposition of two words that, because they are synonyms, associated terms, or even contraries, complement each other to evoke one single idea. The juxtaposed terms, used as metaphor, suggest specific or essential traits of the being they refer to, introducing a mode of poetry as an almost habitual form of expression.

1. According to the passage, some abstract universal ideas can be expressed in Nahuatl by

a) Putting various meaningful elements together in one word

b) Taking away from a word any reference to particular instances

c) Turning each word of a phrase into a poetic metaphor

d) Giving a word a new and opposite meaning

e) Removing a word from its associations with other words.

Ans. (a).

2. It can be inferred solely from the information in the passage that

a) Metaphors are always used in Nahuatl to express abstract conceptual relationships

b) There are many languages that, like Greek or German, allow extensive compounding

c) The abstract terms of the Nahuatl language are habitually used in poetry

d) Some record or evidence of the though of the tlamatinime exists

e) All abstract universal ideas are ideas of complex relations.

Ans. (d).

3. A main purpose of the passage is to

a) Argue against a theory of poetic expression by citing evidence about the Nahuatl

b) Delineate the function of the tlamatinime in Nahuatl society

c) Explore the rich metaphorical heritage the Nahuatl received from the toltecs

d) Describe some conceptual and aesthetic resources of the Nahuatl language

e) Explain the abstract philosophy of the Nahuatl thinkers.

Ans. (d).

Learning and Protein Synthesis

Few areas of neuron behavioural research seemed more promising is the early sixties than that investigating the relationship between protein synthesis and learning. The conceptual framework for the research was derived directly from molecular biology, which had shown that genetic information is stored in nucleic acids and expressed in proteins why not acquired information as well.

The first step towards establishing a connection between protein synthesis and learning seemed to be to block memory (cause adhesion) by interrupting the production of proteins. We were fortunate in finding a non lethal dosage of puromycin that could, it first appealed, thoroughly inhibit brain protein synthesis as well as reliability produce amnesia.

Before the actual connection between protein synthesis and learning could be established however we began to have douche about whether inhibition of protein synthesis was in fact the method by which puromycin produced amnesia. First, ocher drugs, glutavimides themselves potent protein synthesis inhibitors either failed to cause amnesia in some situations where it could easily be induced by puromycin or produced an amnesia with a different time course from that of puromycin. Second, puromycin was found to inhabit protein synthesis by breaking certain amino acid chaim, and the resulting fragments were suspected of being the actual cause of amnesia is some eases. Third, puromycin was reported to cause abnormalities in the train, including seizures. Thus, not only were decreased protein synthesis and amnesia dissociated, but alternative mechanism for the amnestic action of puromycin were readily suggested.

So, puromycin turned out to be a disappointment. It came to be regarded as a poor agent for amnesia studies, although, of course, it was poor only in the context of our original paradigm of protein synthesis inhibition. In our frustration, our initial response was simply to change dregs rather than our conceptual orientation. After many such disappointments, however, it now appears unlikely, that we will make a firm connection between protein synthesis and learning merely by pursuing the approaches of the past our experience with drugs has shown that all the amnestic agents, often interfere with memory in ways that seem unrelated to their inhibition of protein synthesis. More importantly, the notion that the interruption or intensification of protein production in the train can be related in cause and affect fashion to learning non seems simplistic and unproductive. Remove the battery from a car and the car will not go Drive the car a long distance at high speed and the battery will become more highly charged. Neither of these facts proves that the battery power the car, only knowledge of the overall automotive system will reveal it mechanism of locomotion and the role of the battery with in the system.

1. The primary purpose a the passage is to show that extensive experimentation has

a) Mot supported the hypothesis that learning is directly dependent on protein synthesis

b) Cast doubt on the value of puromycin in the newer behavioural study of learning

c) Revealed the importance of amnesia in the neuron behavioural study of learning

d) Demonstrated the importance of amino acid fragmentation in the induction of amnesia.

e) Not yet demonstrated the applicability of molecular biology to behavioural research.

Ans. (a).

2. According to the passage, neuron behaviourists initially based their belief that protein synthesis was related to learning on which of the following?

a) Specific research into learning on which of the following
b) Traditional theories about learning
c) Historic experiments on the effects puromycin
d) Previous discoveries in molecular biology
e) Now technique in protein synthesis.

Ans. (d).

3. This passage was most likely excepted from

a) A book review in a leading journal devoted to genetic research.
b) A diary kept by a practicing neuron behavioural research
c) An article summarizing a series of scientific investigations in neuron behavioural research.
d) A news paper article on recent advances in the biochemistry of learning
e) A technical article on experimental techniques in the field of molecular biology.

Ans. (c).

4. It can be inferred from the passage that after puromycin was perceived to be a disappointment, researches did which of the following?

a) They continued to experiment with puromycin until a neuron anatomical framework was developed.
b) They continued to experiment with puromycin, but also tried other protein synthesis inhibitors

c) They ceased to experiment with puromycin and shifted to other promising protein synthesis inhibitors.

d) They ceased to experiment with puromycin and reexamined through experiments the relationship between genetic information and acquired information.

e) They continued to experiment with puromycin, but applied their results to other facts of memory research.

Ans. (c).

5. In the example of the car (lines 62-70) the battery is meant to represent which of the following elements in the neuron behavioural research programme?

a) glutarimides

b) acquired information

c) puromycin

d) amnesia

e) protein synthesis

Ans. (e).

6. The passage all of the following as effects of puromycin except

a) Fragmentation of amino-acid chaim

b) Inhibition of protein synthesis

c) Brain seizures

d) Memory loss

e) Destruction of genetic information

Ans. (e).

7. Which of the following statements would be most likely to come after the last sentences of the passage?

a) It is important in the future, therefore for behavioural bio-chemist to focus on the several components of the total learning system.

b) The ambivalent status of current research, however should not deter neuron behaviourists from exploring the deeper connection between protein production and learning.

c) The failures of the past, however must not impede further research into the amnestic of protein-synthesis inhibitors.

d) It is important in the future, therefore, for behavioural biochemist to emphasise more strongly place of their specific findings within the overall protein synthesis model of learning.

e) It is a legacy of this research, therefore, that molecular biology's genetic models have led to disagreement among neuron behaviourists.

Ans. (a).

Shift of Labour

In any country, the wages commanded by the labourers who have comparable skills but who work in various industries are determined by the productivity of the least productive unit of labour, i.e. the unit of labour which works in the industry which has catatest economic disadvantages. We will represent the various opportunities of employment in a country like United States by Symbols. A standing for a group of industries in which we have exceptional economic advantage over foreign countries; B for a group in which our advantages are less; E , one in which they are still less; D, the group of industries in which they are the least of all.

When our population is so small that all our labour can be engaged in the group represented by A, productivity of labour and (therefore wages) will be at their maximum. when our population increases so that some of the labour will have to work in group B, the wages of all labour must decline to the level of productivity in that group. But no employer, without government aid, will yet be able to afford to hire labour to exploit the opportunities, represented by E and D, unless there is a further increase in population.

But suppose that the political party in power holds the belief that we should produce everything that we consume, that the opportunities represented by E and D should also be exploited. The commodities, that the industries composing C and D will produce have been hitherto obtained from abroad in exchange for commodities produce by A and B. The government now renders this difficult by imposing high duties upon the former class of commodities. This means that workers in A and B must pay higher prices for what they buy, but do not receive higher prices for what they sell.

After the duty has gone into effect and the prices of commodities that can be produced by C and D have rich sufficiently enterprises will be able to hire labour at the wages prevailing in A and B and establish industries in C and D. So far as the remaining labours in A and B buy the products of C and D ,the difference between the price which they pay for these product and the price they would pay it they were permitted to import those products duty-free is a tax paid not to the government, but to the producers in C and D, to enable the later to remain in business. It is on uncompensated deduction from the natural earnings of the labourers in A and B. nor are the workers in C and D paid as much, estimated in purchasing power as they would have received if they had been allowed to remain in A and B under the earlier conditions.

1. The author's main point is that

   a) The government ought to subsidize C and D

   b) Wages ought to be independent of international trade

   c) It is impossible to attain national self sufficiency

   d) The varying productivity of the various industries leads tot he inequalities in wages of workers in these industries

   e) A policy that draws labour from the fields of catater natural productiveness to fields of lower natural productiveness tends to redirect purchasing power.

   Ans. (e).

2. No employer, without government aid will yet be able to afford to hire labour to exploit the opportunities represented by C and D because

a) The population has increased

b) Productivity of labour is not at the maximum

c) Productivity would drop correspondingly with the wages of labour

d) We cannot produce everything we consume

e) Enterprises would have to pay wages equivalent to those obtained by workers in A and B while producing under catater disadvantages.

Ans. (e).

3. When C and D are established, workers in these industries

a) Receives wages equal to those workers in A and B

b) Receives higher wages than do the workers in A and B

c) Are not affected so adversely by the levying of duties as are workers in A and B

d) Must be paid by government funds collected from the duties on imports.

e) Receive lower wages than do the workers in A and B.

Ans. (a).

4. We cannot exploit C and D unless

a) The producers in E and D are compensated for the disadvantages under which they operate.

b) We export large quantities of commodities produced by A and B

c) The prices of commodities produced by A and B are raised

d) The productivity of labour in all industries is increased

e) We allow duties to be paid to the producers in C and D rather than to the government.

Ans. (a).

■■■

Chapter 4

Practice Exercises

Read the passage given below and answer questions that follow based on the information given in the passage.

Media Merger

First AOL and Time Warner announced their intention to combine. Then came Time Warner/EMI and Tribune/ Times Mirror. Even more significant, however, has been the speculation that these mergers have caused: If these transactions are consummated, a large number of additional media mergers are expected. There is even the possibility of a nightmare scenario-a wave of media mergers so large that within a decade most of our information will be supplied by perhaps six of these huge conglomerates and a fringe of much smaller firms.

It's time to ask two critical questions. Is this kind of media oligopoly what we, as a society, want? And if not, can the antitrust laws effectively prevent the threatened merger wave? The answer to the first question is clear. We do not want a media oligopoly. The answer to the second question, however, is far less certain. We should distrust a media oligopoly because it would give undue control to a small number of individuals. This need not manifest itself in a price rise for the daily newspaper or AOL's monthly fee. Rather, it could consist of a change in editorial viewpoints, a shift in the relative prominence of links to certain websites or a decision not to cover certain topics, because they are not "newsworthy". These problems could exist without any improper intent on the part of the media barons. Even if they try to be fair and objective, they will necessarily bring their own worldview to the job. And in time some of these conglomerates may be controlled by people who are not fair or objective.

At first it might appear that the antitrust laws can be of little help in grappling with the issues presented by large media mergers. The anti-merger laws are commonly understood as protecting price competition, and a relatively small number of firms-to greatly oversimplify, let's say at most half a dozen-are normally thought to be enough to keep a market price-competitive. In industry after industry firms merge until there is only a handful left, and the antitrust enforcers are normally unable to do anything to prevent this. (In former years mergers were governed by an "incipiency" standard that prevented mergers and merger waves well before they would have led to very large or likely anti-competitive problems.) Even if a handful of firms are enough to insure effective competition in most industries, would six conglomerate media firms be sufficient for the diversity of viewpoints necessary to democracy? Would we be reassured if they could somehow guarantee that they would sell their magazines and Internet advertisements at competitive prices?

I am hopeful that the antitrust laws, if correctly and vigorously interpreted, are adaptable enough to meet this challenge. This is because antitrust is not exclusively about price. It is essentially about choice-about giving consumers a competitive range of options in the marketplace so that they can make their own, effective selection from the market's offerings. Consumers should be able to make their choices along any dimension important to them-including price, variety and editorial viewpoint.

Communications media compete in part by offering independent editorial viewpoints and an independent gatekeeper function. Six media firms cannot effectively respond to the demand for choice or diversity competition by extending their product lines, because new media products will inevitably bear, to some degree, the perspective of their corporate parent. For these reasons competition in terms of editorial viewpoint or gate keeping can be guaranteed only by insuring that a media market contains a significantly larger number of firms than is required for price competition in other, more conventional markets.

It is unclear, however, whether this interpretation of the anti-trust laws will be applied by the enforcement agencies and the courts. What is needed, therefore, is a much more careful look at the challenges that will be raised by future media mergers.

This could best be accomplished if Congress created a Temporary Committee to Study Media Mergers and Media Convergence. This committee could include members of Congress; the heads of the Federal Trade Commission, the Federal Communications Commission and the Justice Department's antitrust division; CEOs of media companies; and representatives of consumer groups. The committee would identify problems that may be caused by large media mergers and by media convergence. If the committee concludes that existing antitrust laws are inadequate, it should recommend to Congress that new anti-merger legislation be enacted. This may be the only way to prevent the nightmare scenario of a media oligopoly.

1. A wave of media mergers could

a) be a threat to democracy

b) result in limiting editorial viewpoints

c) result in misuse of certain laws

d) both (a) and (b)

e) none of the above

Ans. (d).

2. According to the passage, what could be the most significant outcome of media oligopoly?

a) An increase in the cost of newspapers

b) The fact that in the long run, there will be a shift of power to people who might not be

c) balanced and fair in the way they deal with the media

d) Certain websites may get more prominence than others

e) There will be no competition among the newspapers

f) There will soon exist only six media conglomerates

Ans. (b).

3. Which of the following statements, according to the author, are true

a) Half a dozen firms are enough to keep the market price-competitive

b) Half a dozen companies are not enough to provide a democratic media

c) Enforcement agencies may not interpret the ant-trust laws correctly

d) Half a dozen companies will be inadequate to meet the consumer demand for product diversity

i. (a, b)

ii. (a, b, c)

iii. (a, b, c, d)

iv. (b, c, d)

v. (a, c, d)

Ans. (iii).

4. The current anti-trust laws

a) are not sufficient to deal with issues relating to large scale media mergers

b) can prevent mergers from happening

c) will be effective if properly interpreted

d) favour a particular company or group of companies

e) none of the above

Ans. (c).

5. To get a clear picture of the challenges posed by media mergers, the author recommends:

a) creation of strict laws

b) strengthening the enforcement agencies

c) creation of a study committee by the congress

d) none of the above

e) all of the above

Ans. (c).

The First Computer Programmer

Ada Lovelace was the daughter of the poet Lord Byron. She was taught by Mary Somerville, a well-known researcher and scientific author, who introduced her to Charles Babbage in June 1833. Babbage was an English mathematician, who first had the idea for a programmable computer.

In 1842 and 1843, Ada translated the work of an Italian mathematician, Luigi Menabrea, on Babbage's Analytical Engine. Though mechanical, this machine was an important step in the history of computers; it was the design of a mechanical general-purpose computer. Babbage worked on it for many years until his death in 1871. However, because of financial, political, and legal issues, the engine was never built. The design of the machine was very modern; it anticipated the first completed general-purpose computers by about 100 years.

When Ada translated the article, she added a set of notes which specified in complete detail a method for calculating certain numbers with the Analytical Engine, which have since been recognised by historians as the world's first computer program.

She also saw possibilities in it that Babbage hadn't: she realised that the machine could compose pieces of music. The computer programming language 'Ada', used in some aviation and military programs, is named after her.

1. Ada Lovelace's teacher introduced her to Charles Babbage.

True

False

Ans. True.

2. Babbage programmed the first computer.

True

False

Ans. True.

3. Ada translated the article in 1843.

True

False

Ans. Flase. Ada translated the article in 1842.

4. The Analytical Engine was electronic.

True

False

Ans. True.

5. Luigi Menabrea designed the first computer.

True

False

Ans. True.

6. Babbage finished the machine before he died.

True

False

Ans. True.

7. Babbage's design was way back of time.

True

False

Ans. False. Babbage's design was ahead of its time.

8. Ada's work took years to be recognised as being the first computer program.

True

False

Ans. False. Ada's work was instantly recognised as being the first computer program.

9. Babbage saw that his machine could write music.

True

False

Ans. True.

10. Ada wrote military and aviation computer programs.

True

False

Ans. True.

Airbus Crisis Over

Airbus says it has turned the corner after a crisis connected to production problems and turmoil in the boardroom at its A380 super-jumbo project that has gone on for the past year. Speaking at the Paris air show, Louis Gallois, CEO of the European planemaker, said, "Airbus is back."

Airbus, which announced a raft of orders on the first day of the show, is competing with Boeing, its American rival, for the title of the largest planemaker in the world.

Boeing is expected to reveal the numbers of orders for its 787

Dreamliner soon. Airbus orders unveiled on Monday included Qatar Airways confirming a $16bn order for 80 A350 Airbus planes and ordering three A380 super-jumbos for about $750m.

Boeing and Airbus are also competing for orders from aircraft leasing firms. Orders from these companies – who rank highly among the biggest global buyers of aircraft – are often regarded as an indication of how successful a model will be in the long-term.

Airbus also secured orders from US Airways that are worth $10bn for 22 of its A350 jets, 60 A320s and ten of its A330-200 wide-body planes.

A few months ago, Airbus unveiled a major cost-cutting programme aiming to reduce the workforce in Europe by 10,000, as well as announcing a group restructuring. "I can tell you with full confidence that Airbus is back and fully back, as you have started noting yesterday as demonstrated by our first day announcements," said Mr Gallois on the second day of the air show.

However, Boeing also announced a deal with General Electric (GE) on the show's first day. GE's commercial aviation services placed an order for six 777 Boeing freighters valued at around $1.4bn, to be delivered in the last quarter of 2008.

A Wall Street Journal website report, quoting the Delta operating chief yesterday said that Delta Air Lines were on the verge of ordering as many as 125 Boeing 787 jetliners by the end of this year. However, a spokesman for Delta later said that it had been having conversations "with several aircraft makers" and that "no final decision" had been made on future fleet purchases.

1. The problems at Airbus

a) have been resolved completely.

b) are well on their way to being sorted out.

c) are far from resolved.

Ans. (b).

2. Airbus announced
   a) a large number of orders on the first day of the show.
   b) some orders on the first day of the show.
   c) a few orders on the first day of the show.

   Ans. (a).
3. Qatar Airways ordered
   a) 83 planes on Monday.
   b) 80 planes on Monday.
   c) 3 planes on Monday.

   Ans. (c).
4. US Airways
   a) placed an order for the new super-jumbo.
   b) didn't place an order for the new super-jumbo.
   c) may have placed an order for the new super-jumbo.

   Ans. (b).
5. Boeing
   a) announced sales of the Dreamliner.
   b) may sell some Dreamliners to General Electric.
   c) may sell some Dreamliners to Delta Air Lines.

   Ans. Boeing.
6. The Wall Street Journal website report
   a) was definitely correct.
   b) was possibly correct.
   c) was definitely wrong.

   Ans. (c).

Bio-fuels and the Environment

Leading investors have joined the growing chorus of concern about governments and companies rushing into producing bio fuels as a solution for global warming, saying that many involved in the sector could be jeopardizing future profits if they do not consider the long-term impact of what they are doing carefully.

It is essential to build sustainability criteria into the supply chain of any green fuel project in order to ensure that there is no adverse effect on the surrounding environment and social structures. The report produced by the investors expresses concern that many companies may not be fully aware of the potential pitfalls in the bio-fuel sector.

Production of corn and soya beans has increased dramatically in the last years as an eco-friendly alternative to fossil fuels but environmental and human rights campaigners are worried that this will lead to destruction of rain forests. Food prices could also go up as there is increased competition for crops as both foodstuffs and sources of fuel. Last week, the UN warned that biofuels could have dangerous side effects and said that steps need to be taken to make sure that land converted to grow biofuels does not damage the environment or cause civil unrest. There is already great concern about palm oil, which is used in many foods in addition to being an important biofuel, as rain forests are being cleared in some countries and people driven from their homes to create palm oil plantations.

An analyst and author of the investors' report says that biofuels are not a cure for climate change but they can play their part as long as governments and companies manage the social and environmental impacts thoroughly. There should also be greater measure taken to increase efficiency and to reduce demand.

1. .... are worried about the boom in bio-fuels.

a) Few people

b) Many people

c) Only these leading investors

Ans. (a).

2. Bio-fuel producers .... know about the possible problems.

a) do not

b) might not

c) must not

Ans. (b).

3. Environmentalists believe that increased production of corn and soya

a) has destroyed rain forests.

b) may lead to the destruction of rain forests.

c) will lead to the destruction of rain forests.

Ans. (c).

4. Bio-fuels might

a) drive food prices up.

b) drive food prices down.

c) have little or no impact on food prices.

Ans. (a).

5. The increased production of palm oil

a) just affects the environment.

b) just affects people.

c) affects both people and the environment.

Ans. (c).

6. The author of the report says that bio-fuels.

a) have no role to play in fighting global warming.

b) can be effective in fighting global warming on their own.

c) should be part of a group of measures to fight global warming.

Ans. (b).

Bully for You

The makers of a controversial computer game about bullying have decided to go ahead and launch it despite calls for it to be banned. In the game, players take on the role of a new students at a school and have to fight the bullies, by punching them or hitting them with a baseball bat.

Critics have said that the game encourages violence, but the makers deny this and say that, while there is violence in the game, it is just an amusing look at school life, besides which, the violence in the game is directed against the bullies to protect pupils who are being bullied. The makers also say that players will learn to stand up to bullies.

A British politician, a former minister, has called for it to be banned as it might affect the way young people perceive violence.

Anti-bullying charities have said that the game might make people respond violently to bullies, which might make things more complicated and result in injuries.

1. The makers of the computer game decided not to release it.

True

False

Ans. False.

2. In the game, the player takes on the role of a bully.

True

False

Ans. False.

3. The game is set in a university.

True

False

Ans. False.

4. Everyone agrees that the game encourages violence.

True

False

Ans. False.

5. A British politician has spoken in favour of the game.

True

False

Ans. False.

6. The politician used to be a minister.

True

False

Ans. True.

7. The politician thinks it might make young people look at violence differently.

True

False

Ans. True.

8. The anti-bullying charity thinks the game is good because it might make pupils stand up to bullies.

True

False

Ans. False.

9. The anti-bullying charity thinks that people might get hurt because of this game.

True

False

Ans. True.

10. The makers of the game have changed the contents before releasing it in the UK.

True

False

Ans. False.

Papua New Guinea Reconciliation

In Papua New Guinea, the descendants of cannibals who killed and ate four Fijian missionaries in 1878 have apologised for their ancestors' actions. They held a reconciliation ceremony, which was attended by thousands of people, in the East New Britain province where they were killed.

The missionaries were part of a group of Methodist ministers and teachers who arrived in 1875 to spread Christianity. The murders three years later, by Tolai tribespeople on the Gazelle Peninsula, triggered angry reprisals. The English pastor who was head of the mission, George Brown, avenged the killings by taking part in an expedition that resulted in the deaths of a number of tribespeople and the burning of several villages.

Candles were lit in memory of the four. Fiji's High Commissioner in Papua New Guinea, Ratu Isoa Tikoca, accepted the apologies on behalf of the descendants. "We at this juncture are deeply touched and wish you the greatest joy of forgiveness as we finally end this record disagreement," he said.

The Governor-General Sir Paulias Matane praised the early missionaries for making the country Christian and called for more people to follow the guiding principles of the religion.

1. The descendants of the cannibals are sorry about what happened.

True

False

Ans. True.

2. Few people attended the ceremony.

True

False

Ans. False.

3. The ceremony was held in the UK.

True

False

Ans. False.

4. The missionaries were killed very soon after they arrived.

True

False

Ans. False.

5. No one was punished for the killings.

True

False

Ans. False.

6. The Fijian representative attended.

True

False

Ans. True.

7. Ratu Isoa Tikoca was not moved by the ceremony.

True

False

Ans. False.

8. Candles were lit to remember the missionaries.

True

False

Ans. True.

9. Sir Paulias Matane resents the work of the early missionaries.

True

False

Ans. False.

10. Sir Paulias Matane wishes that more people had religious principles.

True

False

Ans. True.

Introducing Science

The pioneers of the teaching of science imagined that its introduction into education would remove the conventionality, artificiality, and backward-lookingness which were characteristic; of classical studies, but they were gravely disappointed. So, too, in their time had the humanists thought that the study of the classical authors in the original would banish at once the dull pedantry and superstition of medieaval scholasticism. The professional schoolmaster was a match for both of them, and has almost managed to make the understanding of chemical reactions as dull and as dogmatic an affair as the reading of Virgil's Aeneid. The chief claim for the use of science in education is that it teaches a child something about the actual universe in which he is living, in making him acquainted with the results of scientific discovery, and at the same time teaches him how to think logically and inductively by studying scientific method. A certain limited success has been reached in the first of these aims, but practically none at all in the second. Those privileged members of the community who have been through a secondary or public school education may be expected to know something about the elementary physics and chemistry of a hundred years ago, but they probably know hardly more than any bright boy can pick up from an interest in wireless or scientific hobbies out of school hours.

As to the learning of scientific method, the whole thing is palpably a farce. Actually, for the convenience of teachers and the requirements of the examination system, it is necessary that the pupils not only do not learn scientific method but learn precisely the reverse, that is, to believe exactly what they are told and to reproduce it when asked, whether it seems nonsense to them or not. The way in which educated people respond to such quackeries as spiritualism or astrology, not to say more dangerous ones such as racial theories or currency myths, shows that fifty years of education in the method of science in Britain or Germany has produced no visible effect whatever. The only way of learning the method of science is the long and bitter way of personal experience, and, until the educational or social systems are altered to make this possible, the best we can expect is the production of a minority of people who are able to acquire some of the techniques of science and a still smaller minority who are able to use and develop them.

1. The author implies that the 'professional schoolmaster' has

a) no interest in teaching science

b) thwarted attempts to enliven education

c) aided true learning

d) supported the humanists

e) been a pioneer in both science and humanities.

Ans. (b).

2. The author's attitude to secondary and public school education in the sciences is

a) ambivalent

b) neutral

c) supportive

d) satirical

e) contemptuous

Ans. (e).

3. The word 'palpably' most nearly means

a) empirically

b) obviously

c) tentatively

d) markedly

e) ridiculously

Ans. (b).

4. The author blames all of the following for the failure to impart scientific method through the education system except

a) poor teaching

b) examination methods

c) lack of direct experience

d) the social and education systems

e) lack of interest on the part of students

Ans. (e).

5. If the author were to study current education in science to see how things have changed since he wrote the piece, he would probably be most interested in the answer to which of the following questions?

a) Do students know more about the world about them?

b) Do students spend more time in labouratories?

c) Can students apply their knowledge logically?

d) Have textbooks improved?

e) Do they respect their teachers?

Ans. (c).

6. Astrology is mentioned as an example of
 a) a science that needs to be better understood
 b) a belief which no educated people hold
 c) something unsupportable to those who have absorbed the methods of science
 d) the gravest danger to society
 e) an acknowledged failure of science

 Ans. (c).

7. All of the following can be inferred from the text except
 a) at the time of writing, not all children received a secondary school education
 b) the author finds chemical reactions interesting
 c) science teaching has imparted some knowledge of facts to some children
 d) the author believes that many teachers are authoritarian
 e) it is relatively easy to learn scientific method.

 Ans. (e).

Between Boys and Girls

By the time a child is six or seven she has all the essential avoidances well enough by heart to be trusted with the care of a younger child. And she also develops a number of simple techniques. She learns to weave firm square balls from palm leaves, to make pinwheels of palm leaves or frangipani blossoms, to climb a coconut tree by walking up the trunk on flexible little feet, to break open a coconut with one firm well-directed blow of a knife as long as she is tall, to play a number of group games and sing the songs which go with them, to tidy the house by picking up the litter on the stony floor, to bring water from the sea, to spread out the copra to dry and to help gather it in when rain threatens, to go to a neighboring house and bring back a lighted faggot for the chief's pipe or the cook-house fire.

But in the case of the little girls all these tasks are merely supplementary to the main business of baby-tending. Very small boys also have some care of the younger children, but at eight or nine years of age they are usually relieved of it. Whatever rough edges have not been smoothed off by this responsibility for younger children are worn off by their contact with older boys. For little boys are admitted to interesting and important activities only so long as their behaviour is circumspect and helpful. Where small girls are brusquely pushed aside, small boys will be patiently tolerated and they become adept at making themselves useful. The four or five little boys who all wish to assist at the important, business of helping a grown youth lasso reef eels, organize themselves into a highly efficient working team; one boy holds the bait, another holds an extra lasso, others poke eagerly about in holes in the reef looking for prey, while still another tucks the captured eels into his lavalava. The small girls, burdened with heavy babies or the care of little staggerers who are too small to adventure on the reef, discouraged by the hostility of the small boys and the scorn of the older ones, have little opportunity for learning the more adventurous forms of work and play. So while the little boys first undergo the chastening effects of baby-tending and then have many opportunities to learn effective cooperation under the supervision of older boys, the girls' education is less comprehensive. They have a high standard of individual responsibility, but the community provides them with no lessons in cooperation with one another. This is particularly apparent in the activities of young people: the boys organise quickly; the girls waste hours in bickering, innocent of any technique for quick and efficient cooperation.

1. The primary purpose of the passage with reference to the society under discussion is to

a) explain some differences in the upbringing of girls and boys

b) criticise the deficiencies in the education of girls

c) give a comprehensive account of a day in the life of an average young girl

d) delineate the role of young girls

e) show that young girls are trained to be useful to adults

Ans. explain some differences in the upbringing of girls and boys.

2. The word 'brusquely' most nearly means

a) quickly

b) gently

c) nonchalantly

d) abruptly

e) callously

Ans. abruptly.

3. The list of techniques in paragraph one could best be described as

a) household duties

b) rudimentary physical skills

c) important responsibilities

d) useful social skills

e) monotonous tasks

Ans. useful social skills.

4. It can be inferred that the 'high standard of individual responsibility' is

a) developed mainly through child-care duties

b) only present in girls

c) taught to the girl before she is entrusted with babies

d) actually counterproductive

e) weakened as the girl grows older.

Ans. developed mainly through child-care duties.

5. The expression 'innocent of' is best taken to mean

a) not guilty of

b) unskilled in

c) unsuited for

d) uninvolved in

e) uninterested in

Ans. unskilled in.

6. It can be inferred that in the community under discussion all of the following are important except

a) domestic handicrafts

b) well-defined social structure

c) fishing skills

d) formal education

e) division of labour

Ans. formal education.

7. Which of the following if true would weaken the author's contention about 'lessons in cooperation'?

i. Group games played by younger girls involve cooperation

ii. Girls can learn from watching boys cooperating

iii. Individual girls cooperate with their mothers in looking after babies

a) i.only

b) ii. only

c) iii. only

d) i. and ii. only

e) i., ii. and iii.

Ans. (i). and (ii). only.

8. Which of the following is the best description of the author's technique in handling her material?

a) Both description and interpretation of observations.

b) Presentation of facts without comment.

c) Description of evidence to support a theory.

d) Generalisation from a particular viewpoint.

e) Close examination of preconceptions.

Ans. Both description and interpretation of observations.

Florence Nightingale

The name of Florence Nightingale lives in the memory of the world by virtue of the heroic adventure of the Crimea. Had she died – as she nearly did – upon her return to England, her reputation would hardly have been different; her legend would have come down to us almost as we know it today – that gentle vision of female virtue which first took shape before the adoring eyes of the sick soldiers at Scutari. Yet, as a matter of fact, she lived for more than half a century after the Crimean War; and during the greater part of that long period all the energy and all the devotion of her extraordinary nature were working at their highest pitch. What she accomplished in those years of unknown labour could, indeed, hardly have been more glorious than her Crimean triumphs; but it was certainly more important. The true history was far stranger even than the myth. In Miss Nightingale's own eyes the adventure of the Crimea was a mere incident – scarcely more than a useful stepping-stone in her career. It was the fulcrum with which she hoped to move the world; but it was only the fulcrum. For more than a generation she was to sit in secret, working her lever: and her real life began at the very moment when, in popular imagination, it had ended.

She arrived in England in a shattered state of health. The hardships and the ceaseless efforts of the last two years had undermined her nervous system; her heart was affected; she suffered constantly from fainting-fits and terrible attacks of utter physical prostration. The doctors declared that one thing alone would save her - a complete and prolonged rest. But that was also the one thing with which she would have nothing to do. She had never been in the habit of resting; why should she begin now? Now, when her opportunity had come at last; now, when the iron was hot, and it was time to strike? No; she had work to do; and, come what might, she would do it. The doctors protested in vain; in vain her family lamented and entreated, in vain her friends pointed out to her the madness of such a course. Madness? Mad - possessed – perhaps she was. A frenzy had seized upon her. As she lay upon her sofa, gasping, she devoured blue-books, dictated letters, and, in the intervals of her palpitations, cracked jokes. For months at a stretch she never left her bed. But she would not rest. At this rate, the doctors assured her, even if she did not die, she would become an invalid for life. She could not help that; there was work to be done; and, as for rest, very likely she might rest ... when she had done it.

Wherever she went, to London or in the country, in the hills of Derbyshire, or among the rhododendrons at Embley, she was haunted by a ghost. It was the specter of Scutari – the hideous vision of the organisation of a military hospital. She would lay that phantom, or she would perish. The whole system of the Army Medical Department, the education of the Medical Officer, the regulations of hospital procedure ... rest? How could she rest while these things were as they were, while, if the like necessity were to arise again, the like results would follow? And, even in peace and at home, what was the sanitary condition of the Army?

The mortality in the barracks, was, she found, nearly double the mortality in civil life. 'You might as well take 1100 men every year out upon Salisbury Plain and shoot them,' she said. After inspecting the hospitals at Chatham, she smiled grimly. 'Yes, this is one more symptom of the system which, in the Crimea, put to death 16,000 men.' Scutari had given her knowledge; and it had given her power too: her enormous reputation was at her back – an incalculable force. Other work, other duties, might lie before her; but the most urgent, the most obvious, of all was to look to the health of the Army.

1. According to the author, the work done during the last fifty years of Florence Nightingale's life was, when compared with her work in the Crimea, all of the following except

a) less dramatic

b) less demanding

c) less well-known to the public

d) more important

e) more rewarding to Miss Nightingale herself.

Ans. less demanding.

2. The 'fulcrum' refers to her

a) reputation

b) mental energy

c) physical energy

d) overseas contacts

e) commitment to a cause

Ans. reputation.

3. Paragraph two paints a picture of a woman who is

a) an incapacitated invalid

b) mentally shattered

c) stubborn and querulous

d) physically weak but mentally indomitable

e) purposeful yet tiresome

Ans. physically weak but mentally indomitable.

4. The primary purpose of paragraph 3 is to

a) account for conditions in the army

b) show the need for hospital reform

c) explain Miss Nightingale's main concerns

d) argue that peacetime conditions were worse than wartime conditions

e) delineate Miss Nightingale's plan for reform

Ans. explain Miss Nightingale's main concerns.

5. The series of questions in paragraphs 2 and 3 are

a) the author's attempt to show the thoughts running through Miss Nightingale's mind

b) Miss Nightingale questioning her own conscience

c) Miss Nightingale's response to an actual questioner

d) Responses to the doctors who advised rest

e) The author's device to highlight the reactions to Miss Nightingale's plans

Ans. The author's attempt to show the thoughts running through Miss Nightingale's mind.

6. The author's attitude to his material is

a) disinterested reporting of biographical details

b) over-inflation of a reputation

c) debunking a myth

d) uncritical presentation of facts

e) interpretation as well as narration

Ans. interpretation as well as narration.

7. In one of her statements Miss Nightingale intended to

a) criticize the conditions in hospitals

b) highlight the unhealthy conditions under which ordinary soldiers were living

c) prove that conditions in the barracks were as bad as those in a military hospital

d) ridicule the dangers of army life

e) quote important statistics

Ans. highlight the unhealthy conditions under which ordinary soldiers were living.

Mr. Harding's Woes

Mr. Harding was not a happy man as he walked down the palace pathway, and stepped out into the close. His position and pleasant house were a second time gone from him; but that he could endure. He had been schooled and insulted by a man young enough to be his son; but that he could put up with. He could even draw from the very injuries which had been inflicted on him some of that consolation which, we may believe, martyrs always receive from the injustice of their own sufferings. He had admitted to his daughter that he wanted the comfort of his old home, and yet he could have returned to his lodgings in the High Street, if not with exultation, at least with satisfaction, had that been all. But the venom of the chaplain's harangue had worked into his blood, and sapped the life of his sweet contentment.

'New men are carrying out new measures, and are carting away the useless rubbish of past centuries!' What cruel words these had been- and how often are they now used with all the heartless cruelty of a Slope! A man is sufficiently condemned if it can only be shown that either in politics or religion he does not belong to some new school established within the last score of years. He may then regard himself as rubbish and expect to be carted away. A man is nothing now unless he has within him a full appreciation of the new era; an era in which it would seem that neither honesty nor truth is very desirable, but in which success is the only touchstone of merit. We must laugh at everything that is established. Let the joke be ever so bad, ever so untrue to the real principles of joking; nevertheless we must laugh – or else beware the cart. We must talk, think, and live up to the spirit of the times, or else we are nought. New men and new measures, long credit and few scruples, great success or wonderful ruin, such are now the tastes of Englishmen who know how to live! Alas, alas! Under such circumstances Mr. Harding could not but feel that he was an Englishman who did not know how to live. This new doctrine of Mr. Slope and the rubbish cart sadly disturbed his equanimity.

'The same thing is going on throughout the whole country!' 'Work is now required from every man who receives wages!' And had he been living al his life receiving wages, and doing no work? Had he in truth so lived as to be now in his old age justly reckoned as rubbish fit only to be hidden away in some huge dust-hole? The school of men to whom he professes to belong, the Grantlys, the Gwynnes, are afflicted with no such self accusations as these which troubled Mr. Harding. They, as a rule, are as satisfied with the wisdom and propriety of their own conduc as can be any Mr. Slope, or any Bishop with his own.

But, unfortunately for himself, Mr. Harding had little of this self-reliance. When he heard himself designated as rubbish by the Slopes of the world, he had no other resource than to make inquiry within his own bosom as to the truth of the designation. Alas, alas! the evidence seemed generally to go against him.

1. The main cause of Mr. Harding's unhappiness as he leaves the Bishop's Palace is

 a) the loss of his house

 b) the loss of his position

 c) the need to live with his daughter

 d) the thought-provoking words of the chaplain

 e) the injustice he has suffered

 Ans. the thought-provoking words of the chaplain.

2. It can be inferred that Slope is

 a) the chaplain

 b) the Bishop

 c) a foreigner

d) a politician

e) a young writer

Ans. the chaplain.

3. The word 'equanimity' most nearly means

a) status

b) happiness

c) justice

d) complacency

e) composure

Ans. composure.

4. It can be inferred that Mr Harding is especially disturbed because he

a) does not feel himself to be old

b) is offended by the young man's impertinence

c) believes no one else feels as he does

d) believe his life's work has been worthwhile

e) feels there may be some truth in regarding himself as 'rubbish'

Ans. feels there may be some truth in regarding himself as 'rubbish'.

5. Mr. Harding differs from others of his 'school' because they

a) do not believe Slope

b) have never been called 'rubbish'

c) are sure their conduct is irreproachable

d) have already examined their consciences

e) feel that Mr. Harding is not one of them

Ans. are sure their conduct is irreproachable.

6. The tone of the sentence 'New men....live' (lines 34-37) is

a) objective

b) ironic

c) derogatory

d) expository

e) ambivalent

Ans. ironic.

7. The first two sentences of paragraph 3 relate the

a) words of Mr. Slope

b) thoughts of Mr. Harding

c) view of the old school of men

d) viewpoint of the author

e) opinions of all young men

Ans. words of Mr. Slope.

The Rule of the Road

A stout old lady was walking with her basket down the middle of a street in Petrograd to the great confusion of the traffic and with no small peril to herself. It was pointed out to her that the pavement was the place for pedestrians, but she replied: 'I'm going to walk where I like. We've got liberty now.' It did not occur to the dear old lady that if liberty entitled the pedestrian to walk down the middle of the road, then the end of such liberty would be universal chaos. Everybody would be getting in everybody else's way and nobody would get anywhere. Individual liberty would have become social anarchy.

There is a danger of the world getting liberty-drunk in these days like the old lady with the basket, and it is just as well to remind ourselves of what the rule of the road means. It means that in order that the liberties of all may be preserved, the liberties of everybody must be curtailed. When the policeman,say, at Piccadilly Circus steps into the middle of the road and puts out his hand, he is the symbol not of tyranny, but of liberty. You may not think so. You may, being in a hurry, and seeing your car pulled up by this insolence of office, feel that your liberty has been outraged. How dare this fellow interfere with your free use of the public highway? Then, if you are a reasonable person, you will reflect that if he did not interfere with you, he would interfere with no one, and the result would be that Piccadilly Circus would be a maelstrom that you would never cross at all. You have submitted to a curtailment of private liberty in order that you may enjoy a social order which makes your liberty a reality.

Liberty is not a personal affair only, but a social contract. It is an accommodation of interests. In matters which do not touch anybody else's liberty, of course, I may be as free as I like. If I choose to go down the road in a dressing-gown who shall say me nay? You have liberty to laugh at me, but I have liberty to be indifferent to you. And if I have a fancy for dyeing my hair, or waxing my moustache (which heaven forbid), or wearing an overcoat and sandals, or going to bed late or getting up early, I shall follow my fancy and ask no man's permission. I shall not inquire of you whether I may eat mustard with my mutton. And you will not ask me whether you may follow this religion or that, whether you may prefer Ella Wheeler Wilcox to Wordsworth, or champagne to shandy.

In all these and a thousand other details you and I please ourselves and ask no one's leave. We have a whole kingdom in which we rule alone, can do what we choose, be wise or ridiculous, harsh or easy, conventional or odd. But directly we step out of that kingdom, our personal liberty of action becomes qualified by other people's liberty. I might like to practice on the trombone from midnight till three in the morning. If I went on to the top of Everest to do it, I could please myself, but if I do it in my bedroom my family will object, and if I do it out in the streets the neighbours will remind me that my liberty to blow the trombone must not interfere with their liberty to sleep in quiet.

There are a lot of people in the world, and I have to accommodate my liberty to their liberties.

We are all liable to forget this, and unfortunately we are much more conscious of the imperfections of others in this respect than of our own. A reasonable consideration for the rights or feelings of others is the foundation of social conduct It is in the small matters of conduct, in the observance of the rule of the road, that we pass judgement upon ourselves, and declare that we are civilized or uncivilized. The great moments of heroism and sacrifice are rare. It is the little habits of commonplace intercourse that make up the great sum of life and sweeten or make bitter the journey.

1. The author might have stated his 'rule of the road' as

a) do not walk in the middle of the road

b) follow the orders of policemen

c) do not behave inconsiderately in public

d) do what you like in private

e) liberty is more important than anarchy

Ans. do not behave inconsiderately in public.

2. The author's attitude to the old lady in paragraph one is

a) condescending

b) intolerant

c) objective

d) sardonic

e) supportive

Ans. condescending.

3. The sentence 'It means....curtailed' is an example of

a) hyperbole

b) cliché

c) simile

d) paradox

e) consonance

Ans. simile.

4. Which sentence best sums up the author's main point?

a) There is a danger....

b) A reasonable....

c) It is in the small matters....

d) The great moments....

e) It is the little....

Ans. A reasonable....

5. A situation analogous to the 'insolence of office' described in paragraph 2 would be

a) a teacher correcting grammar errors

b) an editor shortening the text of an article

c) a tax inspector demanding to see someone's accounts

d) an army office giving orders to a soldier

e) a gaoler locking up a prisoner

Ans. a tax inspector demanding to see someone's accounts.

6. 'Qualified' most nearly means

a) accredited

b) improved

c) limited

d) stymied

e) educated

Ans. limited.

7. The author assumes that he may be as free as he likes in

a) all matters of dress and food

b) any situation which does not interfere with the liberty of others

c) anything that is not against the law

d) his own home

e) public places as long as no one sees him

Ans. any situation which does not interfere with the liberty of others.

8. In the sentence ' We are all liable....' the author is

a) pointing out a general weakness

b) emphasising his main point

c) countering a general misconception

d) suggesting a remedy

e) modifying his point of view

Ans. pointing out a general weakness.

Love of Poetry

I have yet to meet a poetry-lover under thirty who was not an introvert, or an introvert who was not unhappy in adolescence. At school, particularly, maybe, if, as in my own case, it is a boarding school, he sees the extrovert successful, happy, and good and himself unpopular or neglected; and what is hardest to bear is not unpopularity, but the consciousness that it is deserved, that he is grubby and inferior and frightened and dull. Knowing no other kind of society than the contingent, he imagines that this arrangement is part of the eternal scheme of things, that he is doomed to a life of failure and envy. It is not till he grows up, till years later he runs across the heroes of his school days and finds them grown commonplace and sterile, that he realises that the introvert is the lucky one, the best adapted to an industrial civilization the collective values of which are so infantile that he alone can grow, who has educated his fantasies and learned how to draw upon the resources of his inner life. At the time, however, his adolescence is unpleasant enough. Unable to imagine a society in which he would feel at home, he turns away from the human to the nonhuman: homesick he will seek, not his mother, but mountains or autumn woods, and the growing life within him will express itself in a devotion to music and thoughts upon mutability and death. Art for him will be something infinitely precious, pessimistic, and hostile to life. If it speaks of love it must be love frustrated, for all success seems to him noisy and vulgar; if it moralizes, it must counsel a stoic resignation, for the world he knows is well content with itself and will not change.

Deep as first love and wild with all regret,
O death in life, the days that are no more.
Now more than ever seems it sweet to die
To cease upon the midnight with no pain.

That to the adolescent is the authentic poetic note and whoever is the first in his life to strike it, whether Tennyson, Keats, Swinburne, Housman or another, awakens a passion of imitation and an affectation which no subsequent refinement or sophistication of his taste can entirely destroy. In my own case it was Hardy in the summer of 1923; for more than a year I read no one else and I do not think that I was ever without one volume or another or the beautifully produced Wessex edition in my hands: I smuggled them into class, carried them about on Sunday walks, and took them up to the dormitory to read in the early morning, though they were far too unwieldy to be read in bed with comfort. In the autumn of 1924 there was a palace revolution after which he had to share his kingdom with Edward Thomas,until finally they were both defeated by Elliot at the battle of Oxford in 1926. Besides serving as the archetype of the Poetic, Hardy was also an expression of the contemporary scene. He was both my Keats and my Sandburg.

To begin with, he looked like my father: that broad unpampered moustache, bald forehead, and deeply lined sympathetic face belonged to that other world of feeling and sensation. Here was a writer whose emotions, if sometimes monotonous and sentimental in expression, would be deeper and more faithful than my own, and whose attachment to the earth would be more secure and observant.

1. According to the author, poetry lovers under thirty generally

a) have a strong sense of their own inferiority during school years

b) are always products of boarding schools

c) have an unhappy home life

d) are outgoing as adolescents

e) long to return to early childhood

Ans. have a strong sense of their own inferiority during school years.

2. The author's main purpose is apparently to

a) describe what lead to his being an introvert

b) explore the reasons for his early taste in poetry

c) explain what lead to his becoming a poet

d) account for the unhappy adolescent's aesthetic sense

e) criticize a system that makes young people feel unhappy and neglected

Ans. explore the reasons for his early taste in poetry.

3. The word 'contingent' most nearly means

a) juvenile

b) scholarly

c) competitive

d) immediate

e) intelligent

Ans. immediate.

4. The author regards the introverted adolescent as ultimately lucky because he has

a) become financially successful in an industrialized society

b) ceased to envy others

c) cultivated inner resources that he will need in modern society

d) a better general education than those who were envied in school

e) learned to appreciate nature

Ans. cultivated inner resources that he will need in modern society.

5. To the adolescent the 'authentic poetic note' is one of

a) pain and affirmation

b) hostility and vulgarity

c) contentment and peace

d) purity and love

e) melancholy and acceptance

Ans. melancholy and acceptance.

6. It can be inferred that, for the author, the poetry of Hardy is

a) something with which he is not entirely comfortable

b) a temporary interest soon supplanted by other poetry

c) a secret obsession that he is reluctant to confess

d) his first poetic love that time has not entirely erased

e) a childlike passion

Ans. his first poetic love that time has not entirely erased.

7. The author uses all of the following to make his point except

a) metaphor

b) personal experience

c) generalization

d) classical allusions

e) comparison

Ans. classical allusions.

8. The poetry quoted is most likely included as

a) extracts from the author's own poetry

b) extracts from Hardy's poetry

c) examples of poetry that appeals to the unhappy adolescent

d) the type of poetry much admired by all poetry lovers

e) examples of schoolboy poetry

Ans. examples of poetry that appeals to the unhappy adolescent.

9. It can be inferred that Edward Thomas

a) was once held in high esteem by the author

b) was a better poet than Hardy

c) was writing in 1924

d) had views opposed to Eliot

e) wrote poetry similar to that of Hardy

Ans. was once held in high esteem by the author.

10. The author mentions Carl Sandburg as

a) an example of a modern poet

b) an example of a traditional figure

c) having a poetic appearance

d) a poet to appeal to young people

e) resembling his father

Ans. an example of a modern poet.

11. The author qualifies his appreciation of Hardy by pointing out that Hardy's poetic techniques were

a) sometimes unmoving

b) not always deeply felt

c) occasionally lacking in variety

d) always emotional

e) irrelevant to certain readers

Ans. occasionally lacking in variety.

12. The author feels that Hardy's physical appearance suggested

a) deep and lasting feelings

b) paternal values

c) careworn old age

d) a contemporary writer

e) fatherly concern

Ans. deep and lasting feelings.

Animals and Vegetation

That large animals require a luxuriant vegetation, has been a general assumption which has passed from one work to another; but I do not hesitate to say that it is completely false, and that it has vitiated the reasoning of geologists on some points of great interest in the ancient history of the world. The prejudice has probably been derived from India, and the Indian islands, where troops of elephants, noble forests, and impenetrable jungles, are associated together in every one's mind. If, however, we refer to any work of travels through the southern parts of Africa, we shall find allusions in almost every page either to the desert character of the country, or to the numbers of large animals inhabiting it. The same thing is rendered evident by the many engravings which have been published of various parts of the interior.

Dr. Andrew Smith, who has lately succeeded in passing the Tropic of Capricorn, informs me that, taking into consideration the whole of the southern part of Africa, there can be no doubt of its being a sterile country. On the southern coasts there are some fine forests, but with these exceptions, the traveler may pass for days together through open plains, covered by a poor and scanty vegetation. Now, if we look to the animals inhabiting these wide plains, we shall find their numbers extraordinarily great, and their bulk immense. We must enumerate the elephant, three species of rhinoceros, the hippopotamus, the giraffe, the bos caffer, two zebras, two gnus, and several antelopes even larger than these latter animals. It may be supposed that although the species are numerous, the individuals of each kind are few.

By the kindness of Dr. Smith, I am enabled to show that the case is very different. He informs me, that in lat. 24', in one day's march with the bullock – wagons, he saw, without wandering to any great distance on either side, between one hundred and one hundred and fifty rhinoceroses-the same day he saw several herds of giraffes, amounting together to nearly a hundred. At the distance of a little more than one hour's march from their place of encampment on the previous night, his party actually killed at one spot eight hippopotamuses, and saw many more. In this same river there were likewise crocodiles. Of course it was a case quite extraordinary, to see so many great animals crowded together, but it evidently proves that they must exist in great numbers. Dr. Smith describes the country passed through that day, as 'being thinly covered with grass, and bushes about four feet high, and still more thinly with mimosa-trees.'

Besides these large animals, every one the least acquainted with the natural history of the Cape, has read of the herds of antelopes, which can be compared only with the flocks of migratory birds. The numbers indeed of the lion, panther, and hyena, and the multitude of birds of prey, plainly speak of the abundance of the smaller quadrupeds: one evening seven lions were counted at the same time prowling round Dr. Smith's encampment. As this able naturalist remarked to me, the carnage each day in Southern Africa must indeed he terrific! I confess it is truly surprising how such a number of animals can find support in a country producing so little food. The larger quadrupeds no doubt roam over wide tracts in search of it; and their food chiefly consists of underwood, which probably contains much nutriment in a small bulk. Dr. Smith also informs me that the vegetation has a rapid growth; no sooner is a part consumed, than its place is supplied by a fresh stock.

There can be no doubt, however, that our ideas respecting the apparent amount of food necessary for the support of large quadrupeds are much exaggerated.

The belief that where large quadrupeds exist, the vegetation must necessarily be luxuriant, is the more remarkable, because the converse is far from true. Mr. Burchell observed to me that when entering Brazil, nothing struck him more forcibly than the splendour of the South American vegetation contrasted with that of South Africa, together with the absence of all large quadrupeds. In his Travels, he has suggested that the comparison of the respective weights (if there were sufficient data) of an equal number of the largest herbivorous quadrupeds of each country would be extremely curious. If we take on the one side, the elephants hippopotamus, giraffe, bos caffer, elan, five species of rhinoceros; and on the American side, two tapirs, the guanaco, three deer, the vicuna, peccari, capybara (after which we must choose from the monkeys to complete the number), and then place these two groups alongside each other it is not easy to conceive ranks more disproportionate in size. After the above facts, we are compelled to conclude, against anterior probability, that among the mammalia there exists no close relation between the bulk of the species, and the quantity of the vegetation, in the countries which they inhabit.

1. The author is primarily concerned with

a) discussing the relationship between the size of mammals and the nature of vegetation in their habitats

b) contrasting ecological conditions in India and Africa

c) proving the large animals do not require much food

d) describing the size of animals in various parts of the world

e) explaining that the reasoning of some geologists is completely false

Ans. discussing the relationship between the size of mammals and the nature of vegetation in their habitats.

2. The word 'vitiated' most nearly means

a) infiltrated

b) occupied

c) impaired

d) invigorated

e) strengthened

Ans. impaired.

3. According to the author, the 'prejudice' has lead to

a) errors in the reasoning of biologists

b) false ideas about animals in Africa

c) incorrect assumptions on the part of geologists

d) doubt in the mind of the author

e) confusion in natural history

Ans. incorrect assumptions on the part of geologists.

4. The author uses information provided by Dr. Smith to

i. supply information on quality and quantity of plant life in South Africa

ii. indicate the presence of large numbers of animals

iii. give evidence of numbers of carnivorous animals

a) i only

b) ii only

c) iii only

d) i and ii only

e) i, ii and iii

Ans. i, ii and iii

5. The flocks of migratory birds are mentioned to

a) describe an aspect of the fauna of South Africa

b) illustrate a possible source of food for large carnivores

c) contrast with the habits of the antelope

d) suggest the size of antelope herds

e) indicate the abundance of wildlife

Ans. suggest the size of antelope herds.

6. The 'carnage' refers to the

a) number of animals killed by hunters

b) number of prey animals killed by predators

c) number of people killed by lions

d) amount of food eaten by all species

e) damage caused by large animals

Ans. number of prey animals killed by predators.

7. To account for the 'surprising' number of animals in a 'country producing so little food', Darwin suggests all of the following as partial explanations except

a) food which is a concentrated source of nutrients

b) rapid regrowth of plant material

c) large area for animals to forage in

d) mainly carnivorous animals

e) food requirements have been overestimated

Ans. mainly carnivorous animals.

8. The author makes his point by reference to all of the following except

a) travel books

b) published illustrations

c) private communications

d) recorded observations

e) historical documents

Ans. historical documents.

9. Darwin quotes Burchell's observations in order to

a) counter a popular misconception

b) describe a region of great splendour

c) prove a hypothesis

d) illustrate a well-known phenomenon

e) account for a curious situation

Ans. counter a popular misconception.

10. Darwin apparently regards Dr. Smith as

a) reliable and imaginative

b) intrepid and competent

c) observant and excitable

d) foolhardy and tiresome

e) incontrovertible and peerless

Ans. intrepid and competent.

11. Darwin's parenthetical remark indicates that

a) Burchell's data are not reliable

b) Burchell's ideas are not to be given much weight

c) comparison of the weights of herbivores is largely speculative

d) Darwin's views differ from Burchell's

e) more figures are needed before any comparison can be attempted

Ans. comparison of the weights of herbivores is largely speculative.

12. Anterior probability refers to

a) what might have been expected

b) ideas of earlier explorers

c) likelihood based on data from India

d) hypotheses of other scientists

e) former information

Ans. what might have been expected.

The Ring at Casterbridge

The Ring at Casterbridge was merely the local name of one of the finest Roman amphitheatres, if not the very finest remaining in Britain.

Casterbridge announced old Rome in every street, alley, and precinct. It looked Roman, bespoke the art of Rome, concealed dead men of Rome. It was impossible to dig more than a foot or two deep about the town fields and gardens without coming upon some tall soldier or other of the Empire, who had laid there in his silent unobtrusive rest for a space of fifteen hundred years. He was mostly found lying on his side, in an oval scoop in the chalk, like a chicken in its shell; his knees drawn up to his chest; sometimes with the remains of his spear against his arm; a brooch of bronze on his breast or forehead; an urn at his knees, a jar at his throat, a bottle at his mouth; and mystified conjecture pouring down upon him from the eyes of Casterbridge street boys, who had turned a moment to gaze at the familiar spectacle as they passed by.

Imaginative inhabitants, who would have felt an unpleasantness at the discovery of a comparatively modern skeleton in their gardens, were quite unmoved by these hoary shapes. They had lived so long ago, their time was so unlike the present, their hopes and motives were so widely removed from ours, that between them and the living there seemed to stretch a gulf too wide for even a spirit to pass.

The Amphitheatre was a huge circular enclosure, with a notch at opposite extremities of its diameter north and south. It was to

Casterbridge what the ruined Coliseum is to modern Rome, and was nearly of the same magnitude. The dusk of evening was the proper hour at which a true impression of this suggestive place could he received. Standing in the middle of the arena at that time there by degrees became apparent its real vastness, which a cursory view from the summit at noon-day was apt to obscure. Melancholy, impressive, lonely, yet accessible from every part of the town, the historic circle was the frequent spot for appointments of a furtive kind. Intrigues were arranged there; tentative meetings were there experimented after divisions and feuds. But one kind of appointment – in itself the most common of any – seldom had place in the Amphitheatre: that of happy lovers.

Why, seeing that it was pre-eminently an airy, accessible, and sequestered spot for interviews, the cheerfullest form of those occurrences never took kindly to the soil of the ruin, would he a curious inquiry. Perhaps it was because its associations had about them something sinister. Its history proved that. Apart from the sanguinary nature of the games originally played therein, such incidents attached to its past as these: that for scores of years the town-gallows had stood at one corner; that in 1705 a woman who had murdered her husband was half-strangled and then burnt there in the presence of ten thousand spectators.

Tradition reports that at a certain stage of the burning her heart burst and leapt out of her body, to the terror of them all, and that not one of those ten thousand people ever cared particularly for hot roast after that. In addition to these old tragedies, pugilistic encounters almost to the death had come off down to recent dates in that secluded arena, entirely invisible to the outside world save by climbing to the top of the enclosure, which few townspeople in the daily round of their lives ever took the trouble to do. So that, though close to the turnpike-road, crimes might be perpetrated there unseen at mid-day.

Some boys had latterly tried to impart gaiety to the ruin by using the central arena as a cricket-ground. But the game usually languished for the aforesaid reason – the dismal privacy which the earthen circle enforced, shutting out every appreciative passer's vision, every commendatory remark from outsiders – everything, except the sky; and to play at games in such circumstances was like acting to an empty house. Possibly, too, the boys were timid, for some old people said that at certain moments in the summer time, in broad daylight, persons sitting with a book or dozing in the arena had, on lifting their eyes, beheld the slopes lined with a gazing legion of Hadrian's soldiery as if watching the gladiatorial combat; and had heard the roar of their excited voices; that the scene would remain but a moment, like a lightning flash, and then disappear.

Henchard had chosen this spot as being the safest from observation which he could think of for meeting his long-lost wife, and at the same time as one easily to be found by a stranger after nightfall. As Mayor of the town, with a reputation to keep up, he could not invite her to come to his house till some definite course had been decided on.

1. The amphitheatre is described as a 'suggestive' place because

a) its real size could not be appreciated at a glance

b) it was full of historical associations

c) mysterious meetings took place there

d) it was lonely yet accessible

e) it was best appreciated in the evening.

Ans. it was full of historical associations.

2. The word 'hoary' is closest in meaning to

a) unimaginative

b) buried

c) curled up

d) mummified

e) ancient

Ans. Ancient.

3. The 'curious enquiry' refers to finding out

a) why happy lovers never met there

b) why interviews never took place there

c) what historical events took place there

d) how the amphitheatre came to have sinister associations

e) why the amphitheatre lay in ruins

Ans. why happy lovers never met there.

4. The word 'round' most nearly means

a) route

b) routine

c) meanderings

d) circle

e) journey

Ans. routine.

5. The boys had given up cricket in the Amphitheatre in part because

a) it was too dark

b) crimes commonly took place there

c) there were no spectators or passers-by to applaud their efforts

d) they were afraid of being caught

e) it was too exposed to the weather

Ans. there were no spectators or passers-by to applaud their efforts.

6. The author's primary purpose is to

a) justify his opinion of the Ring

b) attempt to account for the atmosphere of a place

c) chronicle the development of the Amphitheatre

d) describe the location of a Roman relic

e) explain the uses to which historical sites are put

Ans. attempt to account for the atmosphere of a place.

7. The attitude of the local residents to the unearthed remains of dead Romans was one of

a) total apathy

b) confusion and unease

c) trepidation

d) momentary interest

e) revulsion

Ans. momentary interest.

8. The incident of the woman who was burnt is mentioned in order to

a) horrify the reader

b) illustrate one reason for the unsavoury reputation of the place

c) show the bloodthirsty nature of former occupants

d) add realistic details to an imaginary plot

e) show the magnitude of the gulf between the past and the present

Ans. illustrate one reason for the unsavoury reputation of the place.

9. All of the following are said to have taken place at the Ring except

a) ghostly apparitions

b) boxing matches

c) hangings

d) secret assignations

e) theatrical performances

Ans. theatrical performances.

10. It can be inferred from the last paragraph that Henchard

a) is afraid of his wife

b) has something to hide from the townspeople

c) is a stranger to the Ring

d) is about to commit a crime

e) is an infamous resident of Casterbridge

Ans. has something to hide from the townspeople.

11. The ring was 'safest from observation' because

a) no one inside could be seen from outside the arena

b) it was far from the main road

c) people found it a pleasant place only in Summer

d) no one except lovers ever went there after dark

e) it was too inaccessible

Ans. no one inside could be seen from outside the arena.

12. It appears that in general the attitude of Casterbridge residents to the Roman past suggests that they

a) appreciated the art of the Romans

b) feared the ghosts of the buried Roman soldiers

c) felt far removed from the concerns of the Romans

d) were awe-struck by their civilization

e) were proud of their heritage

Ans. felt far removed from the concerns of the Romans.

Click Fraud

Marketing executives in television work with a relatively stable advertising medium. In many ways, the television ads aired today are similar to those aired two decades ago. Most television ads still feature actors, still run 30 or 60 seconds, and still show a product. However, the differing dynamics of the Internet pose unique challenges to advertisers, forcing them to adapt their practices and techniques on a regular basis.

In the early days of Internet marketing, online advertisers employed banner and pop-up ads to attract customers. These techniques reached large audiences, generated many sales leads, and came at a low cost. However, a small number of Internet users began to consider these advertising techniques intrusive and annoying. Yet because marketing strategies relying heavily on banners and pop-ups produced results, companies invested growing amounts of money into purchasing these ad types in hopes of capturing market share in the burgeoning online economy. As consumers became more sophisticated, frustration with these online advertising techniques grew. Independent programmers began to develop tools that blocked banner and pop-up ads. The popularity of these tools exploded when the search engine Google, at the time an increasingly popular website fighting to solidify its place on the Internet with giants Microsoft and Yahoo, offered free software enabling users to block pop-up ads. The backlash against banner ads grew as new web browsers provided users the ability to block image-based ads such as banner ads. Although banner and pop-up ads still exist, they are far less prominent than during the early days of the Internet.

A major development in online marketing came with the introduction of pay-per-click ads. Unlike banner or pop-up ads, which originally required companies to pay every time a website visitor saw an ad, pay-per-click ads allowed companies to pay only when an interested potential customer clicked on an ad. More importantly, however, these ads circumvented the pop-up and banner blockers. As a result of these advantages and the incredible growth in the use of search engines, which provide excellent venues for pay-per-click advertising, companies began turning to pay-per-click marketing in droves. However, as with the banner and pop-up ads that preceded them, pay-per-click ads came with their drawbacks. When companies began pouring billions of dollars into this emerging medium, online advertising specialists started to notice the presence of what would later be called click fraud: representatives of a company with no interest in the product advertised by a competitor click on the competitor's ads simply to increase the marketing cost of the competitor. Click fraud grew so rapidly that marketers sought to diversify their online positions away from pay-per-click marketing through new mediums.

Although pay-per-click advertising remains a common and effective advertising tool, marketers adapted yet again to the changing dynamics of the Internet by adopting new techniques such as pay-per-performance advertising, search engine optimization, and affiliate marketing. As the pace of the Internet's evolution increases, it seems all the more likely that advertising successfully on the Internet will require a strategy that shuns constancy and embraces change.

1. According to the passage, which of the following best describes the practice of click fraud?

a) Clicking on the banner advertisements of rival companies

b) Using software to block advertisements

c) Utilizing search engine optimization to visit the pages of competitors

d) Fraudulently purchasing products online

e) Clicking on the pay-per-click ads of competitors

Ans. Clicking on the pay-per-click ads of competitors.

Passage Combination Exercises

Read the two passages thoroughly and then answer the questions that follow based on the information given in the two passages. Also, at the end think of a name to be given to the combined passages.

Passage I

Had Dr. Johnson written his own Life, in conformity with the opinion which he has given, that every man's life may be best written by himself; had he employed in the preservation of his own history, that clearness of narration and elegance of language in which he has embalmed so many eminent persons, the world would probably have had the most perfect example of biography that was ever exhibited. But although he at different times, in a desultory manner, committed to writing many particulars of the progress of his mind and fortunes, he never had persevering diligence enough to form them into a regular composition. Of these memorials a few have been preserved; but the greater part was consigned by him to the flames, a few days before his death.

As I had the honour and happiness of enjoying his friendship for upwards of twenty years; as I had the scheme of writing his life constantly in view; as he was well apprised of this circumstance, and from time to time obligingly satisfied my enquiries, by communicating to me the incidents of his early years; as I acquired a facility in recollecting, and was very assiduous in recording, his conversation, of which the extraordinary vigour and vivacity constituted one of the first features of his character; and as I have spared no pains in obtaining materials concerning him, from every quarter where I could discover that they were to be found, and have been favoured with the most liberal communications by his friends; I flatter myself that few biographers have entered upon such a work as this, with more advantages; independent of literary abilities, in which I am not vain enough to compare myself with some great names who have gone before me in this kind of writing.

Wherever narrative is necessary to explain, connect, and supply, I furnish it to the best of my abilities; but in the chronological series of Johnson's life, which I trace as distinctly as I can, year by year, I produce, wherever it is in my power, his own minutes, letters, or conversation, being convinced that this mode is more lively, and will make my readers better acquainted with him, than even most of those were who actually knew him, but could know him only partially; whereas there is here an accumulation of intelligence from various points, by which his character is more fully understood and illustrated.

Indeed, I cannot conceive a more perfect mode of writing any man's life, than not only relating all the most important events of it in their order, but interweaving what he privately wrote, and said, and thought; by which mankind are enabled as it were to see him alive, and to 'live over each scene' with him, as he actually advanced through the several stages of his life. Had his other friends been as diligent and ardent as I was, he might have been almost entirely preserved. As it is, I will venture to say that he will be seen in this work more completely than any man who has ever yet lived.

And he will be seen as he really was, for I profess to write, not his panegyric, which must be all praise, but his Life; which, great and good as he was, must not be supposed to be entirely perfect. To be as he was, is indeed subject of panegyric enough to any man in this state of being; but in every picture there should be shade as well as light, and when I delineate him without reserve, I do what he himself recommended, both by his precept and his example:

'If the biographer writes from personal knowledge, and makes haste to gratify the public curiosity, there is danger lest his interest, his fear, his gratitude, or his tenderness, overpower his fidelity, and tempt him to conceal, if not to invent. There are many who think it an act of piety to hide the faults or failings of their friends, even when they can no longer suffer by their detection; we therefore, see whole ranks of characters adorned with uniform panegyric, and not to be known from one another but by extrinsic and casual circumstances. If we owe regard to the memory of the dead, there is yet more respect to be paid to knowledge, to virtue, and to truth.'

Passage II

Nobody ever wrote a dull autobiography. If one may make such a bull, the very dullness would be interesting. The autobiographer has two qualifications of supreme importance in all literary work. He is writing about a topic in which he is keenly interested, and about a topic upon which he is the highest living authority. It may he reckoned, too, as a special felicity that an autobiography, alone of all books, may be more valuable in proportion to the amount of misrepresentation which it contains. We do not wonder when a man gives a false character to his neighbour, but it is always curious to see how a man contrives to present a false testimonial to himself. It is pleasant to he admitted behind the scenes and trace the growth of that singular phantom which is the man's own shadow cast upon the coloured and distorting mists of memory. Autobiography for these reasons is so generally interesting, that I have frequently thought with the admirable Benvenuto Cellini that it should be considered as a duty by all eminent men; and, indeed, by men not eminent. As every sensible man is exhorted to make his will, he should also be bound to leave to his descendants some account of his experience of life. The dullest of us would in spite of themselves say something profoundly interesting, if only by explaining how they came to be so dull—a circumstance which is sometimes in great need of explanation. On reflection, however, we must admit that autobiography done under compulsion would he in danger of losing the essential charm of spontaneity. The true autobiography is written by one who feels an irresistible longing for confidential expansion; who is forced by his innate constitution to unbosom himself to the public of the kind of matter generally reserved for our closest intimacy.

1. It can be inferred that Dr. Johnson

a) wrote many biographies

b) wrote his own autobiography

c) was opposed to autobiography

d) did not want Boswell to write about him

e) encouraged Boswell to destroy his papers

Ans. wrote many biographies.

2. In passage I, the author, Boswell, seems most proud of his

a) literary abilities

b) friendship with an eminent man

c) thoroughness in obtaining biographical materials

d) good memory

e) personal knowledge of the life of Johnson

Ans. thoroughness in obtaining biographical materials.

3. The writer of passage I apparently believes all of the following except

a) it is difficult for any individual to know any man completely

b) letters and conversations are especially interesting

c) other friends should also have recorded Johnson's conversation

d) Johnson was a great man despite his faults

e) it is not necessary to follow a chronological approach to biography

Ans. it is not necessary to follow a chronological approach to biography.

4. 'Panegyric' most nearly means

a) eulogy

b) myth

c) fame

d) portrait

e) caricature

Ans. eulogy.

5. In the quotation in the last paragraph of passage1, Dr. Johnson is concerned that biographers sometimes tend to do all of the following except

a) fabricate details of a man's life

b) put pleasing the public too high in their priorities

c) conceal facts out of a false sense of respect

d) tend to over-praise their subjects

e) speak ill of the dead

Ans. speak ill of the dead.

6. The word 'bull' would most likely mean

a) generalization

b) paradoxical statement

c) general rule

d) confession

e) ridiculous assertion

Ans. paradoxical statement.

7. The 'phantom' is a person's

a) uniquely clear perception of himself

b) distortion of his memories to suit the impression he wishes to create

c) tendency to denigrate others

d) enhancement of autobiography by authentic memories

e) growing awareness of his own importance

Ans. distortion of his memories to suit the impression he wishes to create.

8. The author of passage II mentions Cellini as

a) an eminent yet dull man

b) a biographer of distinction

c) a confidant of the author

d) an authority who has advocated the writing of autobiography

e) a lawyer who thought that wills should contain autobiographical information

Ans. an authority who has advocated the writing of autobiography.

9. The author of passage 2 seems to think that misrepresentation in an autobiography

i. is to be expected

ii. adds to the interest

iii. reveals insight into character

a) i. only

b) ii. only

c) i. and ii. only

d) ii. and iii. only

e) i., ii and iii

Ans. i, ii and iii.

10. In the sentence 'On reflection...', the author

a) qualifies his opinion stated earlier

b) defines the most important attribute of biography

c) introduces his main point

d) enlarges on his theme

e) identifies a problem

Ans. qualifies his opinion stated earlier.

11. The author of passage 2 and Dr. Johnson would probably have agreed that

i. an autobiographer is the greatest authority on his own life

ii. autobiography is always misleading

iii. biography tends to over-praise

a) i. only

b) ii. only

c) iii. only

d) i. and ii. only

e) ii. and iii. only

Ans. i. only.

12. It can be inferred that Boswell would be most surprised by the contention of the author of passage 2 that

a) all eminent men should write an autobiography

b) people may misrepresent the character of others

c) dull men can be profoundly interesting

d) a man is the highest authority on his own life

e) autobiographies are profoundly interesting

Ans. dull men can be profoundly interesting.

13. Boswell and the author of passage two differ in tone and attitude to their subjects in that Boswell

a) is more objective whereas Stephen is more rhetorical

b) is more confident whereas Stephen is more hesitant

c) writes more impersonally, whereas Stephen writes formally

d) is more pompous, whereas Stephen does not always expect to be taken seriously

e) writes in a more literary style, whereas Stephen's writing is more expository

Ans. is more pompous, whereas Stephen does not always expect to be taken seriously.

Passage I

It begins the moment you set foot ashore, the moment you step off the boat's gangway. The heart suddenly, yet vaguely, sinks. It is no lurch of fear. Quite the contrary. It is as if the life-urge failed, and the heart dimly sank. You trail past the benevolent policeman and the inoffensive passport officials, through the fussy and somehow foolish customs – we don't really think it matters if somebody smuggles in two pairs of false-silk stockings – and we get into the poky but inoffensive train, with poky but utterly inoffensive people, and we have a cup of inoffensive tea from a nice inoffensive boy, and we run through small, poky but nice and inoffensive country, till we are landed in the big but unexciting station of Victoria, when an inoffensive porter puts us into an inoffensive taxi and we are driven through the crowded yet strangely dull streets of London to the cosy yet strangely poky and dull place where we are going to stay. And the first half-hour in London, after some years abroad, is really a plunge of misery. The strange, the grey and uncanny, almost deathly sense of dullness is overwhelming. Of course, you get over it after a while, and admit that you exaggerated. You get into the rhythm of London again, and you tell yourself that it is not dull. And yet you are haunted, all the time, sleeping or waking, with the uncanny feeling: It is dull! It is all dull! This life here is one vast complex of dullness! I am dull! I am being dulled! My spirit is being dulled! My life is dulling down to London dullness.

This is the nightmare that haunts you the first few weeks of London. No doubt if you stay longer you get over it, and find London as thrilling as Paris or Rome or New York. But the climate is against me. I cannot stay long enough. With pinched and wondering gaze, the morning of departure, I look out of the taxi upon the strange dullness of London's arousing; a sort of death; and hope and life only return when I get my seat in the boat-train, and hear all the Good-byes! Good-bye! Good-bye!

Thank God to say Good-bye!

Passage II

On the banks of the Thames it is a tremendous chapter of accidents – the London-lover has to confess to the existence of miles upon miles of the dreariest, stodgies commonness.

Thousands of acres are covered by low black houses, of the cheapest construction, without ornament, without grace, without character or even identity. In fact there are many, even in the best quarters, in all the region of Mayfair and Belgravia, of so paltry and inconvenient and above all of so diminutive a type, that you wonder what peculiarly limited domestic need they were constructed to meet. The great misfortune of London, to the eye (it is true that this remark applies much less to the City), is the want of elevation. There is no architectural impression without a certain degree of height, and the London street-vista has none of that sort of pride.

All the same, if there be not the intention, there is at least the accident, of style, which, if one looks at it in a friendly way, appears to proceed from three sources. One of these is simply the general greatness, and the manner in which that makes a difference for the better in any particular spot, so that though you may often perceive yourself to be in a shabby corner it never occurs to you that this is the end of it. Another is the atmosphere, with its magnificent mystifications, which flatters and superfuses, makes everything brown, rich, dim, vague, magnifies distances and minimises details, confirms the inference of vastness by suggesting that, as the great city makes everything, it makes its own system of weather and its own optical laws. The last is the congregation of the parks, which constitute an ornament not elsewhere to be matched and give the place a superiority that none of its uglinesses overcome. They spread themselves with such a luxury of space in the centre of the town that they form a part of the impression of any walk, of almost any view, and, with an audacity altogether their own, make a pastoral landscape under the smoky sky. There is no mood of the rich London climate that is not becoming to them - I have seen them look delightfully romantic, like parks in novels, in the wettest winter – and there is scarcely a mood of the appreciative resident to which they have not something to say. The high things of London, which here and there peep over them, only make the spaces vaster by reminding you that you are after all not in Kent or Yorkshire; and these things, whatever they be, rows of 'eligible' dwellings, towers of churches, domes of institutions, take such an effective gray-blue tint that a clever watercolourist would seem to have put them in for pictorial reasons.

The view from the bridge over the Serpentine has an extraordinary nobleness, and it has often seemed to me that the Londoner twitted with his low standard may point to it with every confidence. In all the town-scenery of Europe there can be few things so fine; the only reproach it is open to is that it begs the question by seeming – in spite of its being the pride of five millions of people – not to belong to a town at all. The towers of Notre Dame, as they rise, in Paris, from the island that divides the Seine, present themselves no more impressively than those of Westminster as you see them looking doubly far beyond the shining stretch of Hyde Park water. Equally admirable is the large, river-like manner in which the Serpentine opens away between its wooded shores. Just after you have crossed the bridge you enjoy on your left, through the gate of Kensington Gardens, an altogether enchanting vista – a footpath over the grass, which loses itself beneath the scattered oaks and elms exactly as if the place were a 'chase.' There could be nothing less like London in general than this particular morsel, and yet it takes London, of all cities, to give you such an impression of the country.

1. 'It' in the first line of passage I refers to a feeling of
   a) foreboding
   b) fear
   c) depression
   d) malaise
   e) relief

   Ans. depression.

2. The author of passage one makes his point mainly by the use of
   a) metaphor and simile
   b) repetition and exclamation
   c) accumulation of details
   d) irony and satire

e) objective observation

Ans. repetition and exclamation.

3. The extensive use of the pronoun 'you' in passage one indicates that the author

a) is speaking to one particular person

b) is describing the experience of someone else

c) believes that his feelings will be shared by many others

d) wishes to add variety to his style

e) is distancing himself from the experience he describes

Ans. believes that his feelings will be shared by many others.

4. Lawrence apparently believes that the 'nightmare' (line 26) is

a) uniquely caused by city life

b) only over when he leaves the country

c) made worse by the weather

d) dispelled by a longer stay in London

e) something that is never entirely conquered

Ans. dispelled by a longer stay in London.

5. The word that James uses in Passage 2 that best conveys Lawrence's 'poky' is

a) diminutive

b) cheapest

c) dreariest

d) stodgiest

e) low

Ans. diminutive.

6. The second paragraph of Passage 2 in relation to the first does which of the following?

a) analyses a problem raised in paragraph one

b) continues the delineation of limitations

c) counters a negative impression

d) enlarges the viewpoint with the aid of wider examples

e) describes more specific locations

Ans. counters a negative impression.

7. The word 'atmosphere' refers to

a) the mood of the place

b) the London air

c) artistic impression

d) the author's mood

e) surroundings

Ans. the London air.

8. By the use of the word 'congregation' the author suggests that the parks are

a) numerous

b) religious

c) too crowded

d) unlimited in extent

e) superior attractions

Ans. numerous .

9. James mentions Notre Dame in order to

a) provide an example of a monument finer than anything that London has to offer

b) highlight the impressive nature of a certain London building and its setting

c) give an example of a sight more suited to a town or city

d) make the image more realistic to the reader

e) prove that London and Paris are both attractive cities

Ans. highlight the impressive nature of a certain London building and its setting.

10. It can be inferred that James would be less likely than Lawrence to

i. complain about the weather

ii. rejoice on leaving the city

iii. find the English countryside dull

a) i. only

b) ii. only

c) i. and ii. only

d) ii. and iii. only

e) i., ii. and iii.

Ans. i., ii. and iii.

11. The contrast between James and Lawrence revealed by the passages involves all of the following except

a) a London lover versus a London hater

b) concern with architectural impression versus apparent indifference to architecture

c) concern with visual impact versus effect on an individual's state of mind

d) appreciation of quiet places and scenic walks versus need for excitement

e) taste for the quaint and limited in scale versus dislike of dreariness and pokiness

Ans. taste for the quaint and limited in scale versus dislike of dreariness and pokiness.

12. To counter Lawrence's charge of 'one vast complex of dullness', James would most likely point out that London

a) is bright and vast

b) offers vistas unmatched in the rest of Europe

c) is always romantic and pastoral

d) juxtaposes the ugly and the visually attractive

e) is uniformly attractive

Ans. juxtaposes the ugly and the visually attractive.

13. The tones of the two passages differ in that Passage 2 is

a) less strident

b) less contemplative

c) less mellow

d) more subjective

e) more emotionally charged

Ans. less strident.

Passage adapted from The Uncommercial Traveller, C Dickens

I chose to wander by Bethlehem Hospital; partly, because it lay on my road round to Westminster; partly, because I had a fancy in my head which could be best pursued within sight of its walls. And the fancy was: Are not the sane and the insane equal at night as the sane lie a dreaming? Are not all of us outside this hospital, who dream, more or less in the condition of those inside it, every night of our lives? Are we not nightly persuaded, as they daily are, that we associate preposterously with kings and queens, and not abilities of all sorts? Do we not nightly jumble events and personages and times and places, as these do daily? Said an afflicted man to me, when I visited a hospital like this, 'Sir, I can frequently fly.' I was half ashamed to reflect that so could I – by night.

I wonder that the great master, when he called Sleep the death of each day's life, did not call Dreams the insanity of each day's sanity.

1. It can be correctly inferred that Bethlehem hospital

i. is very close to Westminster

ii. has patients who are regarded as insane

iii. is a place the author has visited before

a) i. only

b) ii. only

c) iii. only

d) i. and ii.

e) i., ii. and iii.

Ans. ii. only.

2. The author makes his point with the aid of all of the following except

a) rhetorical questions

b) personal anecdote

c) allusion

d) frequent use of metaphor

e) repetition and parallel construction

Ans. frequent use of metaphor.

Passages Adapted From Famous Writings

Here are a few passages adapted from works of famous authors. The readers are required to read and comprehend them and then answer the questions that follow.

Passage from Politics and the English Language

Now, it is clear that the decline of a language must ultimately have political and economic causes: it is not due simply to the bad influence of this or that individual writer. But an effect can become a cause, reinforcing the original cause and producing the same effect in an intensified form, and so on indefinitely.

A man may take to drink because he feels himself to be a

failure, and then fail all the more completely because he drinks. It is rather the same thing that is happening to the English language. It becomes ugly and inaccurate because our thoughts are foolish, but the slovenliness of our language makes it easier for us to have foolish thoughts.

1. The example of the man who takes to drink is used to illustrate which of the following ideas in the paragraph?

a) foolish thoughts

b) the slovenliness of language

c) political and economic causes

d) an effect becoming a cause

e) bad influences

Ans. an effect becoming a cause.

2. The author would most likely agree that

a) individual writers can never have a bad influence on the English language

b) imprecise use of language is likely to make precise thought more difficult

c) the English language is ugly and inaccurate

d) all language declines for political reasons

e) failure generally leads to more failure in a downward spiral

Ans. imprecise use of language is likely to make precise thought more difficult.

Passage from Animal Sanctuaries in Labrador

All the sound reasons ever given for conserving other natural resources apply to the conservation of wildlife – and with three-fold power. When a spendthrift squanders his capital it is lost to him and his heirs; yet it goes somewhere else.

When a nation allows any one kind of natural resource to be

squandered it must suffer a real, positive loss; yet substitutes of another kind can generally be found. But when wildlife is squandered it does not go elsewhere, like squandered money; it cannot possibly be replaced by any substitute, as some inorganic resources are: it is simply an absolute, dead loss, gone beyond even the hope of recall.

The public still has a hazy idea that Nature has an overflowing sanctuary of her own, somewhere or other, which will fill up the gaps automatically. The result is that poaching is commonly regarded as a venial offence, poachers taken red-handed are rarely punished, and willing ears are always lent to the cry that rich sportsmen are trying to take the bread out of the poor settler's mouth. The poor settler does not reflect that he himself, and all other classes alike, really have a common interest in the conservation of any wildlife that does not conflict with legitimate human development.

1. The author of paragraph one probably uses the expression 'three-fold power'

a) because there are three-times as many reasons for conserving wildlife

b) to be more dramatic that saying "double-power"

c) to emphasise the contrast between loss of money, loss of other resources, and loss of wildlife

d) to stress the need for saving money, resources and time

e) to indicate the magnitude of the problem without intending the expression to be taken literally

Ans. to emphasise the contrast between loss of money, loss of other resources, and loss of wildlife.

2. From the context, the word 'venial' in paragraph two most nearly means

a) major

b) criminal

c) frequent

d) trivial

e) natural

Ans. trivial.

3. Both paragraphs apparently imply that

a) there is no source from which wildlife, once exterminated, can be replaced

b) poachers must be punished

c) wildlife has much in common with other natural resources

d) conservation is in conflict with human development

e) preserving wildlife is expensive

Ans. there is no source from which wildlife, once exterminated, can be replaced.

4. It can be inferred that the spendthrift in paragraph one and the poor settler mentioned in paragraph two are alike in that they are

a) in conflict with the aims of conservation

b) inclined to waste natural resources

c) more concerned with the present than the future

d) unable to control their spending

e) unaware of conservation

Ans. more concerned with the present than the future.

Passage from An essay by T H Huxley

The ground is full of seeds that cannot rise into seedlings; the seedlings rob one another of air, light and water, the strongest robber winning the day, and extinguishing his competitors. Year after year, the wild animals with which man never interferes are, on the average, neither more nor less numerous than they were; and yet we know that the annual produce of every pair is from one to perhaps a million young; so that it is mathematically certain that, on the average, as many are killed by natural causes as are born every year, and those only escape which happen to be a little better fitted to resist destruction than those which die. The individuals of a species are like the crew of a foundered ship, and none but good swimmers have a chance of reaching the land.

1. The "robber" in the first sentence is most like which of the following mentioned in the paragraph

a) wild animals

b) produce of every pair

c) individuals of a species

d) crew of a foundered ship

e) good swimmers

Ans. good swimmers.

2. The main point the author conveys is that

a) natural populations of animals in the wild increase in numbers exponentially

b) all members of a species are in violent competition with one another

c) in the struggle to survive, the fittest survive

d) members of one generation of a population are all more or less alike

e) man's interference destroys the natural balance

Ans. in the struggle to survive, the fittest survive.

Passage from An Essay on Drug Addiction

The literature on drug addiction has grown at a rate that defies anyone to keep abreast of the literature, and apparently in inverse proportion to our understanding of the subject. Addiction, or dependence, as it is more fashionable to call it, excites controversy and speculation yet true understanding of the phenomenon remains elusive.

In fact, the area is fraught with speculation and acrimonious debate. Definition of terms such as 'drug', 'addiction', and 'abuse' is obviously less controversial than attempts to explain the nature of drug dependence, yet even the terminology is imprecise and overlain with subjective connotations. At its most basic, a drug, as defined by the World Heath Organization, is simply 'any substance which when taken into the living organism may modify one or more of its functions'. This kind of definition is too wide to be of any use in a discussion of dependence: it covers everything from insulin to aspirin, penicillin to alcohol.

1. The author implies that he thinks the term "dependence" in the context of drugs

a) is more accurate the older term "addiction"

b) has not always been the preferred term

c) is a currently under-used term

d) is an avant-garde aberration

e) is more controversial than the term "addiction"

Ans. has not always been the preferred term.

2. We can infer from the first sentence that

a) not all that has been written on the subject of addiction has added to our understanding

b) no one can have read all the literature on any drug

c) the more that is published the more we are likely to understand

d) the rate of growth should be higher if we are to understand the subject

e) writing about addiction is fashionable

Ans. not all that has been written on the subject of addiction has added to our understanding.

Passage from The South Pole

When the explorer comes home victorious, everyone goes out to cheer him. We are all proud of his achievement — proud on behalf of the nation and of humanity. We think it is a new feather in our cap, and one we have come by cheaply.

How many of those who join in the cheering were there when the expedition was fitting out, when it was short of bare necessities, when support and assistance were most urgently wanted? Was there then any race to be first? At such a time the leader has usually found himself almost alone; too often he has had to confess that his greatest difficulties were those he had to overcome at home before he could set sail. So it was with Columbus, and so it has been with many since his time.

Amundsen has always reached the goal he has aimed at, this man who sailed his little yacht over the whole Arctic Ocean, round the north of America, on the course that had been sought in vain for four hundred years. So, when in 1910 he left the fjord on his great expedition in the Fram, to drift right across the North Polar Sea, would it not have been natural if we had been proud of having such a man to support? But was it so? For a long time he struggled to complete his equipment. Money was still lacking, and little interest was shown in him and his work. He himself gave everything he possessed in the world. But nevertheless had to put to sea loaded with anxieties and debts, as he sailed out quietly on a summer night.

1. In paragraph one, the 'race to be first' refers ironically to the

a) lack of response to urgent appeals for help

b) willingness to give credit

c) lack of support to the explorer before he achieves his goals

d) rush to laud the explorer

e) eagerness of the explorer to be alone

Ans. lack of support to the explorer before he achieves his goals.

2. The 'feather in our cap' refers to

a) our willingness to take unearned credit for a triumph

b) the pride we have in being human

c) our sense of having got a reward for our investment

d) way we respond to all success

e) the way we express our joy

Ans. our willingness to take unearned credit for a triumph.

3. Both paragraphs make their point with the aid of

a) repetition and parallel construction

b) specific details of time and place

c) metaphor

d) reference to historical documents

e) rhetorical questions

Ans. repetition and parallel construction.

4. From both paragraphs taken together, it appears that Amundsen and Columbus shared all of the following except the fact that they

a) were explorers

b) were not always supported when they most needed it

c) achieved feats that should have received accolades

d) had difficulties to face apart from those they faced on their expeditions

e) sailed the seas alone

Ans. sailed the seas alone.

Passage from Our Changing Constitution

Could Washington, Madison, and the other framers of the Federal Constitution revisit the earth in this year 1922, it is likely that nothing would bewilder them more than the recent Prohibition

Amendment. Railways, steamships, the telephone, automobiles, flying machines, submarines – all these developments, unknown in their day, would fill them with amazement and admiration. They would marvel at the story of the rise and downfall of the German Empire; at the growth and present greatness of the Republic they themselves had founded. None of these things, however, would seem to them to involve any essential change in the beliefs and purposes of men as they had known them. The Prohibition Amendment, on the contrary, would evidence to their minds the breaking down of a principle of government which they had deemed axiomatic, the abandonment of a purpose which they had supposed immutable.

1. It can be inferred that the paragraph is intended as

a) an introduction to a discussion of a constitutional amendment

b) a summary of social and political change since the writing of the Federal Constitution

c) an introduction to a history of the Constitution

d) a clarification of the author's view of a controversy

e) a summation of a discussion on political history

Ans. an introduction to a discussion of a constitutional amendment.

2. The author apparently believes that the "principle of government" mentioned in the last sentence is

a) not implicit in the original Constitution

b) to be taken as true for all time

c) apparently violated by the Prohibition Amendment

d) an essential change in the beliefs of the American people

e) something that would bewilder Washington and Madison

Ans. apparently violated by the Prohibition Amendment.

Passage from Animal Sanctuaries in Labrador

I have previously defined a sanctuary as a place where man is passive and the rest of Nature active. But this general definition is too absolute for any special case. The mere fact that man has to protect a sanctuary does away with his purely passive attitude. Then, he can be beneficially active by destroying pests and parasites, like bot-flies or mosquitoes, and by finding antidotes for diseases like the epidemic which periodically kills off the rabbits and thus starves many of the carnivora to death. But, except in cases where experiment has proved his intervention to be beneficial, the less he upsets the balance of Nature the better, even when he tries to be an earthly Providence.

1. The author implies that his first definition of a sanctuary is

a) totally wrong

b) somewhat idealistic

c) unhelpful

d) indefensible

e) immutable

Ans. somewhat idealistic.

2. The author's argument that destroying bot-flies and mosquitoes would be a beneficial action is most weakened by all of the following except.

a) parasites have an important role to play in the regulation of populations

b) the elimination of any species can have unpredictable effects on the balance of nature

c) the pests themselves are part of the food chain

d) these insects have been introduced to the area by human activities

e) elimination of these insects would require the use of insecticides that kill a wide range of insects

Ans. these insects have been introduced to the area by human activities.

Passage from Science & Education, T H Huxley

That Priestley's contributions to the knowledge of chemical fact were of the greatest importance is unquestionable; but it must be admitted that he had no comprehension of the deeper significance of his work; and, so far from contributing anything to the theory of the facts which he discovered, or assisting in their rational explanation, his influence to the end of his life was warmly exerted in favour of error. From first to last, he was a stiff adherent of the phlogiston doctrine which was prevalent when his studies commenced; and, by a curious irony of fate, the man who by the discovery of what he called "dephlogisticated air" furnished the essential datum for the true theory of combustion, of respiration, and of the composition of water, to the end of his days fought against the inevitable corollaries from his own labours.

It is a trying ordeal for any man to be compared with Black and Cavendish, and Priestley cannot be said to stand on their level. Nevertheless his achievements are truly wonderful if we consider the disadvantages under which he laboured.

Without the careful scientific training of Black, without the leisure and appliances secured by the wealth of Cavendish, he scaled the walls of science; and trusting to mother wit to supply the place of training, and to ingenuity to create apparatus out of washing tubs, he discovered more new gases (including oxygen, which he termed "dephlogisticated air") than all his predecessors put together had done.

1. Which pairing best reflects the main emphasis of the two passages? The first focuses mainly on Priestley's

a) discoveries of chemical fact; the second on his ingenuity

b) discovery of "dephlogisticated air"; the second on his discoveries of gases

c) lack of theoretical understanding; the second on his lack of training

d) importance to future science; the second on his status in relation to his contemporaries

e) theoretical misconceptions; the second on his success in the face of disadvantage

Ans. theoretical misconceptions; the second on his success in the face of disadvantage.

2. It can be inferred that "dephlogisticated air" is

i. a misnomer, but relating to something important

ii. a gaseous substance discovered by Priestley

iii. something not fully understood by Preistley

a) i. only

b) ii. only

c) i. and iii.

d) ii. and iii.

e) i, ii and iii

Ans. i, ii and iii.

7. The metaphor "scaled the walls of science" conveys the idea that Priestley

a) climbed to the pinnacle of science

b) fought his way to the top

c) escaped the confines of traditional ideas

d) achieved success in a difficult endeavour

e) clawed his way up against opposition

Ans. achieved success in a difficult endeavour.

3. The attitude of **both** the passages to Priestley's scientific work could be described as

a) firm disapproval

b) wholehearted praise

c) qualified approval

d) determined neutrality

e) ambivalence

Ans. qualified approval.

Passage from an Essay by George Orwell

Much of what goes by the name of pleasure is simply an effort to destroy consciousness. If one started by asking, what is man? what are his needs? how can he best express himself? one would discover that merely having the power to avoid work and live one's life from birth to death in electric light and to the tune of tinned music is not a reason for doing so. Man needs warmth, society, leisure, comfort and security: he also needs solitude, creative work and the sense of wonder. If he recognised this he could use the products of science and industrialism eclectically, applying always the same test: does this make me more human or less human? He would then learn that the highest happiness does not lie in relaxing, resting, playing poker, drinking and making love simultaneously.

1. The author implies that the answers to the questions in sentence two would reveal that human beings

a) are less human when they seek pleasure

b) need to evaluate their purpose in life

c) are being alienated from their true nature by technology

d) have needs beyond physical comforts

e) are always seeking the meaning of life

Ans. have needs beyond physical comforts.

2. The author would apparently agree that playing poker is

a) often an effort to avoid thinking

b) something that gives true pleasure

c) an example of man's need for society

d) something that man must learn to avoid

e) inhuman

Ans. often an effort to avoid thinking.

Passage from an Essay by T H Huxley

Examine the recently laid egg of some common animal, such as a salamander or newt. It is a minute spheroid–an apparently structureless sac, enclosing a fluid, holding granules in suspension. But let a moderate supply of warmth reach its watery cradle, and the plastic matter undergoes changes so rapid, yet so steady and purposeful in their succession, that one can only compare them to those operated by a skilled modeller upon a formless lump of clay. As with an invisible trowel, the mass is divided and subdivided into smaller and smaller portions. And, then, it is as if a delicate finger traced out the line to be occupied by the spinal column, and molded the contour of the body; pinching up the head at one end, the tail at the other, and fashioning flank and limb into due proportions, in so artistic a way, that, after watching the process hour by hour, one is almost involuntarily possessed by the notion, that some more subtle aid to vision than a microscope, would show the hidden artist, with his plan before him, striving with skilful manipulation to perfect his work.

1. The author makes his main point with the aid of

a) logical paradox

b) complex rationalization

c) observations on the connection between art and science

d) scientific deductions

e) extended simile

Ans. extended simile.

2. In the context of the final sentence the word "subtle" most nearly means

a) not obvious

b) indirect

c) discriminating

d) surreptitious

e) scientific

Ans. discriminating.

Passage from The Uncommercial Traveller

There are not many places that I find it more agreeable to revisit when I am in an idle mood, than some places to which I have never been. For, my acquaintance with those spots is of such long standing, and has ripened into an intimacy of so affectionate a nature, that I take a particular interest in assuring myself that they are unchanged. I never was in Robinson Crusoe's Island, yet I frequently return there. I was never in the robbers' cave, where Gil Blas lived, but I often go back there and find the trap-door just as heavy to raise as it used to be. I was never in Don Quixote's study, where he read his books of chivalry until he rose and hacked at imaginary giants, yet you couldn't move a book in it without my knowledge. So with Damascus, and Lilliput, and the Nile, and Abyssinia, and the North Pole, and many hundreds of places — I was never at them, yet it is an affair of my life to keep them intact, and I am always going back to them. The books one reads in childhood create in one's mind a sort of false map of the world, a series of fabulous countries into which one can retreat at odd moments throughout the rest of life, and which in some cases can even survive a visit to the real countries which they are supposed to represent. The pampas, the Amazon, the coral islands of the Pacific, Russia, land of birch-tree and samovar, Transylvania with its boyars and vampires, the China of Guy Boothby, the Paris of du Maurier—one could continue the list for a long time. But one otherimaginary country that I acquired early in life was called America. If I pause on the word "America", and deliberately put aside the existing reality, I can call up my childhood vision of it.

1. The first sentence of passage one contains an element of

a) paradox

b) legend

c) melancholy

d) humour

e) self-deprecation

Ans. paradox.

2. By calling America an "imaginary country" the author of passage two implies that

a) America has been the subject of numerous works for children

b) he has never seen America

c) his current vision of that country is not related to reality

d) America has stimulated his imagination

e) his childhood vision of that country owed nothing to actual conditions

Ans. his childhood vision of that country owed nothing to actual conditions

3. Both passages make the point that

a) imaginary travel is better than real journeys

b) children's books are largely fiction

c) the effects of childhood impressions are inescapable

d) books read early in life can be revisited in the imagination many years later

e) the sight of imaginary places evokes memories

Ans. books read early in life can be revisited in the imagination many years later.

4. Both passages list a series of places, but differ in that the author of passage one

a) has been more influenced by his list of locations

b) never expects to visit any of them in real life, whereas the writer of passage two thinks it at least possible that he might

c) is less specific in compiling his list

d) wishes to preserve his locations in his mind forever, whereas the author of passage two wishes to modify all his visions in the light of reality.

e) revisits them more often

Ans. never expects to visit any of them in real life, whereas the writer of passage two thinks it at least possible that he might.

■■■

CHAPTER 5

Advance Reading Comprehension

It is important that student should be grounded in the techniques required for reading comprehension so as to be able to handle passages with the view not only to determine the factual content but to analyse, grammatically and semantically, as well as literarily, the details of the passage.

Dealing with the Comprehension Passage

Joseph Addison once noted that "Reading is to the mind what exercise is to the body". It follows therefore that reading forms and integral part of one's intellectual or academic life.

At the junior or high school level, students may have problems with both the complexity and the amount of material they have to read. Here are few areas that students, who wish to improve their comprehension power, need to work on.

Skimming and Scanning

Skimming requires a quick reading of the passage to determine the general idea while scanning requires a much slower pace of reading intended to get the main ideas or specific details. In both readings, the reader should understand the purpose and type of text that he is reading as well the content of the passage.

The purpose of the passage is quite important for it gives the reader a clue to comprehension and hence makes him/her better placed to answer the questions on it. Note whether the passage is to persuade, describe, inform, explain, etc.

Non-Verbal Signals

The meaning of a text is not only conveyed by means of words. All texts also contain non-verbal signs as style features like underlining, bold print, italics; or layout features like headings, subheadings, and captions all of which could serve as pointers to meanings.

The structure of the text

The structure of the text could provide a clue to its meaning. Some start with a title and subtitle. After that there is the introduction, the body, followed by a conclusion or summary. The introduction mostly informs the reader about what s/he can expect. The body consists of paragraphs, each dealing with one aspect of the subject matter and linked in a logical manner. The conclusion puts the subject matter in the right perspective.

The structure of paragraphs

A typical paragraph consists of three parts. The first sentence contains the topic sentence, which is the heart of the paragraph. The topic sentence contains the new aspect of the subject of the text. The second part of the paragraph contain sentences which develop the aspect. These sentences may contain arguments, explanations, details, examples and other supporting evidence. The cast sentence of a paragraph is often a summary of the paragraph. An understanding of the structure of the paragraph is a good aid to comprehension.

Punctuation

It is important to note that reading according to punctuation also aids comprehension. Thus, when the reader understands the meaning and usage of punctuation marks, it will be easier for him/her to understand the grammatical structures, and hence come to terms with the meaning of the passage.

The author's viewpoint

Understanding the point of view of the author in relation to the treatment of his/her subject matter is another aid to comprehension. In reading a text, the reader makes inferences or assumptions about the position of the author. This helps in understanding the meaning of the passage. For instance, the reader should try and deduce whether the author is neutral or biased and whether he gave his own opinion or not.

Reader Anticipation: Determining the meaning of words

One of the foremost obstacles to comprehension is the meaning of words used in the passage. Under examination conditions, it is impossible to look up the meaning of words in a dictionary. Students must therefore be able to interpret the meaning of strange or difficult words from the context in which they are used. This is often only possible when the reader understands the relationships between words in meaning and form.

To help disclose the meanings of unknown words it is important to determine the word class, i.e. part of speech to which it belongs, its function in the sentence, its use in certain contexts and its relationship with other words in the sentences.

Summarizing

It is important that the reader make s a good summary of the main or key points obtained from a reading of the passage. She must familiarize him/herself with the passage, determine the main points made about the topic or subject matter and then write these points in his own words when answering the questions on the passage.

Question

At times to get at the heart of the passage and deduce meaning, it is proper for questions to be composed about the topic, title of the passage or heading. For instance, a title of a passage that reads "The effects of smoking" can be turned into "What are the effects of smoking?" in order to guide the reader to determining the answer or focus on the main issues in the passage.

Read Selectively

This implies that the reader must read to find the answers to the question. At times, it is necessary to read the questions on the passage before the passage itself so that as the reader does his reading, s/he is able to pinpoint relevant sections of the passage that answer the question.

Recite

Without looking at the passage, try to recite the answers to the questions, using your own words as much as possible.

Reduce, Record

The reader is advised to make a brief outline of the questions and their answers in keywords or phrases before writing them down on the answer sheet.

Reflect

For a constructive and well-organized answer to a question to be given, it is important that the reader reflects and meditates on the issues dealt with in the passage before putting down the answers. This, at times, may involve comparison and contrast with personal experience, organisation and reorganization of ideas and so on.

Review

Before writing the answers, check over the points that have been selected, their relevance, link with other points made and grammatical constructions in which they are expressed. This should be to provide the reader with the overall organization of the writing and the picture of the whole.

Helpful Testing Hints

More than 50% of the time, the main idea of a passage is stated in the first sentence of the paragraph. Sometimes the main idea or topic sentence comes at the end of the paragraph and, on occasion, anywhere in the paragraph. They may not be stated at all, but simply implied. Make a habit of reading the opening and closing statement of each paragraph. The most effective way to answer the main idea question is to ask yourself what the whole passage is about, not just a portion of it. The answers that cover specific details are either too narrow or too broad. The correct answer is usually a restatement of what is said in the whole passage; therefore, the options that have the same words from the reading are almost always incorrect.

Main Idea Questions

What is the main purpose of the passage?

What does the passage mainly discuss?

With what topic is the passage mainly concerned?

Which of the following does the passage mainly discuss?

Pay attention to signal words and phrases. They help you understand the relationship between the ideas within a paragraph(s).

Cause-and-effect words — as a result, therefore

Time words — meanwhile, before

Contrast words — in contrast, conversely

Addition words — also, in addition

Emphasis words — more important, remember

- Watch for questions that test your knowledge of the relationships between the topic and the supporting ideas. Understand definitions, recognise examples, understand explanations, find similar or unlike characteristics of two things or whatever, learn what produces a result and what its effects are.

- Go over the passages with familiar subjects. Then read the passages whose topics are less familiar.

  Description of the types of questions tested in the comprehension passages

- Main idea questions test your understanding of the whole passage rather the individual parts.
- Specific detail questions are based on the supports presented in the reading. Scan the passage to spot the key words for the specific details. Some specific detail questions are negative and are singled by the words NOT, EXCEPT, MOST, and LEAST. If you cannot find the correct answer for negative specific details, eliminate the choices given in the reading and choose the choice that remains as the correct response.
- Inference questions ask you to draw a logical conclusion from what you read in the passage. The answers to these types of questions are not explicitly stated.
- Language expression questions include pronouns and vocabulary questions.
- Pronoun questions ask you to spot the correct antecedent or noun to which the pronoun refers to. To locate the correct answer to these types of questions,concentrate on the sentence(s) before and a few sentences after the pronoun appears.
- Vocabulary questions ask you the meaning of a word or phrase within the context of the passage.
- Questions about the organisation of the passage, the author's point of view, analogy, or the following paragraph are not as common as the other types.

Sample Passage

Sugar Maple

The sugar maple is a hard maple tree. It can grow as tall as 100 feet and as wide as 4 feet. The sugar maple is commercially valued for its sap, which is used in the making of maple syrup. Two northeastern states, Vermont and New York, rank as major producers of maple syrup. In Canada, Quebec's annual syrup production surpasses 2.5 million gallons. To make pure maple syrup, holes are made in the trunk of the tree at the end of the winter or in early spring. The water-like sap seeps through the holes and runs through a plastic spout that is put into the hole. Afterward, the collected sap is transferred into tubes that are hooked up to a tank kept in the sugar house. Then the sap goes through the boiling process.

Boiling enhances the flavour as well as adding colour to the sap. Once the sugar content of the sap is about 65-66%, the sap is ready to be strained and marketed. The maple syrup found in the supermarkets, however, is usually not pure and has other additives. The colour of pure maple may range from golden honey to light brown. Between 35 to 50 gallons of sap are needed to produce 1 gallon of maple syrup. Also popular for strength and finish of its wood, the sugar maple tree has been put to use in furniture, interior woodwork, flooring, and crates.

1. What is the main purpose of the passage?

a) To examine the economic viability of a tree

b) To list a number of the major producers of maple syrup

c) To provide information on how maple syrup is made

d) To emphasize the use of the maple lumber in furniture and other products

Ans. This is a general inference question. Most of the passage explains the technique used for making maple syrup. The best answer is (c). The choice (a) is inaccurate. The choices (b) and (d) are both specific details but not the main idea of the passage.

2. For which of the following words does the author provide a definition?

a) The sugar maple

b) A tank

c) Additives

d) Furniture

Ans. This specific detail question tests your understanding of a definition. Only the sugar maple is defined. The choices (b), (c), and (d), even though mentioned in the passage, are not defined.

3. According to the passage, which of the following periods is ideal for sapping?

a) Late January through April

b) May to late July

c) August to early October

d) Early November to late December

Ans. This is a specific detail question. Based on the information in the passage, sapping takes place at the end of the winter and in early spring. Therefore, (a) is the best answer.

4. All of the following is true about boiling EXCEPT

a) It enhances the colour.

b) It improves the flavour.

c) It increases the sugar content.

d) It reduces the shelf life of the syrup.

Ans. This specific detail question is negative. In order to answer it correctly, eliminate all the choices a, b, and c that are used in the paragraph; therefore, (d) is the correct choice.

5. What can be inferred about the production of maple syrup?

a) It is rather simple, but time-consuming.

b) It is labour intensive.

c) Its processing demands complicated equipment.

d) The higher the volume, the less predictable the quality is.

Ans. This question tests your inference ability. The answer to the question is not directly stated in the passage. (a) is the best answer. The production technique is quite straightforward, but it takes time. The producers have to depend on the natural flow of the sap.

6. The phrase "to be strained" could best be replaced by

a) To be tried

b) To be purified

c) To be filtered

d) To be solidified

Ans. This is a language expression question. The question is based on the closest synonym for the phrase "to be strained." Even though all the choices are grammatically sound, (c) is the most logical choice according to the context.

7. What is the author's purpose in mentioning "golden honey to light brown"?

a) To provide a visual description

b) To make the reading more technical

c) To illustrate the difference in quality

d) To persuade the reader to buy the product

Ans. This inference question asks the author's purpose. The passage is non-technical; therefore, the choice (b) is inaccurate. The choice (c) is incorrect because the difference in quality is not a concern of the passage. The choice (d) is incorrect considering the author is not persuading the reader to buy any specific product. Therefore, the best choice is (a).

8. The relationship between the wood and the maple tree is similar to the relationship between

a) a vase and a bouquet of flowers

b) a painter and a canvas

c) a novel and a writer

d) an inlet and a sea

Ans. This analogy question tests your understanding of the relationship between the ideas. These types of questions need attention. The analogy here is the relationship between a part and a whole. The choice (a) shows the relationship between cut flowers and a vase. The choice (b) shows the relationship between the performer and the tool. (c) is incorrect because it indicates the relationship between a creator (writer) and the work created (novel). (d) is the correct choice. The relationship between an inlet (a part) and a sea (a whole) is similar to the relationship between the wood (a part) and the maple tree (a whole).

9. Which of the following would best describe the organization of the passage?

a) A persuasive argument in favour of the maple syrup industry is advanced.

b) A comparison and contrast between pure and commercial maple syrup is made.

c) A cause and effect analysis of the maple syrup production is presented.

d) A step-by-step explanation of how maple syrup is made is given.

Ans. This question tests your understanding of how the author organises the information in the passage. Most of the passage explains a step-by-step process of how maple syrup is made; thus, the correct choice is (d). The author does not attempt to convince the reader; consequently, the choice (a) is not true. The passage neither expresses the causes of the maple syrup production nor lists the similarities between pure and commercial maple syrup; therefore, the choices (b) and (c) are incorrect.

10. The following paragraph will probably discuss

a) Ways to eradicate diseases attacking maple trees

b) Other uses of the sugar maple tree

c) Marketing plans for import distribution

d) The diversity of the ecosystem

Ans. This is an inference question. Based on the conclusion we can draw from the passage, the correct choice is (b). Since the sugar maple tree's popularity for strength and finish of its wood is mentioned at the end of the passage, it makes sense to know something about its other uses. The choices (a), (c), and (d) can not be inferred from the passage.

Practice Exercises

Here are a few exercises to help you improve your vocabulary and word selection.

Word Selection

1. Mrs. Gordis graduated from college at the age of 57. Her family was very proud of her ....

a) Internship

b) Achievement

c) Prospect

d) Benefits

Ans. Achievement.

2. Health insurance, dental insurance, and a paid vacation each year are examples of .... that many companies offer their employees.

a) Prospects

b) Achievement

c) Benefits

d) Dot coms

Ans. Benefits.

3. When you're learning a new language, you shouldn't expect .... success. Making progress requires time and effort.

a) Instant

b) Shaky

c) Hot

d) Freshly minted

Ans. Instant.

4. The 2005 Ford Mustang is so .... that there's a six-month waiting list to get a car.

a) freshly minted

b) shaky

c) hot

d) instant

Ans. hot.

Vocabulary

Select the option that best describes the word.

1. Science fiction

a) the study of literature

b) scientific writing about the planets and stars

c) a type of writing that often is about science or the future

d) the story of space exploration

Ans. a type of writing that often is about science or the future.

2. Astronomers

a) people who study outer space; the science of stars, planets, satellites and comets

b) people who go out into space to explore

c) people who write science fiction stories

d) people who tell your future using the stars and planets

Ans. people who study outer space; the science of stars, planets, satellites and comets.

3. Planet

a) a body in space with a long tail

b) a body in space that produces heat and light

c) a body in space that moves and does not produce its own light. Instead it reflects light from the sun

d) a group of planets that has been given a name

Ans. a body in space that moves and does not produce its own light. Instead it reflects light from the sun.

4. Constellation

a) one or more planets that circle around a star such as our sun

b) a group of stars that has been given a name

c) a star that was discovered to have planets

d) a ring that appears around some planets

Ans. a group of stars that has been given a name.

5. Jupiter

a) one of the planets in our solar system

b) a star that was discovered to have planets

c) a special telescope used to view the stars

d) a group of stars that has been given a name

Ans. one of the planets in our solar system.

6. Light year

a) the time it takes a planet to orbit the sun

b) the amount of gravity on the planet

c) a year that is missing a day

d) the distance light travels in one year

e) **Ans.** the distance light travels in one year.

7. Solar system

a) a group of stars that has been given a name

b) a device used to collect the heat from the sun

c) one or more planets that circle around a star such as our sun

d) the universe

Ans. one or more planets that circle around a star such as our sun.

8. Wobble

a) the path a planet follows around the sun

b) to move from side to side

c) a space craft used to study the planets

d) a to move at the speed of light

Ans. to move from side to side.

9. Gravity

a) the force that holds us on the surface of Earth

b) the air and gases around a planet that allows life to exist

c) a body in space that produces heat and light

d) the path a planet follows around the sun

Ans. the force that holds us on the surface of Earth.

Word Selection

1. A group of planets that orbit around a sun is called a ....

a) Gravity

b) Solar system

c) Constellation

d) Reflection

Ans. solar system.

2. The astronomers have been searching for planets for ....

a) Light years

b) 10 years

c) 12 years

d) 100 years

Ans. 12 years.

3. The new planets are .... , like our Jupiter.

a) Huge

b) Far away

c) Small

d) Bright

Ans. Huge.

4. .... are people who study outer space.

a) Andromeda

b) Astronomers

c) Associate

d) Astrologers

Ans. Astronomers.

5. There are .... planets in the new solar system.

a) 2

b) 5

c) 9

d) 3

Ans. 3.

Practice Passages

Astronomers Discover Solar System

What science fiction once told of other worlds far far away, is now fact. Astronomers confirm another solar system like our(s) with multiple planets in the constellation Andromeda.

Geoffrey Marcy is a professor of astronomy and physics at San Francisco State University and says, What we have found now, for the first time ever, is indeed a full fledged system of planets around the star Upsilon Andromeda. It appears to have three planets, one close in, one at a middle distance, and one farther out.

The star is slightly larger than our sun. The planets are huge, like our Jupiter.

Marcy's associate in this research, Debra Fischer, describes the solar system,Here's the inner planet that goes around (every 4.6) days, the middle planet that goes around every 242 days, and then the outer planet that goes around every three and a half to four years.

Astronomically, it's not far away, 44 light years. The sun of that solar system, Upsilon Andromedae is so near and bright, it can be seen by the naked eye during summer and fall.

For twelve years astronomers searched the skies in the belief that if our sun has planets around it surely others do, too.

Geoffrey Marcy says, And then starting three and a half years ago, we began finding for the first time planets singly, one planet here around one star...

When I look up at the stars now at night, I can imagine easily that every one of them has planets around them. Says Debra Fischer.

It was a wobble in the star that led Marcy to the planets. The star wobbles around due to the gravity of the planet much like a dog owner gets yanked around by a little poodle.

Can they support life? (We don't know, because) present technology is notadvanced enough to determine what the planets are made of.

That, Marcy says, is astronomy's next challenge.

1. The sun of the new solar system is so .... it can be seen with the naked eye.

 a) Far away

 b) Many light years away

 c) Near and bright

 d) Much like ours

 Ans. near and bright

2. A light year is ....

 a) The amount of gravity on the planet

 b) The distance light can travel in a year

 c) The distance from one star to another

 d) The time it takes a planet to orbit the sun

 Ans. the distance light can travel in a year

3. What is the connection between how close a planet is to a sun and how long it takes to go around the sun?

 a) A far away planet takes a shorter time to orbit the sun

 b) A far away planet will take twice as long to orbit as a close planet

 c) A close planet will take a shorter time to orbit the sun

 d) There is no connection

 Ans. a close planet will take a shorter time to orbit the sun

4. The new solar system is .... away from Earth.

 a) 44 light years

 b) 4.6 days

c) 242 days

d) 3 1/2 or 4 years

Ans. 44 light years.

5. The sun of the new solar system is called ....

a) Jupiter

b) Upsilon Andromeda

c) Gravity

d) Solar system

Ans. Upsilon Andromeda.

6. What was the reason that the star wobbled?

a) The planet and the star were connected

b) The planet's gravity caused a wobble in the star

c) The telescope caused a wobble

d) The star is moving in an orbit

Ans. the planet's gravity caused a wobble in the star.

7. How are planets and stars different?

a) Stars stay in the same place and planets move

b) Planets stay in the same place and stars move

c) Stars give off heat and light and planets don't

d) Stars stay in the same place and planet move, Star give off heat and light and planet don't.

Ans. Stars stay in the same place and planet move, Star give off heat and light and planet don't.

8. Which of the new planets has an orbit time closest in length to the Earth's orbit?

a) The inner planet

b) The middle planet

c) The outer planet

Ans. The middle planet.

9. One light year equals about 5,800,000,000,000 (5.8 trillion) miles. How far is 44 light years?

a) 255,200,000,000,000

b) 44,000,000,000,000

c) 220,000,000,000,000

d) 25,520,000,000,000

Ans. 255,200,000,000,000.

Some Sounds

A few minutes ago, walking back from lunch, I started to cross the street when I heard the sound of a coin dropping. It wasn't much but, as I turned, my eyes caught the heads of several other people turning too. A woman had dropped what appeared to be a dime.

The tinkling sound of a coin dropping on pavement is an attention-getter. It can be nothing more than a penny. Whatever the coin is, no one ignores the sound of it. It got me thinking about sounds again.

We are besieged by so many sounds that attract the most attention. People in New York City seldom turn to look when a fire engine, a police car or an ambulance comes screaming along the street.

When I'm in New York, I'm a New Yorker. I don't turn either. Like the natives. I hardly hear a siren there.

At home in my little town in Connecticut, it's different. The distant wail of a police car, an emergency vehicle or a fire siren brings me to my feet if I'm seated and brings me to the window if I'm in bed.

It's the quietest sounds that have most effect on us, not the loudest. In the middle of the night, I can hear a dripping tap a hundred yards away through three closed doors. I've been hearing little creaking noises and sounds which my imagination turns into footsteps in the middle of the night for twenty-five years in our house. How come I never hear those sounds in the daytime?

I'm quite clear in my mind what the good sounds are and what the bad sounds are.

I've turned against whistling, for instance. I used to think of it as the mark of a happy worker but lately I've been associating the whistler with a nervous person making compulsive noises.

The tapping, tapping, tapping of my typewriter as the keys hit the paper is a lovely sound to me. I often like the sound of what I write better than the looks of it.

1. The sound of a coin dropping makes people ...

a) think of money.

b) look at each other.

c) pay attention to it.

d) stop crossing the street.

Ans. pay attention to it.

2. People in New York ...

a) don't care about emergencies.

b) are used to sirens.

c) are attracted by sounds.

d) don't hear loud noises.

Ans. are used to sirens.

3. The writer ...

a) sleeps next to the window.

b) has lived in Connecticut for a long time

c) believes in ghosts.

d) is interested in fire engines.

Ans. has lived in Connecticut for a long time.

4. How does the author relate to sounds at night?

a) He imagines sounds that do not exist.

b) He exaggerates quiet sounds.

c) He thinks taps should be turned off.

d) He believes it's rather quiet at night.

Ans. He exaggerates quiet sounds.

5. He dislikes whistling because ...

a) he is tired of it.

b) he used to be happier.

c) it reminds him of tense people.

d) he doesn't like workers.

Ans. it reminds him of tense people.

6. What kind of sound does he find pleasant?

a) tinkling sound of a coin dropping

b) clinking sound of keys

c) tapping of his typewriter

d) creaking sounds

Ans. tapping of his typewriter.

7. How does the writer feel about sounds in general?

a) They make him feel at home.

b) He thinks they should be ignored.

c) He believes they are part of our lives.

d) He prefers silence to loud noises.

Ans. He believes they are part of our lives.

The Great Depression

The worst and longest economic crisis in the modern industrial world, the Great Depression in the United States had devastating consequences for American society. At its lowest depth (1932–33), more than 16 million people were unemployed, more than 5,000 banks had closed, and over 85,000 businesses had failed. Millions of Americans lost their jobs, their savings, and even their homes. The homeless built shacks for temporary shelter—these emerging shantytowns were nicknamed Hoovervilles; a bitter homage to President Herbert Hoover, who refused to give government assistance to the jobless. The effects of the Depression—severe unemployment rates and a sharp drop in the production and sales of goods—could also be felt abroad, where many European nations still struggled to recover from World War I.

Although the stock market crash of 1929 marked the onset of the depression, it was not the cause of it: Deep, underlying fissures already existed in the economy of the Roaring Twenties. For example, the tariff and war-debt policies after World War I contributed to the instability of the banking system. American banks made loans to European countries following World War I. However, the United States kept high tariffs on goods imported from other nations. These policies worked against one another. If other countries could not sell goods in the United States, they could not make enough money to pay back their loans or to buy American goods.

And while the United States seemed to be enjoying a prosperous period in the 1920s, the wealth was not evenly distributed. Businesses made gains in productivity, but only one segment of the population—the wealthy—reaped large profits. Workers received only a small share of the wealth they helped produce. At the same time, Americans spent more than they earned. Advertising encouraged Americans to buy cars, radios, and household appliances instead of saving or purchasing only what they could afford. Easy credit policies allowed consumers to borrow money and accumulate debt. Investors also wildly speculated on the stock market, often borrowing money on credit to buy shares of a company. Stocks increased beyond their worth, but investors were willing to pay inflated prices because they believed stocks would continue to rise. This bubble burst in the fall of 1929, when investors lost confidence that stock prices would keep rising. As investors sold off stocks, the market spiraled downward. The stock market crash affected the economy in the same way that a stressful event can affect the human body, lowering its resistance to infection.

The ensuing depression led to the election of President Franklin D. Roosevelt in 1932. Roosevelt introduced relief measures that would revive the economy and bring needed relief to Americans suffering the effects of the depression. In his 100 days in office, Roosevelt and Congress passed major legislation that saved banks from closing and regained public confidence. These measures, called the New Deal, included the Agricultural Adjustment Act, which paid farmers to slow their production in order to stabilize food prices; the Federal Deposit Insurance Corporation, which insured bank deposits if banks failed; and the Securities and Exchange Commission, which regulated the stock market. Although the New Deal offered relief, it did not end the Depression. The economy sagged until the nation entered World War II. However, the New Deal changed the relationship between government and American citizens, by expanding the role of the central government in regulating the economy and creating social assistance programs.

1. The author's main point about the Great Depression is that

a) government policies had nothing to do with it.

b) the government immediately stepped in with assistance for the jobless and homeless.

c) underlying problems in the economy preceded it.

d) the New Deal policies introduced by Franklin

e) Roosevelt ended it.

Ans. (c) According to the paragraph , Deep, underlying fissures that already existed in the economy led to the Great Depression.

2. This passage is best described as

a) an account of the causes and effects of a major event.

b) a statement supporting the value of federal social policies.

c) a condemnation of outdated beliefs.

d) a polite response to controversial issues.

Ans. (a) The passage is primarily an account that describes the causative factors (for example, tariff and war-debt policies, disproportionate wealth, and the accumulation of debt) that led to the Depression and its effects (for example, business failures, bank closings, homelessness, federal relief programmes).

3. The author cites the emergence of Hoovervilles in paragraph 1 as an example of

a) federally sponsored housing programmes.

b) the resilience of Americans who lost their jobs, savings, and homes.

c) the government's unwillingness to assist citizens in desperate circumstances.

d) the effectiveness of the Hoover administration in dealing with the crisis.

Ans. (c) Paragraph states that shantytowns were called Hoovervilles because citizens blamed their plight on the Hoover administration's refusal to offer assistance.

4. The term policies, as it is used in paragraph 2, most nearly means

a) theories.

b) practices.

c) laws.

d) examples.

Ans. (b) Although policies can refer to regulations or laws (choice c) or guiding principles or theories (choice a), in this context, policies refers to the courses of action that are taken, from which a government or business intends to influence decisions or actions. Choice b is the only answer that implies action.

5. The passage suggests that the 1920s was a decade that extolled the value of

a) thrift.

b) prudence.

c) balance.

d) extravagance.

Ans. (d) The passage describes the decade as one in which spending dominated over prudent measures like saving (paragraph). The wild stock market speculation, also described in that paragraph, is another example of extravagance.

6. The example of the human body as a metaphor for the economy, which is found at the end of paragraph 3, suggests that

a) a stressful event like the stock market crash of 1929 probably made a lot of people sick

b) the crash weakened the economy's ability to withstand other pressures.

c) the crash was an untreatable disease.

d) a single event caused the collapse of the economy.

Ans. (b) The analogy depicts the stock market crash of as a weakening agent to the economy (the way a stressful event may weaken the body's resistance to illness).

7. The content in the last paragraph of the passage would most likely support which of the following statements?

a) The New Deal policies were not radical enough in challenging capitalism.

b) The economic policies of the New Deal brought about a complete business recovery.

c) The Agricultural Adjustment Act paid farmers to produce surplus crops.

d) The federal government became more involved in caring for needy members of society.

Ans. (d) This paragraph clearly states that the New Deal expanded the role of the central government in regulating the economy and creating social assistance programs. Choices (b) and (c) are incorrect and choice a requires an opinion; the author does not offer his or her viewpoint about the New Deal measures.

Atmosphere and Life

The atmosphere forms a gaseous, protective envelope around Earth. It protects the planet from the cold of space, from harmful ultraviolet light, and from all but the largest meteors. After traveling over 93 million miles, solar energy strikes the atmosphere and Earth's surface, warming the planet and creating what is known as the biosphere, the region of Earth capable of sustaining life. Solar radiation in combination with the planet's rotation causes the atmosphere to circulate. Atmospheric circulation is one important reason that life on Earth can exist at higher latitudes because equatorial heat is transported poleward, moderating the climate.

The equatorial region is the warmest part of the earth because it receives the most direct and, therefore, strongest solar radiation. The plane in which the earth revolves around the sun is called the ecliptic. Earth's axis is inclined $23\frac{1}{3}$ degrees with respect to the ecliptic. This inclined axis is responsible for our changing seasons because, as seen from the earth, the sun oscillates back and forth across the equator in an annual cycle. On or about June 21 each year, the sun reaches the Tropic of Cancer, $23\frac{1}{3}$ degrees north latitude. This is the northernmost point where the sun can be directly overhead. On or about December 21 of each year, the sun reaches the Tropic of Capricorn, $23\frac{1}{3}$ degrees south latitude. This is the southernmost point at which the sun can be directly overhead. The polar regions are the coldest parts of the earth because they receive the least direct and, therefore, the weakest solar radiation. Here solar radiation strikes at a very oblique angle and thus spreads the same amount of energy over a greater area than in the equatorial regions. A static envelope of air surrounding the earth would produce an extremely hot, uninhabitable equatorial region, while the polar regions would remain inhospitably cold.

The transport of water vapour in the atmosphere is an important mechanism by which heat energy is redistributed poleward. When water evaporates into the air and becomes water vapour, it absorbs energy. At the equator, air saturated with water vapour rises high into the atmosphere where winds aloft carry it poleward. As this moist air approaches the polar regions, it cools and sinks back to earth. At some point, the water vapour condenses out of the air as rain or snow, releasing energy in the process. The now-dry polar air flows back toward the equator to repeat the convection cycle. In this way, heat energy absorbed at the equator is deposited at the poles and the temperature gradient between these regions is reduced.

The circulation of the atmosphere and the weather it generates is but one example of the many complex, interdependent events of nature. The web of life depends on the proper functioning of these natural mechanisms for its continued existence. Global warming, the hole in the atmosphere's ozone layer, and increasing air and water pollution pose serious, long-term threats to the biosphere. Given the high degree of nature's interconnectedness, it is quite possible that the most serious threats have yet to be recognized.

1. Which of the following best expresses the main idea of the passage?

a) The circulation of atmosphere, threatened by global warming and pollution, protects the biosphere and makes life on Earth possible.

b) If the protective atmosphere around the earth is too damaged by human activity, all life on Earth will cease.

c) Life on Earth is the result of complex interdependent events of nature, and some of these events are a result of human intervention.

d) The circulation of atmosphere is the single most important factor in keeping the biosphere alive, and it is constantly threatened by harmful human activity.

Which of the following best represents the organisation of the passage?

Ans. (a) Choice (b) emphasises only damage to the atmosphere; the passage encompasses more than that. Choice (c) does not mention the atmosphere, which is the main focus of the passage. Choice d is too narrow—the final paragraph of the passage emphasizes that the circulation of the atmosphere is but one example of the complex events that keeps the earth alive.

2. Which of the following is the best definition of the underlined word biosphere as it is used in the passage?

a) the protective envelope formed by the atmosphere around the living earth

b) that part of the earth and its atmosphere in which life can exist

c) the living things on Earth whose existence is made possible by circulation of the atmosphere

d) the circulation of the atmosphere's contribution to life on Earth

Ans. (b) The biosphere, as defined in paragraph, is a region (or part) of the earth; it is not the envelope around the earth, the living things on Earth, or the circulation of the atmosphere (choices a, c, and d).

3. Which of the following sentences from the passage best supports the author's point that circulation of the atmosphere is vital to life on Earth?

a) The equatorial region is the warmest part of the earth because it receives the most direct and, therefore, strongest solar radiation.

b) The circulation of the atmosphere and the weather it generates is but one example of the many complex, interdependent events of nature.

c) [The atmosphere] protects Earth from the cold of space, from harmful ultraviolet light, and from all but the largest meteors.

d) A static envelope of air surrounding the earth would produce an extremely hot, uninhabitable equatorial region, while the polar regions would remain inhospitably cold.

Ans. (d) This question assesses the ability to recognize supported and unsupported claims. Choice a deals with solar radiation, not with circulation of the atmosphere. Choice b is an assertion without specific supporting detail. Choice (c) describes how the atmosphere protects Earth but does not speak of the circulation of the atmosphere. Only choice (d) explains that conditions would be inhospitable at the equator and poles without the circulation of the atmosphere; therefore, it is the best choice.

4. Based on the passage, which of the following is directly responsible for all temperature changes on Earth?

a) variations in the strength of solar radiation

b) variations in the amount of ultraviolet light

c) variation of biologic processes in the biosphere

d) variation in global warming

Ans. (a) This question assesses the ability to see cause and effect. Paragraph deals with how variations in the strength with which solar radiation strikes the earth affects temperature.

None of the other choices is discussed in terms of all temperature changes on Earth.

5. The first paragraph of the passage deals mainly with which of the following effects of the atmosphere on the earth?

a) its sheltering effect

b) its reviving effect

c) its invigorating effect

d) its cleansing effect

Ans. (a) There is no mention in the first paragraph of any reviving or cleansing effect the atmosphere may have (choices (b) and (d). In a sense, enabling the earth to sustain life is invigorating; however, choice a is a better choice because the first two sentences talk about how the atmosphere protects the earth from harmful forces.

Diabetes

There are two types of diabetes, insulin-dependent and non-insulin-dependent. Between 90–95% of the estimated 13–14 million people in the United States with diabetes have non-insulin-dependent, or Type II, diabetes. Because this form of diabetes usually begins in adults over the age of 40 and is most common after the age of 55, it used to be called adult-onset diabetes. Its symptoms often develop gradually and are hard to identify at first; therefore, nearly half of all people with diabetes do not know they have it. For instance, someone who has developed Type II diabetes may feel tired or ill without knowing why. This can be particularly dangerous because untreated diabetes can cause damage to the heart, blood vessels, eyes, kidneys, and nerves. While the causes, short-term effects, and treatments of the two types of diabetes differ, both types can cause the same long-term health problems.

Most importantly, both types affect the body's ability to use digested food for energy. Diabetes does not interfere with digestion, but it does prevent the body from using an important product of digestion, glucose (commonly known as sugar), for energy. After a meal, the normal digestive system breaks some food down into glucose. The blood carries the glucose or sugar throughout the body, causing blood glucose levels to rise. In response to this rise, the hormone insulin is released into the bloodstream and signals the body tissues to metabolize or burn the glucose for fuel, which causes blood glucose levels to return to normal. The glucose that the body does not use right away is stored in the liver, muscle, or fat.

In both types of diabetes, however, this normal process malfunctions. A gland called the pancreas, found just behind the stomach, makes insulin. In people with insulin-dependent diabetes, the pancreas does not produce insulin at all. This condition usually begins in childhood and is known as Type I (formerly called juvenile-onset) diabetes. These patients must have daily insulin injections to survive. People with non-insulin-dependent diabetes usually produce some insulin in their pancreas, but their bodies' tissues do not respond well to the insulin signal and, therefore, do not metabolize the glucose properly, a condition known as insulin resistance.

Insulin resistance is an important factor in non-insulin-dependent diabetes, and scientists are searching for the causes of insulin resistance. They have identified two possibilities. The first is that there could be a defect in the insulin receptors on cells. Like an appliance that needs to be plugged into an electrical outlet, insulin has to bind to a receptor in order to function. Several things can go wrong with receptors. For example, there may not be enough receptors to which insulin may bind, or a defect in the receptors may prevent insulin from binding. The second possible cause of insulin resistance is that, although insulin may bind to the receptors, the cells do not read the signal to metabolize the glucose. Scientists continue to study these cells to see why this might happen.

There's no cure for diabetes yet. However, there are ways to alleviate its symptoms. In 1986, a National Institute of Health panel of experts recommended that the best treatment for non-insulin-dependent diabetes is a diet that helps one maintain a normal weight and pays particular attention to a proper balance of the different food groups. Many experts, including those in the American Diabetes Association, recommend that 50–60% of daily calories come from carbohydrates, 12–20% from protein, and no more than 30% from fat. Foods that are rich in carbohydrates, like breads, cereals, fruits, and vegetables, break down into glucose during digestion, causing blood glucose to rise. Additionally, studies have shown that cooked foods raise blood glucose higher than raw, unpeeled foods. A doctor or nutritionist should always be consulted for more of this kind of information and for help in planning a diet to offset the effects of this form of diabetes.

1. According to the passage, what may be the most dangerous aspect of Type II diabetes?

a) Insulin shots are needed daily for treatment of Type II diabetes.

b) Type II diabetes may go undetected and, therefore, untreated.

c) In Type II diabetes, the pancreas does not produce insulin.

d) Type II diabetes interferes with digestion.

Ans. (b) Paragraph mentions that the symptoms of Type II diabetes may occur gradually and thus be attributed to other causes. Left untreated, diabetes can cause damage to several major organs in the body.

2. Which of the following are the same for Type I and Type II diabetes?

a) Treatments

b) long-term health risks

c) short-term effects

d) causes

Ans. (b) According to the beginning of paragraph , only the long-term health problems are the same for these two different disorders.

3. According to the passage, one place in which excess glucose is stored is the

a) stomach.

b) insulin receptors.

c) pancreas.

d) liver.

Ans. (d) Paragraph mentions that when the body has more glucose than needed, it stores the overflow in muscle tissue, fat, or the liver.

4. A diet dominated by which of the following is recommended for non-insulin-dependent diabetics?

a) protein

b) fat

c) carbohydrates

d) raw foods

Ans. (c) According to the last paragraph, non-insulin-dependent diabetics should stick to a diet consisting of –% carbohydrates. The paragraph also notes that raw foods do not cause as high a blood sugar level as cooked foods.

5. Which of the following is the main function of insulin?

a) It signals tissues to metabolize sugar.

b) It breaks down food into glucose.

c) It carries glucose throughout the body.

d) It binds to receptors.

Ans. (a) Paragraph mentions that, although insulin must bind to a receptor in order to begin working, the main role of insulin is to signal the burning of glucose/sugar for energy. Most hormones function as stimuli for other processes.

6. Which of the following statements best Summarises the main theme of the passage?

a) Type I and Type II diabetes are best treated by maintaining a high-protein diet.

b) Type II diabetes is a distinct condition that can be managed by maintaining a healthy diet.

c) Type I diabetes is an insidious condition most harmful when the patient is not taking daily insulin injections.

d) Adults who suspect they may have Type II diabetes should immediately adopt a high-carbohydrate diet.

Ans. (b) Type II, or non-insulin-dependent, diabetes is the main subject of the passage, which distinguishes Type II from Type I and goes on to stress the importance of diet.

7. Which of the following is mentioned in the passage as a possible problem with insulin receptors in insulin-resistant individuals?

a) Overeating causes the receptors to function improperly.

b) There may be an overabundance of receptors present.

c) A defect causes the receptors to bind with glucose.

d) A defect hinders the receptors from binding with insulin.

Ans. (d) Paragraph of the passage tells us that possible problems with insulin receptors include a paucity of receptors or a defect causing improper binding of the insulin to the receptors. In addition, even though insulin may bind to its receptors, cells may fail to read the signal to metabolize the glucose.

8. According to the passage, in normal individuals, which of the following processes occur immediately after the digestive system converts some food into glucose?

a) The glucose is metabolized by body tissues.

b) Insulin is released into the bloodstream.

c) Blood sugar levels rise.

d) The pancreas manufactures increased amounts of insulin.

Ans. (c) Paragraph states that normally, after the digestive system breaks down food into smaller molecules, including glucose (otherwise known as sugar), the blood-sugar level rises. Insulin is then released from the pancreas, thus signalling tissues to metabolize the glucose.

9. Based on the information in the passage, which of the following best describes people with Type I diabetes?

a) They do not need to be treated with injections of insulin.

b) They comprise the majority of people with diabetes.

c) Their pancreases do not produce insulin.

d) They are usually diagnosed as adults.

Ans. (c) Type I diabetes is the insulin-dependent form of this condition. The minority of diabetics are afflicted with this form. They are diagnosed as children and must take daily injections of insulin to compensate for what their pancreases do not produce.

10. What is the closest meaning of the underlined word offset in the final sentence of the passage?

a) counteract

b) cure

c) soothe

d) erase

Ans. (a) The final paragraph says that there is no cure for diabetes, so choices (b) and (d) are incorrect. Choice (c) is a possibility, but consider the sound of the word soothe. It does not fit with the objective tone of the passage nearly as well as the word counteract.

The Immune System

The immune system is equal in complexity to the combined intricacies of the brain and nervous system. The success of the immune system in defending the body relies on a dynamic regulatory communications network consisting of millions and millions of cells. Organized into sets and subsets, these cells pass information back and forth like clouds of bees swarming around a hive. The result is a sensitive system of checks and balances that produces an immune response that is prompt, appropriate, effective, and self-limiting.

At the heart of the immune system is the ability to distinguish between self and non-self. When immune defenders encounter cells or organisms carrying foreign or non-self molecules, the immune troops move quickly to eliminate the intruders. Virtually every body cell carries distinctive molecules that identify it as self. The body's immune defenses do not normally attack tissues that carry a self-marker. Rather, immune cells and other body cells coexist peaceably in a state known as self-tolerance. When a normally functioning immune system attacks a non-self molecule, the system has the ability to remember the specifics of the foreign body. Upon subsequent encounters with the same species of molecules, the immune system reacts accordingly. With the possible exception of antibodies passed during lactation, this so-called immune system memory is not inherited. Despite the occurrence of a virus in your family, your immune system must learn from experience with the many millions of distinctive non-self molecules in the sea of microbes in which we live. Learning entails producing the appropriate molecules and cells to match up with and counteract each non-self invader.

Any substance capable of triggering an immune response is called an antigen. Antigens are not to be confused with allergens, which are most often harmless substances (such as ragweed pollen or cat hair) that provoke the immune system to set off the inappropriate and harmful response known as allergy. An antigen can be a virus, a bacterium, a fungus, a parasite, or even a portion or product of one of these organisms. Tissues or cells from another individual (except an identical twin, whose cells carry identical self-markers) also act as antigens; because the immune system recognises transplanted tissues as foreign, it rejects them. The body will even reject nourishing proteins unless they are first broken down by the digestive system into their primary, non-antigenic building blocks. An antigen announces its foreignness by means of intricate and characteristic shapes called epitopes, which protrude from its surface. Most antigens, even the simplest microbes, carry several different kinds of epitopes on their surface; some may even carry several hundred. Some epitopes will be more effective than others at stimulating an immune response. Only in abnormal situations does the immune system wrongly identify self as non-self and execute a misdirected immune attack. The result can be a so-called autoimmune disease such as rheumatoid arthritis or systemic lupus erythematosis. The painful side effects of these diseases are caused by a person's immune system actually attacking itself.

1. What is the analogy used to describe the communications network among the cells in the immune system?

a) the immune system's memory

b) immune troops eliminating intruders

c) bees swarming around a hive

d) a sea of microbes

Ans. (c) In the first paragraph, the communication network of the millions of cells in the immune system is compared to bees swarming around a hive.

2. The immune cells and other cells in the body coexist peaceably in a state known as

a) equilibrium.

b) self-tolerance.

c) harmony.

d) tolerance.

Ans. (b) All the answers indicate peaceful coexistence. However, according to the fifth sentence of paragraph, in this instance, the state is referred to as self-tolerance.

3. What is the specific term for the substance capable of triggering an inappropriate or harmful immune response to a harmless substance such as ragweed pollen?

a) antigen

b) microbe

c) allergen

d) autoimmune disease

Ans. (c) See the last paragraph. The substances known as allergens are responsible for triggering an inappropriate immune response to ragweed pollen.

4. How do the cells in the immune system recognise an antigen as foreign or non-self?

a) through an allergic response

b) through blood type

c) through fine hairs protruding from the antigen surface

d) through characteristic shapes on the antigen surface

Ans. (d) The last paragraph of the passage mentions that an antigen announces its foreignness with intricate shapes called epitopes that protrude from the surface.

5. After you have had the chicken pox, your immune system will be able to do all of the following Except

a) prevent your offspring from infection by the chicken pox virus.

b) distinguish between your body cells and that of the chicken pox virus.

c) remember previous experiences with the chicken pox virus.

d) match up and counteract non-self molecules in the form of the chicken pox virus.

Ans. (a) Every individual's immune system must learn to recognise and deal with non-self molecules through experience. However, the last section of paragraph mentions that the immune system is capable of choices (b), (c), and (d).

6. Which of the following best expresses the main idea of this passage?

a) An antigen is any substance that triggers an immune response.

b) The basic function of the immune system is to distinguish between self and non-self.

c) One of the immune system's primary functions is the allergic response.

d) The human body presents an opportune habitat for microbes.

Ans. (b) According to paragraph , the ability to distinguish between self and non-self is the heart of the immune system. This topic is set up in the first paragraph and further elucidated throughout the body of the passage.

7. Why would tissue transplanted from father to daughter have a greater risk of being detected as foreign than a tissue transplanted between identical twins?

a) The age of the twins' tissue would be the same and, therefore, less likely to be rejected.

b) The identical twin's tissue would carry the same self-markers and would, therefore, be less likely to be rejected.

c) The difference in the sex of the father and daughter would cause the tissue to be rejected by the daughter's immune system.

d) The twins' immune systems would remember the same encounters with childhood illnesses.

Ans. (b) The last paragraph mentions that tissues or cells from another individual may act as antigens except in the case of identical twins whose cells carry identical self-markers.

8. What is the meaning of the underlined word intricacies as it is used in the first sentence of the passage?

a) elabourate interconnections

b) confusion of pathways

c) inherent perplexity

d) comprehensive coverage

Ans. (a) The context leads to the meaning: The first sentence speaks of complexity, from which we can infer an elabourate system of interconnections, especially in light of the second sentence. There is no mention of confusion in the passage (choice (b). The word perplexity means bewilderment and is unrelated to the passage (choice (c). Choice (d) is a newspaper and TV term that is unrelated to the passage.

Asthma

No longer is asthma considered a condition with isolated, acute episodes of bronchospasm. Rather, asthma is now understood to be a chronic inflammatory disorder of the airways—that is, inflammation makes the airways chronically sensitive. When these hyper-responsive airways are irritated, airflow is limited, and attacks of coughing, wheezing, chest tightness, and breathing difficulty occur.

Asthma involves complex interactions among inflammatory cells, mediators, and the cells and tissues in the airways. The interactions result in airflow limitation from acute broncho-constriction, swelling of the airway wall, increased mucus secretion, and airway remodeling. The inflammation also causes an increase in airway responsiveness. During an asthma attack, the patient attempts to compensate by breathing at a higher lung volume in order to keep the air flowing through the constricted airways, and the greater the airway limitation, the higher the lung volume must be to keep airways open. The morphologic changes that occur in asthma include bronchial infiltration by inflammatory cells. Key effector cells in the inflammatory response are the mast cells, T lymphocytes, and eosinophils. Mast cells and eosinophils are also significant participants in allergic responses, hence the similarities between allergic reactions and asthma attacks. Other changes include mucus plugging of the airways, interstitial edema, and microvascular leakage. Destruction of bronchial epithelium and thickening of the subbasement membrane is also characteristic. In addition, there may be hypertrophy and hyperplasia of airway smooth muscle, increase in goblet cell number, and enlargement of submucous glands.

Although causes of the initial tendency toward inflammation in the airways of patients with asthma are not yet certain, to date the strongest identified risk factor is atopy. This inherited familial tendency to have allergic reactions includes increased sensitivity to allergens that are risk factors for developing asthma. Some of these allergens include domestic dust mites, animals with fur, cockroaches, pollens, and molds. Additionally, asthma may be triggered by viral respiratory infections, especially in children. By avoiding these allergens and triggers, a person with asthma lowers his or her risk of irritating sensitive airways. A few avoidance techniques include: keeping the home clean and well ventilated, using an air conditioner in the summer months when pollen and mold counts are high, and getting an annual influenza vaccination. Of course, asthma sufferers should avoid tobacco smoke altogether. Cigar, cigarette, or pipe smoke is a trigger whether the patient smokes or inhales the smoke from others. Smoke increases the risk of allergic sensitization in children, increases the severity of symptoms, and may be fatal in children who already have asthma. Many of the risk factors for developing asthma may also provoke asthma attacks, and people with asthma may have one or more triggers, which vary from individual to individual. The risk can be further reduced by taking medications that decrease airway inflammation. Most exacerbations can be prevented by the combination of avoiding triggers and taking anti-inflammatory medications. An exception is physical activity, which is a common trigger of exacerbations in asthma patients. However, asthma patients should not necessarily avoid all physical exertion, because some types of activity have been proven to reduce symptoms. Rather, they should work in conjunction with a doctor to design a proper training regimen, which includes the use of medication.

In order to diagnose asthma, a healthcare professional must

appreciate the underlying disorder that leads to asthma symptoms and understand how to recognise the condition through information gathered from the patient's history, physical examination, 0 measurements of lung function, and allergic status. Because asthma symptoms vary throughout the day, the respiratory system may appear normal during physical examination. Clinical signs are more likely to be present when a patient is experiencing symptoms; however, the absence of symptoms upon examination does not exclude the diagnosis of asthma.

1. According to the passage, what is the name for the familial inclination to have hypersensitivity to certain allergens?

a) interstitial edema

b) hyperplasia

c) hypertrophy

d) atopy

Ans. (d) Many asthma sufferers have an inherited tendency to have allergies, referred to as atopy in the third paragraph.

2. Why does a person suffering from an asthma attack attempt to inhale more air?

a) to prevent the loss of consciousness

b) to keep air flowing through shrunken air passageways

c) to prevent hyperplasia

d) to compensate for weakened mast cells, T lymphocytes, and eosinophils

Ans. (b) The fourth sentence of the second paragraph explains that during an attack the person afflicted with asthma will compensate for constricted airways by breathing a greater volume of air.

3. The passage suggests that in the past, asthma was regarded as which of the following?

a) a result of the overuse of tobacco products

b) a hysterical condition

c) mysterious, unrelated attacks affecting the lungs

d) a chronic condition

Ans. (d) The first sentence of the passage begins, No longer, indicating that in the past asthma was considered an anomalous inflammation of the bronchi. Now asthma is considered a chronic condition of the lungs.

4. Which of the following would be the best replacement for the underlined word exacerbations in this passage?

a) allergies

b) attacks

c) triggers

d) allergens

Ans. (b) An exacerbation is usually defined as an aggravation of symptoms or increase in the severity of a disease. However, in this passage, exacerbations is interchangeable with asthma attacks.

5. The passage mentions all of the following bodily changes during an asthma attack except severe cramping in the chest.

a) heavy breathing.

b) airways blocked by fluids.

c) constricted airways.

Ans. (a) Although cramping may occur during asthma attacks, it is not mentioned in the passage. See the bottom half of the second paragraph for a full explanation of the morphological effects of an attack.

6. Although it is surprising, which of the following triggers is mentioned in the passage as possibly reducing the symptoms of asthma in some patients?

a) using a fan instead of an air conditioner in summer months

b) exposure to second-hand cigarette smoke

c) the love of a family pet

d) performing physical exercise

Ans. (d) The third paragraph discusses triggers in detail. Although using a fan in the summer months sounds good, an air conditioner is recommended when the pollen count is high. Family pets and cigarette smoke are all distinctly inflammatory to asthma sufferers. Only physical activity is touted as a possible symptom reducer.

7. Why might a patient with asthma have an apparently normal respiratory system during an examination by a doctor?

a) Asthma symptoms come and go throughout the day.

b) Severe asthma occurs only after strenuous physical exertion.

c) Doctor's offices are smoke free and very clean.

d) The pollen and mold count may be low that day.

Ans. (a) Because asthma symptoms vary throughout the day, relying on the presence of an attack or even just on the presence of a respiratory ailment to diagnose asthma is flawed logic.

8. Who might be the most logical audience for this passage?

a) researchers studying the respiratory system

b) healthcare professionals

c) a mother whose child has been diagnosed with asthma

d) an antismoking activist

Ans. (b) All the individuals listed would glean a certain amount of knowledge from the passage; however, a healthcare professional would find the broad overview of the effects of asthma, combined with the trigger avoidance and diagnosis information, most relevant. A research scientist would likely have all this information already. A mother with an asthmatic child would probably not be interested in the diagnosis protocol. The antismoking activist probably would not find enough fodder in this article.

9. What is the reason given in this article for why passive smoke should be avoided by children?

a) A smoke-filled room is a breeding ground for viral respiratory infections.

b) Smoke can stunt an asthmatic child's growth.

c) Smoke can heighten the intensity of asthma symptoms.

d) Breathing smoke can lead to a fatal asthma attack.

Ans. (d) According to the last part of the third paragraph, second-hand smoke can increase the risk of allergic sensitization in children.

Eating Disorders

Millions of people in the world are affected by eating disorders. More than 90% of those afflicted are adolescents or young adult women. Although all eating disorders share some common manifestations, anorexia nervosa, bulimia nervosa, and binge eating each have distinctive symptoms and risks.

People who intentionally starve themselves (even while experiencing severe hunger pains) suffer from anorexia nervosa. The disorder, which usually begins around the time of puberty, involves extreme weight loss to at least 15% below the individual's normal body weight. Many people with the disorder look emaciated but are convinced they are overweight. In patients with anorexia nervosa, starvation can damage vital organs such as the heart and brain. To protect itself, the body shifts into slow gear: Menstrual periods stop, blood pressure rates drop, and thyroid function slows. Excessive thirst and frequent urination may occur. Dehydration contributes to constipation, and reduced body fat leads to lowered body temperature and the inability to withstand cold. Mild anemia, swollen joints, reduced muscle mass, and light-headedness also commonly occur in anorexia nervosa.

Anorexia nervosa sufferers can exhibit sudden angry outbursts or become socially withdrawn. One in ten cases of anorexia nervosa leads to death from starvation, cardiac arrest, other medical complications, or suicide. Clinical depression and anxiety place many individuals with eating disorders at risk for suicidal behaviour.

People with bulimia nervosa consume large amounts of food and then rid their bodies of the excess calories by vomiting, abusing laxatives or diuretics, taking enemas, or exercising obsessively. Some use a combination of all these forms of purging. Individuals with bulimia who use drugs to stimulate vomiting, bowel movements, or urination may be in considerable danger, as this practice increases the risk of heart failure. Dieting heavily between episodes of binging and purging is common.

Because many individuals with bulimia binge and purge in secret and maintain normal or above normal body weight, they can often successfully hide their problem for years. But bulimia nervosa patients—even those of normal weight—can severely damage their bodies by frequent binge eating and purging. In rare instances, binge eating causes the stomach to rupture; purging may result in heart failure due to loss of vital minerals such as potassium. Vomiting can cause the esophagus to become inflamed and glands near the cheeks to become swollen. As in anorexia nervosa, bulimia may lead to irregular menstrual periods. Psychological effects include compulsive stealing as well as possible indications of obsessive-compulsive disorder, an illness characterized by repetitive thoughts and behaviours. Obsessive compulsive disorder can also accompany anorexia nervosa. As with anorexia nervosa, bulimia typically begins during adolescence. Eventually, half of those with anorexia nervosa will develop bulimia. The condition occurs most often in women but is also found in men.

Binge-eating disorder is found in about 2% of the general population. As many as one-third of this group are men. It also affects older women, though with less frequency. Recent research shows that binge-eating disorder occurs in about 30% of people participating in medically supervised weight-control programmes.

This disorder differs from bulimia because its sufferers do not purge. Individuals with binge-eating disorder feel that they lose control of themselves when eating. They eat large quantities of food and do not stop until they are uncomfortably full. Most sufferers are overweight or obese and have a history of weight fluctuations. As a result, they are prone to the serious medical problems associated with obesity, such as high cholesterol, high blood pressure, and diabetes. Obese individuals also have a higher risk for gallbladder disease, heart disease, and some types of cancer. Usually they have more difficulty losing weight and keeping it off than do people with other serious weight problems. Like anorexic and bulimic sufferers who exhibit psychological problems, individuals with binge-eating disorder have high rates of simultaneously occurring psychiatric illnesses, especially depression.

1. Fatalities occur in what percent of people with anorexia nervosa?

a) 2%

b) 10%

c) 15%

d) 30%

Ans. (b) See the third paragraph: "One in ten" (% of) cases of anorexia end in death.

2. Which of the following consequences do all the eating disorders mentioned in the passage have in common?

a) heart ailments

b) stomach rupture

c) swollen joints

d) diabetes

Ans. (a) See the second and third paragraphs for reference to heart problems with anorexia, the fourth and fifth paragraphs for discussion of heart problems with bulimia, and the last paragraph, where heart disease is mentioned, as a risk in obese people who suffer from binge-eating disorder.

3. According to the passage, people with binge-eating disorder are prone to all of the following except

a) loss of control.

b) depression.

c) high blood pressure.

d) high cholesterol.

Ans. (c) Near the end of the last paragraph, the passage indicates that binge-eating disorder patients experience high blood pressure.

4. Which of the following is not a statement about people with eating disorders?

a) People with anorexia nervosa commonly have a blood-related deficiency.

b) People with anorexia nervosa perceive themselves as overweight.

c) The female population is the primary group affected by eating disorders.

d) Fifty per cent of people with bulimia have had anorexia nervosa.

Ans. (d) It is the other way around: % of people with anorexia develop bulimia, as stated near the end of the fifth paragraph.

5. People who have an eating disorder but nevertheless appear to be of normal weight are most likely to have

a) obsessive-compulsive disorder.

b) bulimia nervosa.

c) binge-eating disorder.

d) anorexia nervosa.

Ans. (b) The first sentence of the fifth paragraph tells us that bulimia sufferers are often able to keep their problem a secret, partly because they maintain a normal or above-normal weight.

6. Glandular functions of eating-disorder patients slow down as a result of

a) lowering body temperatures.

b) excessive thirst and urination.

c) protective measures taken by the body.

d) the loss of essential minerals.

Ans. (c) In the second paragraph, the thyroid gland function is mentioned as slowing down—one effort on the part of the body to protect itself.

7. The inability to eliminate body waste is related to

a) dehydration.

b) an inflamed esophagus.

c) the abuse of laxatives.

d) weight-control programmes.

Ans. (a) According to the second paragraph, dehydration contributes to constipation.

8. According to the passage, which of the following is true of bulimia patients?

a) They may demonstrate unpredictable social behaviour.

b) They often engage in compulsive exercise.

c) They are less susceptible to dehydration than are anorexia patients.

d) They frequently experience stomach ruptures.

Ans. (b) As stated in the opening sentence of the fourth paragraph, bulimia patients may exercise obsessively.

9. Which of the following represent up to two-thirds of the binge eating disorder population?

a) older males

b) older females

c) younger males

d) younger females

Ans. (d) See the second sentence of the sixth paragraph. If as many as one-third of the binge-eating disorder population are men, it stands to reason that up to two-thirds are younger women, given that we have learned that about % of all eating disorder sufferers are adolescent and young adult women.

A Greyhound

Greyhound racing is the sixth most popular spectator sport in the United States. Over the last decade, a growing number of racers have been adopted to spend their retirement as household pets, once their racing careers are over.

Many people hesitate to adopt a retired racing greyhound because they think only very old dogs are available. Actually, even champion racers only work until they are about three-and-a-half years old. Because greyhounds usually live to be 12 to 15 years old, their retirement is much longer than their racing careers.

People worry that a greyhound will be more nervous and active than other breeds and will need a large space to run. These are false impressions. Greyhounds have naturally sweet, mild dispositions, and while they love to run, they are sprinters rather than distance runners and are sufficiently exercised with a few daily laps around a fenced-in backyard.

Greyhounds do not make good watchdogs, but they are very good with children, get along well with other dogs (and usually cats as well), and are affectionate and loyal. They are intelligent, well-behaved dogs, usually housebroken in only a few days. A retired racing greyhound is a wonderful pet for almost anyone.

Based on the tone of the passage, the author's main purpose is to teach prospective owners how to transform their racing greyhound into a good pet.

Show how the greyhound's nature makes it equally good as racer and pet. encourage people to adopt retired racing greyhounds. objectively present the pros and cons of adopting a racing greyhound.

1. According to the passage, adopting a greyhound is a good idea for people who

a) do not have children.

b) live in apartments.

c) do not usually like dogs.

d) already have another dog or a cat.

Ans. (c) The tone of the passage is enthusiastic in its recommendation of the greyhound as pet and, thereby, encourages people to adopt one. It does not give advice on transforming a greyhound (choice (a). Except to say that they love to run, the passage does not spend equal time on describing the greyhound as racer (choice (b). The author's tone is not objective (choice (d), but rather enthusiastic.

2. Which of the following is implied by the passage?

a) The public is more aware of greyhounds than they used to be.

b) Greyhounds are more competitive than other dogs.

c) Greyhound racing should not be allowed.

d) People who own pet rabbits should not adopt greyhounds.

Ans. (d) See the last paragraph. The passage does not mention (b) or (c). Choice a is clearly wrong; the passage states the opposite.

3. One drawback of adopting a greyhound is that

a) greyhounds are not good with children.

b) greyhounds are old when they retire from racing.

c) the greyhound's sensitivity makes it temperamental.

d) greyhounds are not good watch dogs.

Ans. (a) See the first paragraph. Choices (b), (c), and (d) are not touched on in the passage.

4. This passage is most like an advertisement because it

a) uses statistics to prove its point.

b) does not present information to substantiate its claims.

c) says nothing negative about greyhounds.

d) encourages people to do something.

Ans. (d) See the last paragraph. Choices (a), (b), and (c) are contradicted in the passage.

5. According to the passage, a retired racing greyhound available for adoption will most likely be

a) happy to be retiring.

b) easily housebroken.

c) a champion, or else it would have been euthanized.

d) less high-strung than those that are not available for adoption.

Ans. (d) The enthusiastic tone of the passage seems meant to encourage people to adopt retired greyhounds. Choice (a) is wrong because there is only one statistic in the passage (in the first sentence), and it is not used to prove the point that greyhounds make good pets. Choice (b) is wrong because the author substantiates every point with information. Choice (c) is wrong because the passage does make the negative point that greyhounds do not make good watchdogs.

Ancient Greeks and their Beliefs

The lives of the Ancient Greeks revolved around eris, a concept by which they defined the universe. They believed that the world existed in a condition of opposites. If there was good, then there was evil, if there was love, then there was hatred; joy, then sorrow;

war then peace; and so on. The Greeks believed that good eris occured when one held a balanced outlook on life and coped with problems as they arose. It was a kind of ease of living that came from trying to bring together the great opposing forces in nature. Bad eris was evident in the violent conditions that ruled men's lives. Although these things were found in nature and sometimes could not be controlled, it was believed that bad eris occurred when one ignored a problem, letting it grow larger until it destroyed not only that person, but his family as well. The Ancient Greeks saw eris as a goddess: Eris, the Goddess of Discord, better known as Trouble.

One myth that expresses this concept of bad eris deals with the marriage of King Peleus and the river goddess Thetis. Zeus, the supreme ruler, learns that Thetis would bear a child strong enough to destroy its father. Not wanting to father his own ruin, Zeus convinces Thetis to marry a human, a mortal whose child could never challenge the gods. He promises her, among other things, the greatest wedding in all of Heaven and Earth and allows the couple to invite whomever they please. This is one of the first mixed marriages of Greek Mythology and the lesson learned from it still applies today. They do invite everyone ... except Eris, the Goddess of Discord. In other words, instead of facing the problems brought on by a mixed marriage, they turn their backs on them. They refused to deal directly with their problems and the result is tragic. In her fury, Eris arrives, ruins the wedding, causes a jealous feud between the three major goddesses over a golden apple, and sets in place the conditions that lead to the Trojan War. The war would take place 20 years in the future, but it would result in the death of the only child of the bride and groom, Achilles. Eris would destroy the parents' hopes for their future, leaving the couple with no legitimate heirs to the throne.

Hence, when we are told, "If you don't invite trouble, trouble comes," it means that if we don't deal with our problems, our problems will deal with us ... with a vengeance! It is easy to see why the Greeks considered many of their myths learning myths, for this one teaches us the best way to defeat that which can destroy us.

1. According to the passage, the ancient Greeks believed that the concept of eris defined the universe

 a) as a hostile, violent place.

 b) as a condition of opposites.

 c) as a series of problems.

 d) as a mixture of gods and man.

 Ans. (b) See the end of the next to last sentence in the passage. Choices (a), (c), and (d) are not to be found in the passage.

2. Most specifically, bad eris is defined in the passage as

 a) the violent conditions of life.

 b) the problems man encounters.

 c) the evil goddess who has a golden apple.

 d) the murderer of generations.

 Ans. (b) This is stated explicitly in the second sentence of the passage. Choice (a) is incorrect because only bad eris was defined as violent. Choice (c) deals with problems that belong in the domain of mankind, not the universe. Choice (d) has no support in the passage.

3. It can be inferred that Zeus married Thetis off because

 a) he needed to buy the loyalty of a great king of mankind.

 b) he feared the gods would create bad eris by competing over her.

 c) he feared the Trojan War would be fought over her.

 d) he feared having an affair with her and, subsequently, a child by her.

 Ans. (a) Again, this is a definition explicitly stated in the sixth sentence. Choice (b) is incorrect because a choice dealing with mankind alone is too narrow for a definition of eris, which deals with the entire universe. Choice (c) is incorrect because it only deals with one action of the personified concept in goddess form. Choice (d) has no support.

4. It can also be inferred that Zeus did not fear a child sired by King Peleus because

a) he knew that the child could not climb Mt. Olympus.

b) he knew that the child would be killed in the Trojan War.

c) he knew that no matter how strong a mortal child was, he couldn't overthrow an immortal god.

d) he knew that Thetis would always love him above everyone else.

Ans. (d) This is stated in the third sentence of paragraph. Zeus did not want to sire [father] a child who could eventually overthrow him. According to the passage, he felt it was safer to arrange for the child's father to be a mortal. There is no support in the passage for any of the other choices.

5. According to the passage, Achilles

a) defeated Zeus during the Trojan War.

b) dies during the Trojan War.

c) was born 20 years after the war because of the disruption Eris caused at the wedding.

d) was the illegitimate son of Peleus.

Ans. (c) This answer follows the logic of the previous answer. A mortal child could never challenge the gods implies that Zeus feared that if the child were immortal, it would overthrow him. The other choices mention individual words that appear in the passage but have no support.

6. Which of the following statements is the message offered in the myth?

a) Do not consider a mixed marriage.

b) Do not anger the gods.

c) Do not ignore the problems that arise in life.

d) Do not take myths seriously.

Ans. (b) The second to the last line in paragraph tells us that Achilles was the son of Thetis and Peleus, and that the war will result in his death. Choice (a) is incorrect because there is no other mention of Zeus or events in the Trojan War other than Achilles' death. Choice (c) is incorrect because Eris purposely created the conditions that would lead to the war to kill the child of the bride and groom. Choice (d) is incorrect because Achilles is the son of Thetis and Peleus, the bride and groom of the myth.

Passage adapted from 'The Necklace' by Guy de Maupassant

She was one of those pretty, charming women who are born, as if by an error of Fate, into a petty official's family. She had no dowry, no hopes, nor the slightest chance of being loved and married by a rich man—so she slipped into marriage with a minor civil servant. Unable to afford jewels, she dressed simply: But she was wretched, for women have neither caste nor breeding—in them beauty, grace, and charm replace pride of birth. Innate refinement, instinctive elegance, and wit give them their place on the only scale that counts, and these make humble girls the peers of the grandest ladies.

She suffered, feeling that every luxury should rightly have been hers. The poverty of her rooms—the shabby walls, the worn furniture, the ugly upholstery caused her pain. All these things that another woman of her class would not even have noticed, made her angry. The very sight of the little Breton girl who cleaned for her awoke rueful thoughts and the wildest dreams in her mind. She dreamt of rooms with Oriental hangings, lighted by tall, bronze torches, and with two huge footmen in knee breeches made drowsy by the heat from the stove, asleep in the wide armchairs. She dreamt of great drawing rooms upholstered in old silks, with fragile little tables holding priceless knickknacks, and of enchanting little sitting rooms designed for tea-time chats with famous, sought-after men whose attentions all women longed for.

She sat down to dinner at her round table with its three-day-old cloth, and watched her husband lift the lid of the soup tureen and delightedly exclaim: "Ah, a good homemade beef stew! There's nothing better!" She visualized elegant dinners with gleaming silver and gorgeous china. She yearned for wall hangings peopled with knights and ladies and exotic birds in a fairy forest. She dreamt of eating the pink flesh of trout or the wings of grouse. She had no proper wardrobe, no jewels, nothing. And those were the only things that she loved—she felt she was made for them. She would have so loved to charm, to be envied, to be admired and sought after.

1. Which word best describes the actual living conditions of the couple in the selection?

   a) destitute

   b) poor

   c) comfortable

   d) wealthy

   Ans. (c) The husband had a civil servant's job and received a steady salary; the wife had a servant who cleaned for her. The couple lived in a dwelling that had several rooms. This implies that they lived comfortably. Choice (a) is incorrect because they obviously were not impoverished. Choice (b) is incorrect because the wife had a maid. Choice (d) is incorrect because this was the life the wife wanted to have, but instead had shabby walls, worn furniture etc.

2. Which line best demonstrates the couple's true economic standing?

   She had no dowry, no hopes, not the slightest chance of being married by a rich man …

   The poverty of her rooms—the shabby walls, the worn furniture, the ugly upholstery caused her pain.

She sat down to dinner at her round table with its three-day old cloth, and watched her husband lift the lid of the soup tureen ...

The very sight of the little Breton girl who cleaned for her awoke rueful thoughts and the wildest dreams in her mind.

Ans. (d) This question relates to the previous one. This choice presents the fact that the wife had a maid. Choice (a) does not deal with the couple's economic standing, but only the wife's before she was married. Choice (b) is tempting, but the poverty of her rooms is more in her eyes than a truthful economic indicator. How poverty stricken can she be if she has a maid? Choice c deals with a tablecloth that has been used three days in a row. It has nothing to do with economic standing because it could have been washed by the maid or the wife, and the situation would have been remedied.

3. According to the selection, what can be stated about the marriage of this woman?

a) She married but was ashamed of the insignificant position her husband held.

b) She married on the rebound after a wealthy suitor had abandoned her.

c) She married for love without realising the consequences to her social standing.

d) She never loved her husband.

Ans. (a) It is obvious from the description of the wife's thoughts in the first paragraph that she wished she had married a rich man. Instead, she slipped into marriage with a minor civil servant. The woman is ashamed of her marriage and of her husband's occupation to the point of making it sound like an accident, as one may slip on a wet floor. Choices (b), (c), and (d) are incorrect because the wife loving anything other than expensive things is never mentioned in the passage.

4. What can be inferred about the values of both husband and wife?

a) They share the same values.

b) The husband values family and simple comforts of home, whereas his wife views these comforts as cause for her anguish.

c) The husband has ceased to enjoy the simple things and only strives to quench his wife's insatiable desire for luxury.

d) The husband believes that a wholesome meal can solve all problems, while his wife believes it is the presentation of the meal that counts.

Ans. (b) The husband's delight with the homemade stew only seems to send his wife into another bout of daydreams to escape her middle-class prison. Choice (a) is blatantly incorrect, because the husband obviously enjoys homemade beef stew while the wife dreams of wings of grouse. Choice (c) is incorrect because the husband is either unaware of his wife's anguish or doesn't let it affect his delight in his dinner. Choice (d) is irrelevant to the passage.

5. The main idea of the passage is

a) to have the reader feel great sympathy for the wife.

b) to have the reader feel great sympathy for the husband.

c) to show the class distinctions that were so obvious during the setting of the story.

d) to show the reader how selfish and self-centered the wife is.

Ans. (d) This is reinforced by the last two sentences of the passage. The wife admits she only loves rich things, believes she was made for them, and focuses all her desires on being admired and sought after, thinking only of herself at all times. Choice (a) is incorrect because the author paints a negative picture of the wife. Although choice (b) is tempting, the author does not develop the husband enough for him to become the focus of the passage. Choice (c) is incorrect because it is not developed in the passage. The focus is on the wife, not on class distinctions in general.

6. What part of speech does de Maupassant employ to weave the rich images he presents through the wife's descriptions?

a) adjectives

b) adverbs

c) nouns

d) verbs

Ans. (a) Adjectives are the words that describe nouns. These are the words that truly add dimension to the descriptions of the home and the daydreams of the wife. Innate, instinctive, grandest, gorgeous, gleaming, and pink are some of the adjectives that enrich the nouns of the wife's dreams. Shabby, worn, ugly, and homemade are adjectives that add to the undesirable view she has of her present situation. None of the other choices add such richness to the passage.

Angioplasty

Arteries of the heart blocked by plaque can reduce the flow of blood to the heart possibly resulting in heart attack or death. Plaque is actually fat and cholesterol that accumulates on the inside of the arteries. The arteries of the heart are small and can be blocked by such accumulations. There is a medical procedure that creates more space in the blocked artery by inserting and inflating a tiny balloon into the blood vessel. It is called coronary balloon angioplasty. Angioplasty means "blood vessel repair." When the balloon is inflated, it compresses the plaque against the wall of the artery, creating more space and improving the flow of blood.

Many doctors choose this technique, because it is less invasive than bypass surgery. Yes, both involve entering the body cavity, but in bypass surgery, the chest must be opened, the ribs must be cut, and the section of diseased artery must be removed and replaced. To replace it, the patient's body is opened, once again, to acquire a healthy section of artery. Usually, this blood vessel is removed from an artery located in the calf of the leg. This means the patient now has two painful incisions that must heal at the same time. There is far more risk in such bypass surgery than in angioplasty, which involves threading a thin tube, called a catheter, into the circulatory system and working it to the damaged artery.

Angioplasty may take between 30 minutes to 3 hours to complete. It begins with a distinctive dye that is injected into the bloodstream. A thin catheter is then inserted into the femoral artery of the leg, near the groin. The doctor monitors the path of the dye using x-rays. He moves the tube through the heart and into the plaque-filled artery. He inflates the balloon, creating more space, deflates the balloon, and removes the tube. It is important to note that the plaque has not been removed; it has just been compressed against the sides of the artery. Sometimes, a stent may be implanted, a tiny tube of stainless steel that is expandable when necessary. Its function is to keep the artery open.

There is good news and there is bad news. The good news is that the statistics compiled are superb. Ninety per cent of all angioplasty procedures are successful. The risk of dying during an operation of this type is less than 2%. The risk of heart attack is also small: 3–5%. Yet heart surgeons do not take any risk lightly; therefore, a team of surgeons stands ready to perform bypass surgery if needed. The length of hospitalization is only three days. The bad news is twofold. First, this procedure treats the condition but does not eradicate the cause. In 20% of the cases, there is a recurrence of plaque. Second, angioplasty is not recommended for all patients. The surgeons must consider the patient's age, physical history, how severe the blockage is, and, finally, the degree of damage to the artery before they make their determination.

1. When coronary arteries are blocked by plaque, one of the results could be

   a) stroke.

   b) heart attack.

c) hospitalization.

d) femoral artery deterioration.

Ans. (b) This answer is explicitly stated in the first sentence of the selection. Choices (a) and (d) are not mentioned as a result of plaqueladen arteries. Choice (c) is too general to be the best answer.

2. According to the passage, angioplasty is defined as

a) a tiny balloon.

b) a plaque-laden artery.

c) blood vessel repair.

d) bypass surgery.

Ans. (c) This answer is explicitly stated in the sixth sentence of paragraph. Choice (a) only names one medical instrument used during the procedure. Choice (b) offers the reason for the angioplasty, because it is done to compress the plaque in an artery. Choice (d) offers a procedure that would be chosen as an alternative to angioplasty.

3. It can be inferred from the passage that invasive most closely means

a) entering the body cavity.

b) causing infection.

c) resulting in hospitalization.

d) requiring a specialist's opinion.

Ans. (a) The first and second sentences of paragraph state how both procedures, angioplasty and bypass surgery, are invasive because "both involve entering the body cavity." None of the other choices are supported or implied as a definition for invasive.

4. The angioplasty procedure begins with

a) a thin catheter being inserted into the femoral artery.

b) a balloon being inflated in the heart.

c) a special dye being injected into the bloodstream.

d) a healthy artery being removed from the calf.

Ans. (c) The procedure is detailed in paragraph. It begins with injecting a special dye. Choices (a) and (b) follow later in the procedure, whereas choice (d) deals with bypass surgery rather than the angioplasty procedure.

5. It can be inferred from the passage that

a) a healthy artery is removed and awaits possible bypass surgery.

b) patients have trouble accepting the idea that a tiny balloon will cure the problem.

c) 3–5% of the patients refuse to undergo this procedure.

d) surgeons do not take even a 2% chance of death lightly.

Ans. (d) This answer can be found in paragraph. a team of surgeons stands ready to perform bypass surgery even though the risk factor of death is only %. Choice (a) is not supported in the passage. Choices (c) and (d) are incorrect because the passage does not discuss patient reaction at all.

6. Which one of the following statements is true?

a) The plaque that has caused the problem is not removed during angioplasty.

b) The risk of dying during an angioplasty procedure is 3–5%.

c) The coronary balloon angioplasty is a separate procedure from inflating a balloon into a blocked artery.

d) All of the above statements are true.

Ans. (a) This choice is supported in the last sentence of paragraph. Choice (b) is incorrect: Choice (c) is a complete misunderstanding of the text. Inflating a balloon into a blocked artery is coronary balloon angioplasty. Because two answers are incorrect, (d) is not a viable choice.

History of Time

For centuries, time was measured by the position of the sun with the use of sundials. Noon was recognised when the sun was the highest in the sky, and cities would set their clock by this apparent solar time, even though some cities would often be on a slightly different time. Daylight Saving Time (DST), sometimes called summer time, was instituted to make better use of daylight. Thus, clocks are set forward one hour in the spring to move an hour of daylight from the morning to the evening and then set back one hour in the fall to return to normal daylight.

Benjamin Franklin first conceived the idea of daylight saving during his tenure as an American delegate in Paris in 1984 and wrote about it extensively in his essay, "An Economical Project." It is said that Franklin awoke early one morning and was surprised to see the sunlight at such an hour. Always the economist, Franklin believed the practice of moving the time could save on the use of candlelight, as candles were expensive at the time.

In England, builder William Willett (1857–1915) became a strong supporter for Daylight Saving Time upon noticing blinds of many houses were closed on an early sunny morning. Willet believed everyone, including himself, would appreciate longer hours of light in the evenings. In 1909, Sir Robert Pearce introduced a bill in the House of Commons to make it obligatory to adjust the clocks. A bill was drafted and introduced into Parliament several times but met with great opposition, mostly from farmers. Eventually, in 1925, it was decided that summer time should begin on the day following the third Saturday in April and close after the first Saturday in October.

The U.S. Congress passed the Standard Time Act of 1918 to establish standard time and preserve and set Daylight Saving Time across the continent. This act also devised five time zones throughout the United States: Eastern, Central, Mountain, Pacific, and Alaska. The first time zone was set on "the mean astronomical time of the seventy-fifth degree of longitude west from Greenwich" (England). In 1919, this act was repealed.

President Roosevelt established year-round Daylight Saving Time (also called War Time) from 1942–1945. However, after this period, each state adopted its own DST, which proved to be disconcerting to television and radio broadcasting and transportation. In 1966, President Lyndon Johnson created the Department of Transportation and signed the Uniform Time Act. As a result, the Department of Transportation was given the responsibility for the time laws. During the oil embargo and energy crisis of the 1970s, President Richard Nixon extended DST through the Daylight Saving Time Energy Act of 1973 to conserve energy further. This law was modified in 1986, and Daylight Saving Time was reset to begin on the first Sunday in April (to spring ahead) and end on the last Sunday in October (to fall back).

1. As it is used in paragraph 3, the word obligatory most nearly means

   a) approved.

   b) sparse.

   c) aberrant.

   d) requisite.

   Ans. (d) Choices (b) and (c), meaning scattered and erratic respectively, are not supported in the passage. Choice (a) may be considered a synonym, but it is not the best choice. The best choice is (d), requisite.

2. Who first established the idea of DST?

   a) President Richard Nixon

   b) Benjamin Franklin

   c) Sir Robert Pearce

   d) President Lyndon Johnson

   Ans. (b) Paragraph of the passage clearly states that Benjamin Franklin first considered the concept of DST.

3. Who opposed the bill that was introduced in the House of Commons in the early 1900s?

a) Sir Robert Pearce

b) farmers

c) television and radio broadcasting companies

d) the U.S. Congress

Ans. (b) Paragraph states that the bill (which was introduced by Sir Robert Pearce in) met with great opposition, mostly from farmers.

4. Which of the following statements is true of the U.S. Department of Transportation?

a) It was created by President Richard Nixon.

b) It set standards for DST throughout the world.

c) It constructed the Uniform Time Act.

d) It oversees all time laws in the United States.

Ans. (d) This choice is directly supported by paragraph.

5. Which of the following would be the best title for this passage?

a) The History and Rationale of Daylight Saving Time

b) Lyndon Johnson and the Uniform Time Act

c) The U.S. Department of Transportation and Daylight Saving Time

d) Daylight Saving Time in the United States

Ans. (a) Choices (b) and (c) are incorrect because they each refer to specific points raised in the passage, but not throughout the passage. Choice (d) is too broad to represent the best title. Only choice a describes the point of the entire passage.

6. The Daylight Saving Time Energy Act of 1973 was responsible for

a) preserving and setting Daylight Saving Time across the continent.

b) instituting five time zones in the United States.

c) extending Daylight Saving Time in the interest of energy conservation.

d) conserving energy by giving the Department of Transportation authority over time laws.

Ans. (c) Paragraph clearly states that during the oil embargo and energy crisis of the s, President Richard Nixon extended DST through the Daylight Saving Time Energy Act of to conserve energy further.

Milton Hershey

Milton Hershey was born near the small village of Derry Church, Pennsylvania, in 1857. It was a humble beginning that did not foretell his later popularity. Milton only attended school through the fourth grade; at that point, he was apprenticed to a printer in a nearby town. Fortunately for all chocolate lovers, Milton did not excel as a printer. After a while, he left the printing business and was apprenticed to a Lancaster, Pennsylvania candy maker. It was apparent he had found his calling in life, and at the age of eighteen, he opened his own candy store in Philadelphia. In spite of his talents as a candy maker, the shop failed after six years.

It may come as a surprise to current Milton Hershey fans, but his first candy success came with the manufacture of caramel. After the failure of his Philadelphia store, Milton headed for Denver, where he learned the art of making caramels. There he took a job with a local manufacturer who insisted on using fresh milk in making his caramels; Milton saw that this made the caramels especially tasty. After a time in Denver, Milton once again attempted to open his own candy-making businesses, in Chicago, New Orleans, and New York City. Finally, in 1886, he went to Lancaster, Pennsylvania, where he raised the money necessary to try again. This company—the Lancaster Caramel Company—established Milton's reputation as a master candy-maker.

In 1893, Milton attended the Chicago International Exposition, where he saw a display of German chocolate-making implements.

Captivated by the equipment, he purchased it for his Lancaster candy factory and began producing chocolate, which he used for coating his caramels. By the next year, production had grown to include cocoa, sweet chocolate, and baking chocolate. The Hershey Chocolate company was born in 1894 as a subsidiary of the Lancaster Caramel Company. Six years later, Milton sold the caramel company, but retained the rights, and the equipment, to make chocolate. He believed that a large market of chocolate consumers was waiting for someone to produce reasonably priced candy. He was right.

Milton Hershey returned to the village where he had been born, in the heart of dairy country, and opened his chocolate manufacturing plant. With access to all the fresh milk he needed, he began producing the finest milk chocolate. The plant that opened in a small Pennsylvania village in 1905 is today the largest chocolate factory in the world. The confections created at this facility are favourites around the world.

The area where the factory is located is now known as Hershey, Pennsylvania. Within the first decades of its existence, the town of Hershey thrived, as did the chocolate business. A bank, a school, churches, a department store, even a park and a trolley system all appeared in short order; the town soon even had a zoo. Today, a visit to the area reveals the Hershey Medical Center, Milton Hershey School, and Hershey's Chocolate World—a theme park where visitors are greeted by a giant Reeses Peanut Butter Cup. All of these things—and a huge number of happy chocolate lovers—were made possible because a caramel maker visited the Chicago Exposition of 1893!

1. According to information contained in the passage, the reader can infer which of the following?

a) Chocolate is popular in every country in the world.

b) Reeses Peanut Butter Cups are manufactured by the Hershey Chocolate Company.

c) Chocolate had never been manufactured in the United States before Milton Hershey did it.

d) The Hershey Chocolate Company now makes more money from Hershey's Chocolate World than from the manufacture and sale of chocolate.

Ans. (b) This is an inference question. The writer indicates that visitors to Hershey's Chocolate World are greeted by a giant Reeses Peanut Butter Cup, so it is logical to assume that these are manufactured by Hershey. Although the writer mentions the popularity of chocolate internationally, you cannot assume that it is popular in every country (choice (a), nor is there any indication that Milton Hershey was the first person to manufacture chocolate in the United States (choice (c). Choice (d) is not discussed in the passage at all.

2. Which of the following best defines the word subsidiary as used in paragraph 3?

a) a company owned entirely by one person

b) a company founded to support another company

c) a company that is not incorporated

d) a company controlled by another company

Ans. (d) This question tests your ability to use context clues to determine the intended meaning of a word. In paragraph, the passage says, The Hershey Chocolate company was born in as a subsidiary of the Lancaster Caramel Company. This indicates that a subsidiary is one controlled by another company, choice (d). Although it may be true that Milton Hershey owned each company in its entirety (choice (a), that is not clear from the material. There is also no indication that the chocolate company was created to support the caramel company (choice (b). Finally, the passage contains no discussion of whether or not any of Hershey's companies were incorporated (choice (c).

3. The writer's main purpose in this passage is to

a) recount the founding of the Hershey Chocolate Company.

b) describe the process of manufacturing chocolate.

c) compare the popularity of chocolate to other candies.

d) explain how apprenticeships work.

Ans. (a) Choice (a) is the best choice because it is the most complete statement of the material. Choices (c) and (d) focus on small details of the passage; choice (b) is not discussed in the passage.

4. According to the passage, Milton Hershey sold his caramel company in

a) 1894.

b) 1900.

c) 1904.

d) 1905.

Ans. (b) Paragraph states that Hershey sold the caramel company six years after the founding of the chocolate company. The chocolate company was founded in; the correct choice is (b).

5. The mention of the Chicago International Exposition of 1893 in the passage indicates that

a) the exposition in Chicago is held once every three years.

b) the theme of the exposition of 1893 was "Food from Around the World."

c) the exposition contained displays from a variety of countries.

d) the site of the exposition is now a branch of the Hershey Chocolate Company.

Ans. (c) The Chicago International Exposition was where Hershey saw a demonstration of German chocolate-making techniques, which indicates, along with the word international in its title, that the exposition contained displays from a variety of countries, choice (c). None of the other choices can be inferred from the information in the passage.

6. Which of the following words best fits in the blank in paragraph 1 of the passage?

a) dramatic

b) modest

c) undignified

d) rewarding

Ans. (b) There is nothing inherently dramatic, undignified, or rewarding discussed in paragraph. Modest is the word that best fits being born in a small village and having the unremarkable early life described; it is also a word that provides a contrast to the mention of Milton's later popularity.

Making Miracles Happen

By using tiny probes as neural prostheses, scientists may be able to restore nerve function in quadriplegics and make the blind see or the deaf hear. Thanks to advanced techniques, a single, small, implanted probe can stimulate individual neurons electrically or chemically and then record responses. Preliminary results suggest that the microprobe telemetry systems can be permanently implanted and replace damaged or missing nerves.

The tissue-compatible microprobes represent an advance over the typical aluminum wire electrodes used in studies of the cortex and other brain structures. Researchers accumulate much data using traditional electrodes, but there is a question of how much damage they cause to the nervous system. Microprobes, which are about as thin as a human hair, cause minimal damage and disruption of neurons when inserted into the brain.

In addition to recording nervous-system impulses, the microprobes have minuscule channels that open the way for delivery of drugs, cellular growth factors, neurotransmitters, and other neuroactive compounds to a single neuron or to groups of neurons. Also, patients who lack certain biochemicals could receive doses via prostheses. The probes can have up to four channels, each with its own recording/stimulating electrode.

1. One similar feature of microprobes and wire electrodes is
   a) a minimal disturbance of neurons.
   b) the density of the material.
   c) the capacity for multiple leads.
   d) their ability to generate information.

   Ans. (d) The second sentence of paragraph states that probes record responses. Paragraph says that electrodes accumulate much data.

2. Which of the following best expresses the main idea of the passage?
   a) Microprobes require further techno-logical advances before they can be used in humans.
   b) Wire electrodes are antiquated as a means for delivering neuro active compounds to the brain.
   c) Microprobes have great potential to help counteract neural damage.
   d) Technology now exists that may enable repair of the nervous system.

   Ans. (c) The tone throughout the passage suggests the potential for microprobes. They can be permanently implanted, they have advantages over electrodes, they are promising candidates for neural prostheses, they will have great accuracy, and they are flexible.

3. All of the following are mentioned in the passage as potential uses for prostheses except
   a) transportation of medication.
   b) induction of physical movement.
   c) transportation of growth factor.
   d) removal of bio chemicals from the cortex.

   Ans. (d) According to the third paragraph, people who lack biochemicals could receive doses via prostheses. However, there is no suggestion that removing biochemicals would be viable.

4. The initial function of microprobe channels is to

a) create pathways.

b) disrupt neurons.

c) replace ribbon cables.

d) study the brain.

Ans. (a) The first sentence of the third paragraph says that microprobes have channels that open the way for delivery of drugs. Studying the brain (choice (d) is not the initial function of channels, though it is one of the uses of the probes themselves.

Medical Wastes

Medical waste has been a growing concern because of recent incidents of public exposure to discarded blood vials, needles (sharps), empty prescription bottles, and syringes. Medical waste can typically include general refuse, human blood and blood products, cultures and stocks of infectious agents, labouratory animal carcasses, contaminated bedding material, and pathological wastes.

Wastes are generally collected by gravity chutes, carts, or pneumatic tubes, each of which has its own advantages and disadvantages. Chutes are limited to vertical transport, and there is some risk of exhausting contaminants into hallways if a door is left open during use. Another disadvantage of gravity chutes is that the waste container may get jammed while dropping, or it may be broken upon hitting the bottom. Carts are primarily for horizontal transport of bagged or containerized wastes. The main risk here is that bags may be broken or torn during transport, potentially exposing the worker to the wastes. Using automated carts can reduce the potential for exposure. Pneumatic tubes offer the best performance for waste transport in a large facility. Advantages include high-speed movement, movement in any direction, and minimal intermediate storage of untreated wastes. However, some objects cannot be conveyed pneumatically.

Off-site disposal of regulated medical wastes remains a viable option for smaller hospitals (those with less than 150 beds). Some preliminary on-site processing, such as compaction or hydro pulping, may be necessary prior to sending the waste off site. Compaction reduces the total volume of solid wastes, often reducing transportation and disposal costs, but it does not change the hazardous characteristics of the waste. Compaction may not be economical if transportation and disposal costs are based on weight rather than volume.

Hydropulping involves grinding the waste in the presence of an oxidizing fluid, such as hypochlorite solution. The liquid is separated from the pulp and discharged directly into the sewer unless local limits require additional pretreatment prior to discharge. The pulp can often be disposed of at a landfill. One advantage is that waste can be rendered innocuous and reduced in size within the same system. Disadvantages are the added operating burden, difficulty of controlling fugitive emissions, and the difficulty of conducting microbiological tests to determine whether all organic matters and infectious organisms have been destroyed from the waste.

On-site disposal is a feasible alternative for hospitals generating two tons or more per day of total solid waste. Common treatment techniques include steam sterilization and incineration. Although other options are available, incineration is currently the preferred method for on-site treatment of hospital waste.

Steam sterilisation is limited in the types of medical waste it can treat, but is appropriate for labouratory cultures and/or substances contaminated with infectious organisms. The waste is subjected to steam in a sealed, pressurized chamber. The liquid that may form is drained off to the sewer or sent for processing. The unit is then reopened after a vapour release to the atmosphere, and the solid waste is removed for further processing or disposal. One advantage of steam sterilisation is that it has been used for many years in hospitals to sterilise instruments and containers and to treat small quantities of waste. However, since sterilization does not change the appearance of the waste, there could be a problem in gaining acceptance of the waste for landfilling.

A properly designed, maintained, and operated incinerator achieves a relatively high level of organism destruction. Incineration reduces the weight and volume of the waste as much as 95% and is especially appropriate for pathological wastes and sharps. The most common incineration system for medical waste is the controlled-air type. The principal advantage of this type of incinerator is low particulate emissions. Rotary-kiln and grate-type units have been used, but use of grate-type units has been discontinued because of high air emissions. The rotary kiln also puts out high emissions, and the costs have been prohibitive for smaller units.

1. Which of the following organisational schemes is most prevalent in the passage?

a) chronological order

b) comparison-contrast

c) order by topic

d) hierarchical order

Ans. (b) Throughout, the passage compares and contrasts the various methods of medical waste disposal.

2. One disadvantage of the compaction method of waste disposal is that it

a) cannot reduce transportation costs.

b) reduces the volume of solid waste material.

c) does not allow hospitals to confirm that organic matter has been eliminated.

d) does not reduce the weight of solid waste material.

Ans. (d) See the last sentence of paragraph. Compaction may well reduce transportation costs (choice (a)) according to paragraph. That it reduces the volume of waste (choice (b)) is an advantage, not a disadvantage. Compaction is not designed to eliminate organic matter, so confirming that it has been eliminated (choice (c)) is not an issue.

3. For hospitals that dispose of waste on their own premises, the optimum treatment method is

a) incineration.

b) compaction.

c) sterilization.

d) hydropulping.

Ans. (a) See the last sentence of paragraph, which states that incineration is ... the preferred method for on-site treatment.

4. According to the passage, which of the following could be safely disposed of in a landfill but might not be accepted by landfill facilities?

a) hydropulped material

b) sterilised waste

c) incinerated waste

d) labouratory cultures

Ans. (b) See the last sentence of paragraph, which points out that steam sterilization does not change the appearance of the waste, thus perhaps raising questions at a landfill.

5. The two processes mentioned in the passage that involve the formation of liquid are

a) compaction and hydropulping.

b) incineration and compaction.

c) hydropulping and sterilization.

d) sterilization and incineration.

Ans. (c) Paragraph states that liquid is separated from pulp in the hydropulping process. Paragraph says that liquid may form during the sterilization process.

6. According to the passage, two effective methods for treating waste caused by infectious matter are

a) steam sterilization and incineration.

b) hydropulping and steam sterilization.

c) incineration and compaction.

d) hydropulping and incineration.

Ans. (a) This response relies on an understanding of pathological wastes, which are wastes generated by infectious materials. Paragraph points out that incineration is especially appropriate for pathological wastes. Previously, paragraph had said that steam sterilisation is appropriate for substances contaminated with infectious organisms.

7. Hospitals can minimise employee contact with dangerous waste by switching from

a) a manual cart to a gravity chute.

b) an automated cart to a hydropulping machine.

c) a gravity chute to a manual cart.

d) a manual cart to an automated cart.

Ans. (d) The second paragraph says that the main risk of pushing carts is potential exposure from torn bags but that automated carts can reduce that potential.

8. The process that transforms waste from hazardous to harmless and diminishes waste volume is

a) sterilization.

b) hydropulping.

c) oxidizing.

d) compacting.

Ans. (b) See the next to last sentence of paragraph. Sterilisation does not change the appearance of waste. Although compacting does change the volume of the waste, it is not appropriate for eliminating hazardous materials.

9. The underlined word exhausting, as it is used in the second paragraph of the passage, most nearly means

a) debilitating.

b) disregarding.

c) detonating.

d) discharging.

Ans. (d) See the second sentence of paragraph: ... there is some risk of exhausting contaminants into hallways, meaning waste might be discharged.

10. Budgetary constraints have precluded some small hospitals from purchasing

a) pneumatic tubes.

b) rotary kilns.

c) sterilization equipment.

d) controlled-air kilns.

Ans. (b) See the last sentence of the passage, which states that the costs have been prohibitive for smaller units when using rotary kilns.

11. The underlined phrase fugitive emissions in the fourth paragraph most nearly means

a) contaminants that are extremely toxic.

b) contaminants that are illegally discharged.

c) contaminants that escape the disposal process.

d) contaminants that come from micro-biological testing.

Ans. (c) Although the contaminants may sometimes be extremely toxic (choice (a)), the word fugitive here is the key to the meaning. The words fugitive emissions are used in the context of the disposal process of hydropulping. To be a fugitive means to run away or to escape, so the logical choice, given this context, is choice (c). There is nothing anywhere in the passage about criminal activity, so choice (b) is not a likely answer. Choice (d) is wrong because the microbiological testing of which the passage speaks pertains to ensuring that all waste is disposed of.

Animals and Intelligence

An upsurge of new research suggests that animals have a much higher level of brainpower than previously thought. If animals do have intelligence, how do scientists measure it? Before defining animals' intelligence, scientists defined what is not intelligence. Instinct is not intelligence. It is a skill programmed into an animal's brain by its genetic heritage. Rote conditioning is also not intelligence. Tricks can be learned by repetition, but no real thinking is involved. Cuing, in which animals learn to do or not to do certain things by following outside signals, does not demonstrate intelligence. Scientists believe that insight, the ability to use tools, and communication using human language are all effective measures of the mental ability of animals.

When judging animal intelligence, scientists look for insight, which they define as a flash of sudden understanding. When a young gorilla could not reach fruit from a tree, she noticed crates scattered about the lawn near the tree. She piled the crates into a pyramid, then climbed on them to reach her reward. The gorilla's insight allowed her to solve a new problem without trial and error.

The ability to use tools is also an important sign of intelligence. Crows use sticks to pry peanuts out of cracks. The crow exhibits intelligence by showing it has learned what a stick can do. Likewise, otters use rocks to crack open crab shells in order to get at the meat. In a series of complex moves, chimpanzees have been known to use sticks and stalks in order to get at a favourite snack—termites. To make and use a termite tool, a chimp first selects just the right stalk or twig. He trims and shapes the stick, then finds the entrance to a termite mound. While inserting the stick carefully into the entrance, the chimpanzee turns it skilfully to fit the inner tunnels. The chimp attracts the insects by shaking the twig. Then it pulls the tool out without scraping off any termites. Finally, he uses his lips to skim the termites into his mouth.

Many animals have learned to communicate using human language. Some primates have learned hundreds of words in sign language. One chimp can recognise and correctly use more than 250 abstract symbols on a keyboard. These symbols represent human words. An amazing parrot can distinguish five objects of two different types. He can understand the difference between the number, colour, and kind of object. The ability to classify is a basic thinking skill. He seems to use language to express his needs and emotions. When ill and taken to the animal hospital for his first overnight stay, this parrot turned to go. "Come here!" he cried to a scientist who works with him. "I love you. I'm sorry. Wanna go back?"

The research on animal intelligence raises important questions. If animals are smarter than once thought, would that change the way humans interact with them? Would humans stop hunting them for sport or survival? Would animals still be used for food, clothing, or medical experimentation? Finding the answer to these tough questions makes a difficult puzzle even for a large-brained, problem-solving species like our own.

1. Crows use sticks to pry peanuts out of cracks. Which of the following is the kind of intelligence or conditioning the situation describes?

a) rote learning

b) tools

c) communication

d) instinct

Ans. (b) The crow is using the stick as a tool to assist it in getting food.

2. The underlined word upsurge, as it is used in the first paragraph of the passage, most nearly means

a) an increasingly large amount.

b) a decreasing amount.

c) a well-known amount.

d) an immeasurable amount.

Ans. (a) In the first paragraph, upsurge (a swelling of the ocean) is used as an analogy to illustrate the large and increasing amount of research in animal intelligence.

3. The concluding paragraph of this passage infers which of the following?

a) There is no definitive line between those animals with intelligence and those without.

b) Animals are being given opportunities to display their intelligence.

c) Research showing higher animal intelligence may fuel debate on ethics and cruelty.

d) Animals are capable of untrained thought well beyond mere instinct.

Ans. (c) The questions in this paragraph ask the reader to consider the use of animals in our world and questions whether knowing that they have more intelligence than previously thought might make a difference in human treatment of them.

4. According to the passage, which of the following is true about animals communicating through the use of human language?

a) Parrots can imitate or repeat a sound.

b) Dolphins click and whistle.

c) Crows screech warnings to other crows.

d) Chimpanzees and gorillas have been trained to use sign language or geometric shapes that stand for words.

Ans. (d) This choice is the only one that shows animals using human language.

5. In paragraph 3, what conclusion can be reached about the chimpanzee's ability to use a tool?

a) It illustrates high intelligence because he is able to get his food and eat it.

b) It illustrates instinct because he faced a difficult task and accomplished it.

c) It illustrates high intelligence because he stored knowledge away and called it up at the right time.

d) It illustrates high intelligence because termites are protein packed.

Ans. (c) Although each conclusion is an example of some intelligence, the most accurate conclusion the reader should make is that this action shows high intelligence. The complexity of what the chimpanzee is doing to get his food and the many thinking activities he must accomplish in order to realise his goal of getting the termites—learning a new skill, selecting and shaping a tool, remembering stored knowledge, using the correct knowledge in order to take proper action for the situation—shows intelligence.

6. Which of the following is not a sign of animal intelligence?

a) shows insight

b) cues

c) uses tools

d) makes a plan

Ans. (b) Cuing does not demonstrate animal intelligence because the animal learns to do or not to do certain things by following outside signals.

Photosynthesis

Photosynthesis is the process that plants use to convert sunlight into the food that they need to survive and grow. Most plants create some form of sugar from the sunlight, and this sugar is used by the plant as its primary food source.

Plants actually need only three things to create this sugar: sunlight, carbon dioxide, and water. The sunlight reacts with the plant's chlorophyll, a green chemical which is used to convert water and carbon dioxide into sugar.

As a general rule, photosynthesis occurs in a plant's leaves. The leaf contains chlorophyll, which reacts when sunlight strikes the leaf. It is also the chlorophyll which gives the leaf its typical green colour, since photosynthesis absorbs most light rays except green, which are reflected outwards.

The process of photosynthesis produces more than just sugar, however. One byproduct of the process is oxygen, which is "exhaled" by the plant into the atmosphere. In fact, plant photosynthesis is one of the primary sources of oxygen generation on our planet, making plant life essential to almost all living things on earth.

1. According to paragraph 4, which of the following is a byproduct of photosynthesis?

a) green pigment

b) water

c) carbon dioxide

d) oxygen

Ans. (d) Photosynthesis produces sugar in a plant, and oxygen is a byproduct. The other choices may be involved in photosynthesis, but they are not byproducts.

2. The underlined word essential, as used in paragraph 4, most nearly means

a) necessary.

b) optional.

c) fragrant.

d) growing.

Ans. (a) The passage states that photosynthesis produces oxygen, which is necessary for life on earth. None of the other choices fit the context.

3. The passage explains that photosynthesis is

a) done in the plant stem.

b) what makes plants edible.

c) the way that plants feed themselves.

d) the source of carbon dioxide in the atmosphere.

Ans. (c) The passage states that photosynthesis produces sugar, which the plant uses for food.

4. According to the passage, why do plant leaves look green?

a) Leaves are actually not green.

b) Photosynthesis absorbs all colours except green.

c) Sugar is green.

d) Photosynthesis requires green light to produce sugar.

Ans. (b) The final sentence in paragraph states that green light is reflected by photosynthesis.

5. After reading the passage, what can you conclude about photosynthesis?

a) Chlorophyll is part of the ozone layer.

b) Photosynthesis is the process that feeds a plant.

c) Plants need oxygen to survive.

d) The roots of a plant provide water.

Ans. (b) This choice is the only one that can be concluded from the passage.

6. After reading the passage, what can you infer about photosynthesis?
   a) Human life would not survive without plants.
   b) Chlorophyll tastes sweet.
   c) Sunlight has both good and bad effects on plants.
   d) Too much water can interfere with photosynthesis.

   Ans. (a) Paragraph states that photosynthesis produces oxygen; without oxygen, human life could not exist on earth.

Lincoln's Desire to Read

Abraham Lincoln served as the 16th President of the United States, yet he never went to college. In fact, Lincoln had nearly no formal education whatsoever, attending schools for less than a year throughout his childhood. Yet this should not be construed to mean that Lincoln was ignorant or unlearned; on the contrary, he was one of the most well-read leaders of the time. The fact is that Abraham Lincoln educated himself by studying books of religion, philosophy, and literature, and he continued his voracious reading throughout his life.

A lack of public school education did not prevent Lincoln from becoming a great leader. He led the United States through four years of civil war, which threatened to divide the nation into two separate countries. He was a powerful opponent of slavery, and it was largely through his leadership that slavery was abolished in this country.

Lincoln's determination to educate himself through diligent reading also led to his reputation as a great orator—and even today his speeches are quoted and studied worldwide. He serves as an example of a great leader—and a great reader. His love of books and good literature enabled Abe Lincoln to rise to world renown.

1. What is the main idea of this passage?
   a) Abraham Lincoln was the 16th President of the United States.

b) Abraham Lincoln demonstrated the value of reading.

c) Abraham Lincoln was a Republican.

d) Abraham Lincoln freed the slaves.

Ans. (b) Although all choices are true statements, only b states the main idea.

2. Lincoln accomplished all of the following Except

a) preventing the United States from being divided.

b) ending slavery.

c) becoming a great leader.

d) establishing the Lincoln Memorial.

Ans. (d) Statements (a), (b), and (c) appear in the passage; this statement does not.

3. A voracious reader is

a) likely to become President.

b) a person who makes reading a regular habit.

c) someone who never went to school.

d) probably poor.

Ans. (b) The passage only gives evidence that supports this answer.

4. The underlined word construed, as used in paragraph 1, most nearly means

a) tormented.

b) taken apart.

c) unscrewed.

d) interpreted.

Ans. (d) To construe something is to interpret it in a specific way.

5. According to the passage, what lesson can be learned from the life of Abraham Lincoln?

a) Education is not important.

b) All books are worth reading.

c) Good reading habits can help a person do great things.

d) Politicians are always good role models.

Ans. (c) The passage uses Abraham Lincoln to illustrate the importance of good reading habits. It does not state that all books are worth reading, nor does it imply that education is unimportant.

6. How does Lincoln still affect students today?

a) His face is on money.

b) His speeches are still quoted and studied today.

c) People grow beards to look like him.

d) Students quit school in hopes of becoming president.

Ans. (b) This is the only choice that the passage supports.

Working Women

In an unfinished but highly suggestive series of essays, the late Sarah Eisentein has focused attention on the evolution of working women's values from the turn of the century to the First World War. Eisenstein argues that turn-of-the-century women neither wholly accepted nor rejected what she calls the dominant "ideology of domesticity," but rather took this and other available ideologies-feminism, socialism, trade unionism-and modified or adapted them in light of their won experiences and needs. In thus maintaining that wages-work helped to produce a new "consciousness" among women, Eisenstein to some extent challenges the recent, controversial proposal by Leslie Tentler that for women the work experience only served to reinforce the attractiveness of the dominant ideology. According to the Tentler, the degrading conditions under which many female wage earners worked made them view the family as a source of power and esteem available nowhere else in their social world. In contrast, Eisenstein's study insists that wage-work had other implications for women's identities and consciousness. Most importantly, her work aims to demonstrate that wage-work enabled women to become aware of themselves as a distinct social group capable of defining their collective circumstance. Eisenstein insists that as a group working-class women were not able to come to collective consciousness of their situation until they began entering the labour force, because domestic work tended to isolate them from one another.

Unfortunately, Eisenstein's unfinished study does not develop these ideas in sufficient depth or detail, offering tantalizing hints rather than an exhaustive analysis. Whatever Eisenstein's overall plan may have been, in its current form her study suffers from the limited nature of the sources she depended on. She use the speeches and writings of reformers and labour organisers, who she acknowledges were far from representative, as the voice of the typical woman worker. And there is less than adequate attention given to the differing values of immigrant groups that made up a significant proportion of the population under investigation. While raising important questions, Eisenstein's essays do not provide definitive answer, and it remains for others to take up the challenges they offer.

1. The primary purpose of the passage is to

a) criticise a scholar's assumptions and methodology

b) evaluate an approach to women's study

c) compare two sociological theories

d) correct a misconception about feminist theory

e) defend an unpopular ideology

Ans. This question asks you to identify the primary purpose of the passage as a whole. Choice (b) is the best answer. The passage gives an overview of Eisenstein's approach to women's history and then offers an evaluation of that approach. Choice (a) is not correct: while the passage mentions certain criticisms of Eisenstein's work, it is not her underlying assumptions that are being challenged. Furthermore, the criticisms do not constitute the primary concern of the passage. Choice (c) is not correct: while two theories are mentioned, a passage whose primary purposes were to compare those two theories would have to discuss the second theory in greater detail. Choice (d) and (e) are incorrect because the passage does not suggest that there have been misconceptions about feminist theory, and no particular ideology is being defended.

2. It can be inferred from the passage that, in Eisenstein's view, working women at the turn of the century had which of the following attitudes toward the dominant ideology of their time?

a) They resented the dominant ideology as degrading.

b) They preferred the dominant idology to other available ideologies.

c) They began to view the dominant idology to other availbale ideologies.

d) They accepted some but not all aspects of the dominant ideology.

e) They believed that the dominant ideology isolated them from one another.

Ans. This question requires you to make an inference, based on Eisenstein's argument, regarding her view of the attitudes of the women she studies. The best answer is (d). The first paragraph of the passage notes Eisenstein's argument that women neither wholly accepted nor rejected the dominant ideology of the time, and that they modified this and other ideologies to suit their needs. Choice (a) is incorrect. The dominant ideology is one among several ideologies that Eisenstein argues were adapted and modified by working women; the passage does not suggest that Eisenstein believed that working women resented that ideology or considered it degrading. Choice (b) is incorrect because Eisenstein's argument is that women took aspects of several available ideologies and modified them; there is no suggestion that any one ideology was preferred over others. Choice (c) can be eliminated because according to the passage, it is Tentler, not Eisenstein, who argues that working conditions increased the attractiveness of the dominant ideology. Choice (e) is not correct. Eisenstein argues that domestic work tended to isolate women from one another; there is no indication in the passage that the women themselves believed the dominant ideology was responsible for this.

3. Which of the following best describes the organisation of the first paragraph of the passage?

a) A chronological acount of a historical development is presented, and then furture develpments are predicted.

b) A term is defined according to several different schools of thought, and then a new definition is formulated.

c) A theory is presented, an alternative viewpoint is introduced, and then the reasoning behind the initial theory is summarized.

d) A tentative proposal is made, reasons for and against it are weighed, and then a modified version of the proposal is offered.

e) A controversy is described, its historical implications are assessed, and then a compromise is suggested.

Ans. This question asks you to identify the structure of the first paragraph of the passage. The best answer is (c). The first paragraph presents Eisenstein' theory, then makes note of Tentler's opposing views, then continues with further explication of Eisenstein's argument. Choice (a) can be eliminated because the paragraph discusses a certain historical development, the evolution of working women's values, but it does not make prediction about future developments. Choice (b) is not correct because the paragraph is not concerned with contrasting definitions of any term. Choice (d) and (e) are not correct because the paragraph does not discuss a tentative proposal that requires evaluation or a controversy that calls for resolution.

4. Which of the following would the author of the passage be most likely to approve as a continuation of Eisenstein's study?

a) An oral history of promotion women labour organizers

b) An analysis of letters and diaries written by typical female wage earners at the turn of the century

c) An assessment of what different social and political groups defined as the dominant ideology in the early twentieth century

d) A theoretical study of how socialism and feminism influenced one another at the turn of the century

e) A documentary account of labour's role in the introduction of women into the labour force

Ans. To answer this question you must decide which answer would best provide the sort of information that the author feels is lacking in Eisenstein's study. The author's critique of Eisenstein's argument is found primarily in the second paragraph. Choice (b) is the best answer because the author points out that Eisenstein's study is flawed in that it relies on sources that are not representative of the average female worker. An analysis of writings by typical female wage earners would help to rectify this problem. Choice (a) is not correct. Eisenstein's study already focuses on labour organisers; it is unlikely that the author feels that even more attention to this group is necessary. Choice (c) is not correct because the passage does not suggest that three were disagreements among social and political groups as to the definition of the dominant ideology. Choices (d) and (e) are incorrect because Eisenstein's study is not concerned with the interaction between socialism and feminism, nor with labour's particular role in the introduction of women into the workforce.

Zonation of Coastal Mangrove Forests

Neotropical coastal mangrove forests are usually "zonal," with certain mangrove species found predominantly in the seaward portion of the habitat and other mangrove species on the more landward portions of the coast. The earliest research on mangrove forests produced descriptions of species distribution from shore to land, without exploring the causes of the distributions.

The idea that zonation is caused by plant succession was first expressed by J. H. Davis in a study of Florida mangrove forests. According to Davis' scheme, the shoreline is being extended in a seaward direction because of the "land-building" role of mangroves, which, by trapping sediments over time, extend the shore. As a habitat gradually becomes more inland as the shore extends, the "land-building" species are replaced. This continuous process of accretion and succession would be interrupted only by hurricanes or storm flushings.

Recently the universal application of Davis's succession paradigm has been challenged. It appears that in areas where weak currents and weak tidal energies allow the accumulation of sediments, mangroves will follow land formation and accelerate the rate of soil accretion; succession will proceed according to Davis's scheme. But on stable coastlines, the distribution of mangrove species results in other patterns of zonation; "land building" does not occur.

To find a principle that explains the various distribution patterns, several researchers have looked to salinity and its effects on mangrove. While mangroves can develop in fresh water, they can also thrive in salinities as high as 2.5 times that of seawater. However, those mangrove species found in freshwater habitats do well only in the absence of competition, thus suggesting that salinity tolerance is a critical factor in competitive success among mangrove species. Research suggests that mangroves will normally dominate highly saline regions, although not because they require salt. Rather, they are metabolically efficient (and hence grow well) in portions of an environment whose high salinity excludes plants adapted to lower salinities. Tides create different degrees of salinity along a coastline. The characteristic mangrove species of each zone should exhibit a higher metabolic efficiency at that salinity than will any potential invader, including other species of mangrove.

1. The primary of the purpose of the passage is to

a) refute the idea that the zonation exhibited in mangrove forests is caused by adaption to salinity

b) describe the pattern of zonation typically found in Florida mangrove forests

c) argue that Davis' succession paradigm cannot be successfully applied to Florida mangrove forests

d) discuss hypotheses that attempt to explain the zonation of coastal mangrove forests

e) establish that plants that do well in saline forest environments require salt to achieve maximum metabolic efficiency

Ans. This question asks you to identify the primary purpose of the passage as a whole. The best answer is (d). The passage discusses two hypothesis concerning zonation of mangrove forests. Choice (a) can be eliminated because the passage presents as a viable hypothesis the idea that mangrove zonation may be caused by adaptation to salinity. Choice (b) is incorrect because the passage is concerned with the causes of zonation patterns, not simple with a description of those patterns. Both (c) and (e) contradict information that is presented in the passage.

2. According to the passage, the earliest research on mangrove forest produced which of the following?

a) Data that implied random patterns of mangrove species distribution

b) Descriptions of species distribtutions suggesting zonation

c) Descriptions of the development of mangrove forests over time

d) Reclassification of species formerly thought to be identical

e) Data that confirmed the "land-building" role of mangroves

Ans. This question asks you to identify information provided in the passage about early research on mangrove forests. That research is discussed in the first paragraph. Choice (b) is the best answer. Early research on mangrove forests is characterized as having produced descriptions of species distribution from shore to land. Such a distribution is described in the first sentence of the passage as "zonal." Choice (a) is not correct. Early research described mangrove distribution from shore to land. This implies a regular pattern of distribution, not a random one. Choices (c) and (d) are not correct because there is no indication in the passage that early studies of mangrove forests were concerned with the plants' chronological development or with the reclassification of species. Choice (e) is incorrect because the passage does not say that the research in question did anything except describe species distribution.

3. It can be inferred from the passage that Davis' paradigm does not apply to which of the following?

a) The shoreline of Florida mangrove forests first studies by Davis

b) A shoreline in an area with weak currents

c) A shoreline in an area with weak idal energy

d) A shoreline extended by "land-building" species of mangrove

e) A shoreline in which few sediments can accumulate

Ans. Here you are asked to make an inference based on information that is stated in the passage. Note that the best answer will refer to a situation where Davis's paradigm does not apply. Choice (e) is the best answer. Davis' succession paradigm states that mangroves trap sediments over time, thus extending the shore. A shoreline where few sediments could accumulate would be unable to develop according to such a scheme. Choice (a) is not correct. Davis first expressed his theory of "land-building" in his study of Florida mangrove forests. Thus his paradigm presumably applies to the shoreline of those forests. Choices (b) and (c) are incorrect because the passage states that areas with weak currents and weak tidal energies are areas where land formation will progress according to Davis' paradigm. Choice (d) is not correct because Davis' paradigm describes the "land-building" process of mangroves, so a shoreline that had been extended by that process would fall within the paradigm.

4. Information in the passage indicates that the author would most probably regard which of following statements as Incorrect?

a) Coastal mangrove forests are usually zonal.

b) Hurricanes interrupt the process of accretion and succession that extends existing shorelines.

c) Species of plants that thrive in a saline habitat require salt to flourish.

d) Plants with the highest metabolic efficiency in a given habitat tend to exclude other plants from that habitat.

e) Shoreline in areas with weak currents and trides are more likely to be extended through the process of accumulation of sediment than are shorleines with strong currents and tides.

Ans. Here you are asked to make an inference about the likely view of the author of the passage. Note that the best answer must be a statement that the author would most likely judge to be Incorrect. Choice (c) is best. The author points out that while mangroves normally thrive in highly saline regions, this is not because they require salt. That assertion contradicts the claim made in this answer, so the author would likely regard the claim made in this answer as incorrect. Choice (a) is incorrect because it paraphrases an assertion the author makes in the first sentence of the passage. Choice (b) is incorrect because it paraphrases an assertion the author makes in the last sentence of the second paragraph. Choice (d) is incorrect because the passage does not provide sufficient information to determine whether the author would agree with this statement. Choice (e) is not correct. The author notes that areas with weak currents and tides are likely to be extended through land formation. Thus the author would consider the assertion made here to be correct, not incorrect.

Backward Integration

Modern manufacturers, who need reliable sources of materials and technologically advanced components to operate profitably, face an increasingly difficult choice between owning the producers of these items (a practice known as backward integration) and buying from independent producers. Manufacturers who integrate may reap short-term rewards, but they often restrict their future capacity for innovative product development.

Backward integration removes the need for some purchasing and marketing functions, centralizers overhead, and permits manufacturers to eliminate duplicated efforts in research and development. Where components are commodities (ferrous metals or petroleum, for example), backward integration almost certainly boosts profits. Nevertheless, because product innovation means adopting the most technologically advanced and cost-effective ways of making components, backward integration may entail a serious risk for a technologically active company—for example, a producer of sophisticated consumer electronics.

A company that decides to make rather than buy important parts can lock itself into an outdated technology. Independent suppliers may be unwilling to share innovations with assemblers with whom they are competing. Moreover, when an assembler sets out to master the technology of producing advanced components, the resulting demands on its resources may compromise its ability to assemble these components successfully into end products. Long-term contracts with suppliers can achieve many of the same cost benefits as backward integration without compromising a company's ability to innovate.

However, moving away from backward integration is not a complete solution either. Developing innovative technologies requires independent suppliers of components to invest huge sums in research and development. The resulting low profit margins on the sale of components threaten the long-term financial stability of these firms. Because the ability of end-product assemblers to respond to market opportunities depends heavily on suppliers of components, assemblers are often forced to integrate by purchasing the suppliers of components just to keep their suppliers in business.

1. According to the passage, all of the following are benefits associated with backward integration Except:

a) improvement in the management of overhead expenses

b) enhancement of profit margins on sales of components

c) simplification of purchasing and marketing operations

d) reliability of a source of necessary components

e) elimination of unnecessary research efforts

Ans. This question asks you to identify which one of the five answer choices is not mentioned in the passage as a benefit associated with backward integration. The best answer is (b). The passage does not indicate how backward integration affects the profit margins on sales of components by independent suppliers. Choices (a), (c), and (e) are mentioned in the passage as a benefit of backward integration. Choice (d) is incorrect because the passage indicates that backward integration is a way of having a reliable source of necessary components.

2. According to passage, when an assembler buys a firm that makes some important component of the end product that the assembler produces, independent suppliers of the same component may

a) withhold technological innovations from the assembler

b) experience improved profit margins of on sales of their products

c) lower their prices to protect themselves from competition

d) suffer finanical difficluties and go out of business

e) stop developing new versions of the component

Ans. This question asks you to identify information presented in the passage about independent suppliers of product components. Choice (a) is the best answer. The passage asserts that independent supplies making the same components as assemblers may not share technological innovations with assemblers. Choices (b), (c), (d), and (e) can be eliminated because there is no indication in the passage as assemblers experience improved profit margins, lower their prices, suffer financial difficulties, or stop developing new versions of the component.

3. Which of the following best describes the way the last paragraph functions in the context of the passage?

a) The last in a series of arguments supporting the central argument of the passage is presented.

b) A viewpoint is presented which qualifies one presented earlier in the passage.

c) Evidence is presented in support of the argument developed in the preceding paragrap.

d) Questions arising from the earlier discussion are identified as points of departure for further study of the topic.

e) A specific example is presented to illustrate the main elements of argument presented in the earlier paragraphs.

Ans. This question asks you to choose the statement that best describes the function of the last paragraph of the passage. The best answer is (b). At the end of the third paragraph, the author indicates that assemblers benefit from contracting with, rather than owning, independent suppliers. In the last paragraph, however, the author indicates that contracting with independent suppliers can itself present problems. Thus the last paragraph qualifies the viewpoint presented at the end of the third paragraph. Choice (a) is not the correct answer because the passage makes several points about backward integration, but does not present a central argument about this topic. Choice (c) is not the correct answer because the final paragraph qualifies rather than supports an argument made in the third paragraph about contracting with independent suppliers. Choices (d) and (e) are incorrect because the final paragraph does not identify questions or present a specific example.

4. According to the passage, which of the following relationships between profits and investments in research and development holds true for producers of technologically advanced components?

a) Modest investments are required and the profit margins on component sales are lowl.

b) Modest investments are required but the profit margins on component sales are quite high.

c) Despite the huge investments that are required, the profit margins on components sales are high.

d) Because huge investments are required, the profit margins on component sales are low.

e) Long-term contractual relationships with purchasers of components ensure a high ratio of profits to investment costs.

Ans. This question asks you to identify information presented in the passage about the relationship between profits and investments for producers of technologically advanced components. The best answer is (d). The passage indicates that the high investments required to develop technologically advanced components. Choice (a) is incorrect because the passage indicates that large, not modest, investments in research and development are required. Choices (b) and (c) are incorrect because the passage indicates that profit margins for producers of technologically advanced components are low, not high as these answer choice assert. Choice (e) is incorrect: although the author claims that long-term contracts with suppliers are beneficial to assemblers, the passage does not indicate that long-term contracts with purchasers lead to high profits for producers of technologically advanced components.

■■■

CHAPTER 6

Miscellaneous Practice Exercises

Tragedy

There are two theories that have often been used to explain ancient and modern tragedy. Neither quite explains the complexity of the tragic process or the tragic hero, but each explains important elements of tragedy, and, because their conclusions are contradictory, they represent extreme views. and of the limitation of human effort. But this theory of tragedy is an oversimplification, primarily because it confuses the tragic condition with the tragic process: the theory does not acknowledge that fate, in a tragedy, normally becomes external to the hero only after the tragic process has as a heroism that creates the splendour and exhilaration that is unique to tragedy. The tragic hero quality of an honest person, but the external antagonist of the criminal. Secondarily, this theory of tragedy does not distinguish tragedy from irony. Irony does not need an exceptional central figure: the original destiny never quite fades out of the tragedy. as a rule, the more ignoble the hero the sharper the irony, when irony alone is the objective. It is heroism that creates the splendor and exhilaration that is unique to tragedy. The tragic hero normally has an extraordinary, often a nearly divine, destiny almost within grasp, and the glory of the original destiny never quite fades out of the tragedy.

The second theory of tragedy states that the act that sets the tragic process in motion must be primarily a violation of normal law, whether human or divine; in short, that the tragic hero must have a flaw that has an essential connection with sin. Again it is true that the great majority of tragic heroes do possess hubris, or a proud and passionate mind that seems to make the hero's downfall morally explicable. But such hubris is only the precipitating agent of catastrophe, just as in comedy the cause)f the happy ending is usually some act of humility often performed by a noble character who is meanly disguised.

This theory of tragedy as morally explicable runs into the question of whether an innocent sufferer in a tragedy, such as Iphigenia, or Socrates in Plato Apology, is a tragic figure. They are, of course, even though it is not very easy to find crucial moral flaws in them. Cordelia shows sincerity and high spirit in refusing to flatter her faber, and Cordelia is 30 hanged. Tragedy, in short, is ambiguous and cannot be reduced to the opposition between human effort. and external fate, just as it cannot be reduced to the opposition between good and evil.

1. The primary purpose of the passage is to

a) compare and criticise two theories of tragedy.

b) develop a new theory of tragedy.

c) Summarise the thematic content of tragedy.

d) reject one theory of tragedy and offer another theory in its place.

e) distinguish between tragedy and iron

Ans. The passage juxtaposes two contradictory theories of tragedy. See the first sentence of para 1. Hence, (a).

2. The author states that the theories discussed in the passage "represent extreme views" because their conclusions are

a) unpopular

b) complex

c) paradoxical

d) contradictory.

e) imaginative

Ans. contradictory.

3. Which of the following comparisons of the tragic with the ironic hero is best supported by information contained in the passage?

a) Tragic hero's fate is an external condition, but an ironic hero's fate is an internal one.

b) A tragic hero must be controlled by fate, but an ironic hero cannot be.

c) A tragic hero's moral flaw surprises the, audience, but an ironic hero's sin does not.

d) A tragic hero and an ironic hero cannot both be virtuous figures in the same tragedy.

e) A tragic hero is usually extraordinary, but an ironic hero may be cowardly or even villainous.

Ans. A tragic hero is usually extraordinary, but an ironic hero may be cowardly or even villainous.

4. The author contrasts an honest person and a criminal primarily in order to

a) prove that fate cannot be external to the tragic hero.

b) establish a criterion that allows a distinction to be made between irony and tragedy.

c) develop the distinction between the tragic condition and the tragic process.

d) introduce the concept of sin as the cause of tragic action.

e) argue that the theme of omnipotent external fate is shared by comedy and tragedy.

Ans. develop the distinction between the tragic condition and the tragic process.

5. According to the. author, Cordellia is an example of a figure who

a) transcended both the laws of 'fate and the laws of society.

b) sinned, but whose sin did not set the tragic process in motion.

c) disobeyed a moral law, but was not punished for doing so.

d) submitted willingly to fate, even though her submission caused her death.

e) did not set the tragic process in motion, but is still a tragic figure.

Ans. did not set the tragic process in motion, but is still a tragic figure.

6. In the author's opinion, an act of humility in comedy is most analogous to

a) a catastrophe in tragedy.

b) an ironic action in tragedy.

c) a tragic hero's pride and passion

d) a tragic hero's aversion to sin.

e) a tragic hero's pursuit of an unusual destiny.

Ans. a tragic hero's pride and passion.

English as a National Foreign Language

India has two national languages for central administrative purposes: Hindi and English. Hindi is the national, official, and main link language of India. English is an associate official language. The Indian Constitution also officially approves twenty-two regional languages for official purposes.

Dozens of distinctly different regional languages are spoken in India, which share many characteristics such as grammatical structure and vocabulary. Apart from these languages, Hindi is used for communication in India. The homeland of Hindi is mainly in the north of India, but it is spoken and widely understood in all urban centers of India. In the southern states of India, where people speak many different languages that are not much related to Hindi, there is more resistance to Hindi, which has allowed English to remain a lingua franca to a greater degree.

Since the early 1600s, the English language has had a toehold on the Indian subcontinent, when the East India Company established settlements in Chennai, Kolkata, and Mumbai, formerly Madras, Calcutta, and Bombay respectively. The historical background of India is never far away from everyday usage of English. India has had a longer exposure to English than any other country which uses it as a second language, its distinctive words, idioms, grammar and rhetoric spreading gradually to affect all places, habits and culture.

In India, English serves two purposes. First, it provides a linguistic tool for the administrative cohesiveness of the country, causing people who speak different languages to become united. Secondly, it serves as a language of wider communication, including a large variety of different people covering a vast area. It overlaps with local languages in certain spheres of influence and in public domains.

Generally, English is used among Indians as a 'link' language and it is the first language for many well-educated Indians. It is also the second language for many who speak more than one language in India. The English language is a tie that helps bind the many segments of our society together. Also, it is a linguistic bridge between the major countries of the world and India.

English has special national status in India. It has a special place in the parliament, judiciary, broadcasting, journalism, and in the education system. One can see a Hindi-speaking teacher giving their students instructions during an educational tour about where to meet and when their bus would leave, but all in English. It means that the language permeates daily life. It is unavoidable and is always expected, especially in the cities.

The importance of the ability to speak or write English has recently increased significantly because English has become the de facto standard. Learning English language has become popular for business, commerce and cultural reasons and especially for internet communications throughout the world. English is a language that has become a standard not because it has been approved by any 'standards' organization but because it is widely used by many information and technology industries and recognized as being standard. The call centre phenomenon has stimulated a huge expansion of internet-related activity, establishing the future of India as a cyber-technological super-power. Modern communications, videos, journals and newspapers on the internet use English and have made 'knowing English' indispensable.

The prevailing view seems to be that unless students learn English, they can only work in limited jobs. Those who do not have basic knowledge of English cannot obtain good quality jobs. They cannot communicate efficiently with others, and cannot have the benefit of India's rich social and cultural life. Men and women who cannot comprehend and interpret instructions in English, even if educated, are unemployable. They cannot help with their children's school homework everyday or decide their revenue options of the future.

A positive attitude to English as a national language is essential to the integration of people into Indian society. There would appear to be virtually no disagreement in the community about the importance of English language skills. Using English you will become a citizen of the world almost naturally. English plays a dominant role in the media. It has been used as a medium for inter-state communication and broadcasting both before and since India's independence. India is, without a doubt, committed to English as a national language. The impact of English is not only continuing but increasing.

1. According to the writer, the Indian constitution recognises
   a) 22 official languages.
   b) Hindi as the national language.

c) 2 national, official languages.

d) 2 national languages.

Ans. 22 official languages.

2. English's status as a lingua franca is helped by

a) its status in northern India.

b) the fact that it is widely understood in urban centres.

c) the fact that people from the south speak languages not much related to Hindi.

d) it shares many grammatical similarities with Hindi.

Ans. the fact that people from the south speak languages not much related to Hindi.

3. In paragraph 3, 'toehold' means that English

a) dominated India.

b) changed the names of some cities in India.

c) has had a presence in India.

d) has been in India longer than any other language.

Ans. has had a presence in India.

4. Hindi-speaking teachers

a) might well be heard using English.

b) only use English.

c) only use English for instructions.

d) do not use English.

Ans. might well be heard using English.

5. In paragraph eight, it says 'the prevailing view', which suggests that

a) the view is correct.

b) the view is held by the majority.

c) the view is incorrect.

d) the view is held by the minority.

Ans. the view is held by the majority.

6. English in India

a) is going to decrease.

b) has decreased since independence.

c) causes disagreement.

d) is going to have a greater importance.

Ans. is going to have a greater importance.

Changes in Trade

Many United States companies have, unfortunately, made the search for legal protection from import competition into a major line of work. Since 1980 the United States International Trade Commission (ITC) has received about 280 complaints alleging damage from imports that benefit from subsidies by foreign governments. Another 340 charge that foreign companies "dumped" their products in the United States at "less than fair value." Even when no unfair practices are alleged, the simple claim that an industry has been injured by imports is sufficient grounds to seek relief.

Contrary to the general impression, this quest for import relief has hurt more companies than it has helped. As corporations begin to function globally, they develop an intricate web of marketing, production, and research relationships. The complexity of these relationships makes it unlikely that a system of import relief laws will meet the strategic needs of all the units under the same parent company.

Internationalization increases the danger that foreign companies will use import relief laws against the very companies the laws were designed to protect. Suppose a United States-owned company establishes an overseas plant to manufacture a product while its competitor makes the same product in the United States. If the competitor can prove injury from the imports—and that the United States company received a subsidy from a foreign government to build its plant abroad—the United States company's products will be uncompetitive in the United States, since they would be subject to duties.

Perhaps the most brazen (marked by contemptuous boldness) case occurred when the ITC investigated allegations that Canadian companies were injuring the United States salt industry by dumping rock salt used to de-ice roads. The bizarre aspect of the complaint was that a foreign conglomerate with United States operations was crying for help against a United States company with foreign operations. The "United States" company claiming injury was a subsidiary of a Dutch conglomerate, while the "Canadian" companies included a subsidiary of a Chicago firm that was the second-largest domestic producer of rock salt.

1. The passage is chiefly concerned with

a) arguing against the increased Internationalization of United States corporations

b) warning that the application of laws affecting trade frequently has unintended consequences

c) demonstrating that foreign-based firms receive more subsidies from their governments than United States firms receive from the United States government

d) advocating the use of trade restrictions for "dumped" products but not for other imports

e) recommending a uniform method for handling claims of unfair trade practices

Ans. warning that the application of laws affecting trade frequently has unintended consequences

2. It can be inferred from the passage that the minimal basis for a complaint to the International Trade Commission is which of the following?

a) A foreign competitor has received a subsidy from a foreign government.

b) A foreign competitor has substantially increased the volume of products shipped to the United States.

c) A foreign competitor is selling products in the United States at less than fair market value.

d) The company requesting import relief has been injured by the sale of imports in the United States.

e) The company requesting import relief has been barred from exporting products to the country of its foreign competitor.

Ans. The company requesting import relief has been injured by the sale of imports in the United States.

3. The last paragraph performs which of the following functions in the passage?

a) It summarizes the discussion thus far and suggests additional areas of research.

b) It presents a recommendation based on the evidence presented earlier.

c) It discusses an exceptional case in which the results expected by the author of the passage were not obtained.

d) It introduces an additional area of concern not mentioned earlier.

e) It cites a specific case that illustrates a problem presented more generally in the previous paragraph.

Ans. It cites a specific case that illustrates a problem presented more generally in the previous paragraph.

4. The passage warns of which of the following dangers?

a) Companies in the United States may receive no protection from imports unless they actively seek protection from import competition.

b) Companies that seek legal protection from import competition may incur legal costs that far exceed any possible gain.

c) Companies that are United States-owned but operate

internationally may not be eligible for protection from import competition under the laws of the countries in which their plants operate.

d) Companies that are not United States-owned may seek legal protection from import competition under United States import relief laws.

e) Companies in the United States that import raw materials may have to pay duties on those materials.

Ans. Companies that are not United States-owned may seek legal protection from import competition under United States import relief laws.

5. The passage suggests that which of the following is most likely to be true of United States trade laws?

a) They will eliminate the practice of "dumping" products in the United States.

b) They will enable manufacturers in the United States to compete more profitably outside the United States.

c) They will affect United States trade with Canada more negatively than trade with other nations.

d) Those that help one unit within a parent company will not necessarily help other units in the company.

e) Those that are applied to international companies will accomplish their intended result.

Ans. Those that help one unit within a parent company will not necessarily help other units in the company.

6. It can be inferred from the passage that the author believes which of the following about the complaint mentioned in the last paragraph?

a) The ITC acted unfairly toward the complainant in its investigation.

b) The complaint violated the intent of import relief laws.

c) The response of the ITC to the complaint provided suitable relief from unfair trade practices to the complainant.

d) The ITC did not have access to appropriate information concerning the case.

e) Each of the companies involved in the complaint acted in its own best interest.

Ans. The complaint violated the intent of import relief laws.

7. According to the passage, companies have the general impression that International Trade Commission import relief practices have

a) caused unpredictable fluctuations in volumes of imports and exports

b) achieved their desired effect only under unusual circumstances

c) actually helped companies that have requested import relief

d) been opposed by the business community

e) had less impact on international companies than the business community expected

Ans. actually helped companies that have requested import relief

8. According to the passage, the International Trade Commission is involved in which of the following?

a) Investigating allegations of unfair import competition

b) Granting subsidies to companies in the United States that have been injured by import competition

c) Recommending legislation to ensure fair

d) Identifying international corporations that wish to build plants in the United States

e) Assisting corporations in the United States that wish to compete globally.

Ans. Investigating allegations of unfair import competition.

Archaeology as a Profession

Archaeology as a profession faces two major problems. First, it is the poorest of the poor. Only paltry sums are available for excavating and even less is available for publishing the results and preserving the sites once excavated. Yet archaeologists deal with priceless objects every day. Second, there is the problem of illegal excavation, resulting in museum-quality pieces being sold to the highest bidder.

I would like to make an outrageous suggestion that would at one stroke provide funds for archaeology and reduce the amount of illegal digging. I would propose that scientific archeological expeditions and governmental authorities sell excavated artifacts on the open market. Such sales would provide substantial funds for the excavation and preservation of archaeological sites and the publication of results. At the same time, they would break the illegal excavator's grip on the market, thereby decreasing the inducement to engage in illegal activities.

You might object that professionals excavate to acquire knowledge, not money. Moreover, ancient artifacts are part of our global cultural heritage, which should be available for all to appreciate, not sold to the highest bidder. I agree. Sell nothing that has unique artistic merit or scientific value. But, you might reply, everything that comes our of the ground has scientific value. Here we part company. Theoretically, you may be correct in claiming that every artifact has potential scientific value. Practically, you are wrong.

I refer to the thousands of pottery vessels and ancient lamps that are essentially duplicates of one another. In one small excavation in Cyprus, archaeologists recently uncovered 2,000 virtually indistinguishable small jugs in a single courtyard. Even precious royal seal impressions known as/melekh handles have been found in abundance—more than 4,000 examples so far.

The basements of museums are simply not large enough to store the artifacts that are likely to be discovered in the future.

There is not enough money even to catalogue the finds; as a result, they cannot be found again and become as inaccessible as if they had never been discovered. Indeed, with the help of a computer, sold artifacts could be more accessible than are the pieces stored in bulging museum basements. Prior to sale, each could be photographed and the list of the purchasers could be maintained on the computer A purchaser could even be required to agree to return the piece if it should become needed for scientific purposes. It would be unrealistic to suggest that illegal digging would stop if artifacts were sold on the open market.

But the demand for the clandestine product would be substantially reduced. Who would want an unmarked pot when another was available whose provenance was known, and that was dated stratigraphically by the professional archaeologist who excavated it?

1. The primary purpose of the passage is to propose
 a) an alternative to museum display of artifacts
 b) a way to curb illegal digging while benefiting the archaeological profession
 c) a way to distinguish artifacts with scientific value from those that have no such value
 d) the governmental regulation of archaeological sites
 e) a new system for cataloguing duplicate artifacts

 Ans. a way to curb illegal digging while benefiting the archaeological profession

2. The author implies that all of the following statements about duplicate artifacts are true EXCEPT:
 a) A market for such artifacts already exists.
 b) Such artifacts seldom have scientific value.
 c) There is likely to be a continuing supply of such artifacts.
 d) Museums are well supplied with examples of such artifacts.

e) Such artifacts frequently exceed in quality those already catalogued in museum collections.

Ans. Such artifacts frequently exceed in quality those already catalogued in museum collections.

3. Which of the following is mentioned in the passage as a disadvantage of storing artifacts in museum basements?

a) Museum officials rarely allow scholars access to such artifacts.

b) Space that could be better used for display is taken up for storage.

c) Artifacts discovered in one excavation often become separated from each other.

d) Such artifacts are often damaged by variations in temperature and humidity.

e) Such artifacts' often remain uncatalogued and thus cannot be located once they are put in storage.

Ans. Such artifacts' often remain uncatalogued and thus cannot be located once they are put in storage.

4. The author mentions the excavation in Cyprus (lines 31-34) to emphasize which of the following points?

a) Ancient lamps and pottery vessels are less valuable, although more rare, than royal seal impressions.

b) Artifacts that are very similar to each other present cataloguing difficulties to archaeologists.

c) Artifacts that are not uniquely valuable, and therefore could be sold, are available in large quantities.

d) Cyprus is the most important location for unearthing large quantities of salable artifacts.

e) Illegal sales of duplicate artifacts are wide-spread, particularly on the island of Cyprus.

Ans. Artifacts that are not uniquely valuable, and therefore could be sold, are available in large quantities.

5. The author's argument concerning the effect of the official sale of duplicate artifacts on illegal excavation is based on which of the following assumptions?

a) Prospective purchasers would prefer to buy authenticated artifacts.

b) The price of illegally excavated artifacts would rise.

c) Computers could be used to trace sold artifacts.

d) Illegal excavators would be forced to sell only duplicate artifacts.

e) Money gained from selling authenticated artifacts could be used to investigate and prosecute illegal excavators.

Ans. Prospective purchasers would prefer to buy authenticated artifacts.

Pesticides and Species Interdependence

Species interdependence in nature confers many benefits on the species involved, but it can also become a point of weakness when one species involved in the relationship is affected by a catastrophe. Thus, flowering plant species dependent on insect pollination, as opposed to self-pollination or wind pollination, could be endangered when the population of insect-pollinators is depleted by the use of pesticides.

In the forests of New Brunswick, for example, various pesticides have been sprayed in the past 25 years in efforts to control the spruce budworm, an economically significant pest. Scientists have now investigated the effects of the spraying of Matacil, one of the anti-budworm agents that is least toxic to insect-pollinators. They studied Matacil's effects on insect mortality in a wide variety of wild insect species and on plant fecundity, expressed as the percentage of the total flowers on an individual plant that actually developed fruit and bore seeds. They found that the most pronounced mortality after the spraying of Matacil occurred among the smaller bees and one family of flies, insects that were all important pollinators of numerous species of plants growing beneath the tree canopy of forests. The fecundity of plants in one common indigenous species, the red-osier dogwood, was significantly reduced in the sprayed areas as compared to that of plants in control plots where Matacil was not sprayed. This species is highly dependent on the insect-pollinators most vulnerable to Matacil. The creeping dogwood, a species similar to the red-osier dogwood, but which is pollinated by large bees, such as bumblebees, showed no significant decline in fecundity. Since large bees are not affected by the spraying of Matacil, these results add weight to the argument that spraying where the pollinators are sensitive to the pesticide used decreases plant fecundity.

The question of whether the decrease in plant fecundity caused by the spraying of pesticides actually causes a decline in the overall population of flowering plant species still remains unanswered. Plant species dependent solely on seeds for survival or dispersal are obviously more vulnerable to any decrease in plant fecundity that occurs, whatever its cause. If, on the other hand, vegetative growth and dispersal (by means of shoots or runners) are available as alternative reproductive strategies for a species, then decreases in plant fecundity may be of little consequence. The fecundity effects described here are likely to have the most profound impact on plant species with all four of the following characteristics: a short life span, a narrow geographic range, an incapacity for vegetative propagation, and a dependence on a small number of insect-pollinator species. Perhaps we should give special attention to the conservation of such plant species since they lack key factors in their defenses against the environmental disruption caused by pesticide use.

1. Which of the following best summarizes the main point of the passage?

a) Species interdependence is a point of weakness for some plants, but is generally beneficial to insects involved in pollination.

b) Efforts to control the spruce budworm have had deleterious effects on the red-osier dogwood.

c) The used of pesticides may be endangering certain plant species dependent on insects for pollination.

d) The spraying of pesticides can reduce the fecundity of a plant species, but probably does not affect its overall population stability.

e) Plant species lacking key factors in their defenses against human environmental disruption will probably become extinct.

Ans. The used of pesticides may be endangering certain plant species dependent on insects for pollination.

2. According to the author, a flowering plant species whose fecundity has declined due to pesticide spraying may not experience an overall population decline if the plant species can do which of the following?

a) Reproduce itself by means of shoots and runners.

b) Survive to the end of the growing season.

c) Survive in harsh climates.

d) Respond to the fecundity decline by producing more flowers.

e) Attract large insects as pollinators.

Ans. Reproduce itself by means of shoots and runners.

3. The passage suggests that the lack of an observed decline in the fecundity of the creeping dogwood strengthens the researchers conclusions regarding pesticide use because the

a) creeping dogwood is a species that does not resemble other forest plants

b) creeping dogwood is a species pollinated by a broader range of insect species than are most dogwood species

c) creeping dogwood grows primarily in regions that were not sprayed with pesticide, and so served as a control for the experiment

d) creeping dogwood is similar to the red-osier dogwood, but its insect pollinators are known to be insensitive to the pesticide used in the study

e) geographical range of the creeping dogwood is similar to that of the red-osier dogwood, but the latter species relies less on seeds for reproduction

Ans. creeping dogwood is similar to the red-osier dogwood, but its insect pollinators are known to be insensitive to the pesticide used in the study.

4. The passage suggests that which of the following is true of the forest regions in New Brunswick sprayed with most anti-budworm pesticides other than Matacil?

a) The fecundity of some flowering plants in those regions may have decreased to an even greater degree than in the regions where Matacil is used.

b) Insect mortality in those regions occurs mostly among the larger species of insects, such as bumblebees.

c) The number of seeds produced by common plant species in those regions is probably comparable to the number produced where Matacil is sprayed.

d) Many more plant species have become extinct in those regions than in the regions where Matacil is used.

e) The spruce budworm is under better control in those regions than in the regions where Matacil is sprayed.

Ans. The fecundity of some flowering plants in those regions may have decreased to an even greater degree than in the regions where Matacil is used.

■■■

Other Books on

WORD POWER SERIES

1.	Effective English Comprehention Read Fast, Understand Better! (New)	150/-
2.	Latest Essays for College & Competitive Examinations (New)	150/-
3.	Dictionary of New Words (New)	125/-
4.	Art of English Conversation Speak English Fluently (New)	125/-
5.	Teach Yourself English Grammer & Composition (New)	125/-
6.	Common & Uncommon Proverbs (New)	125/-
7.	Effective Editing Help Yourself in Becoming a Good Editor (New)	125/-
8.	Effective English A Boon for Learners (New)	125/-
9.	Essays for Primary Classes	55/-
10.	Essays for Junior Classes	55/-
11.	Essays for Senior Classes	55/-
12.	Dictionary of Synonyms and Antonyms	125/-
13.	Dictionary of Idioms and Phrases	125/-
14.	Common Phrases	125/-
15.	How to Write & Speak Correct English	125/-
16.	Meaningful Quotes	150/-
17.	Punctuation Book	125/-
18.	Top School Essays	95/-
19.	How to Write Business Letters with CD	250/-
20.	Everyday Grammar	125/-
21.	Everyday Conversation	125/-
22.	Letters for All Occasions	95/-
23.	School Essays & Letters for Juniors	75/-

24.	Common Mistakes in English	95/-
25.	The Power of Writing	150/-
26.	Learn English in 21 Lessons	95/-
27.	First English Dictionary	95/-
28.	Boost Your Spelling Power	110/-
29.	Self-Help to English Conversation	110/-
30.	The Art of Effective Communication	125/-
31.	A Book of Proverbs & Quotations	95/-
32.	Word Power Made Easy	95/-
33.	English Grammar Easier Way	125/-
34.	General English for Competitive Examinations	125/-
35.	Spoken English	95/-
36.	School Essays, Letters Writing and Phrases	95/-
37.	How to Write & Speak Better English	95/-
38.	Quote Unquote (A Handbook of Famous Quotations)	125/-
39.	Improve Your Vocabulary	125/-
40.	Common Errors in English	110/-
41.	The Art of Effective Letter Writing	110/-
42.	Synonyms & Antonyms	95/-
43.	Idioms	95/-
44.	Business Letters	95/-

Unit No. 220, 2nd Floor, 4735/22,
Prakash Deep Building,Ansari Road, Darya Ganj,
New Delhi- 110002, Ph.: 32903912, 23280047, 09811594448
• E-mail : lotus_press@sify.com, www.lotuspress.co.in